This book is created on the initiative and with the support of the Statens Kunstfond's (the Danish National Endowment for the Arts) committee for architecture presiding 1999-2001.

Editors: Carsten Juel-Christiansen & Gilbert Hansen
Translation: Dan A. Marmorstein
Translation consultant: Regitze Hess
Production and graphic design: Gilbert Hansen,
Architectural Magazine **B**
Printer: Linde Tryk, Aarhus

Publisher: Fonden til udgivelse af Arkitekturtidsskrift **B** /
The Architectural Magazine **B**
Copenhagen, Denmark
E-mail: b-arki@inet.uni2.dk
ISBN 87-987280-4-0
© The authors and
Fonden til udgivelse af Arkitekturtidsskrift **B**,
2000 (unless otherwise statet).

Transitions
space in the dispersed city

Foreword	4
Introduction	5
Of Other Spaces: Utopias and Heterotopias	9
The Room, the Street and Human Agreement	15
Excerpts from "The Evil Demon of Images"	21
On Atopi	26
Project theme: Transitions, the introductory draft for the assignment	30
Sites	32
The Collective Space	
Steen Høyer	35
Jens Kvorning	65
Tage Lyneborg	81
The Space's Middle Ground	
Kristine Jensen	101
Svein Tønsager	119
Niels Grønbæk	143
The Edge of the Space	
Anders Abraham	161
Anders Munck	189
Poul Ingemann	205
Resume – the works set into perspective	220

FOREWORD

The present publication is a re-printing, in a somewhat re-edited form, and translated into English, of the volume originally entitled "Overgang - rum i den spredte by". The present volume, "Transitions - space in the dispersed city", is being published in synchronicity with Denmark's exhibition-contribution to the 7th International Architecture Biennial in Venice, in the year 2000.

The original Danish version was created on the initiative of the Statens Kunstfond's (the Danish National Endowment for the Arts) specially-appointed committee for architecture which presided in the period 1996-98.
The foreword to the original version reads: "In our present century, urban formation has gradually and almost imperceptibly changed in character, Changed economic and infrastructural fundamental structures, changed conditions of production, changed ideals concerning settlement, the exclusion of strategic population localizations and many other mutually connected parameters have displaced the delineation of the frontier between city and countryside. These changes in the urban formation's conditions, often transpiring in conflict with the open cultural landscape, have fashioned the background for and reflected themselves in the debate around means and ends in our landscape's transformation. In stimulating this publication, the Statens Kunstfond's architecture committee is attempting to provide the circumstances for a thorough testing of the city's new spatial qualities and possibilities. A circle of architects, each of whom has committedly turned his/ her attention toward the city's spatial formation, has been invited - on the basis of the project theme formulated by the architect, Professor Carsten Juel-Christiansen - to proceed with encircling the problem's formulation, and to come forth with architectonic responses."

Inasmuch as the content of "Overgang - rum i den spredte by" revealed itself to converge ever so cogently with the theme of the 7th International Architecture Biennial, "The City - less aesthetics, more ethics", the presiding architecture committee of the Statens Kunstfond, upon a commission by the Cultural Ministry, resolved to set into effect the exhibition of contributions from the book, and appointed Professor Carsten Juel-Christiansen commissioner for the exhibition project. All nine contributions have been re-formulated as material specifically articulated for the Venice exhibition, in either selected parts or in edited form.
The present publication can thus be regarded as constituting an extended and in-depth exhibition catalogue of the Danish contribution to the 7th International Architecture Biennial.
As was the case with the publication of the original Danish version, the present volume is being put into print by The Architectural Magazine **B**, under the persevering and indefatigable editorial hand of architect Gilbert Hansen.
The contents of the book have been translated from Danish into English by composer Dan A. Marmorstein.

Statens Kunstfond's
architecture committee 1999-2001
Claus Bonderup
Kjeld Vindum
Lone Wiggers

INTRODUCTION

Carsten Juel-Christiansen

Were we to summarize this book, its contents could be apprehended as embodying a sincere hope that architectonic coherence, spatial quality and human dignity were assertions that could fluently be conjoined with the design of the city. It must not be construed here that all these values are not already present but indeed, a rather extensive series of entirely different considerations are demanding to be satisfied with the result that there no longer seems to be any qualitative goal in fastening our gaze on the city's space.

That which motivates the authors of this book is not the loss of the city's historic image as such but rather a critique of the dearth of values that architecture will come to represent if every consideration concerning architectonic coherence in the city is severed beforehand by narrowly defined interests. Implicit in this critique is also a resistance to looking at society as a mass production of accepted individuality; such a view would inevitably result in getting the city to look like an exhibition of single-family houses with a transparent life-style hierarchy serving as ground plan. The narrative of the urban image, then, is seated neither in subjecting architecture to the control of the production apparatus nor in leaving it to the whims of individual consumer tastes (and in these times, these can certainly be said to be two sides of the same coin). It can emerge, however, if the relation between life and space is formulated as a matter of common concern.

The works in the book have been created against this background: the present day city is permeated by the systems that envelop contemporary life. The mechanisms that regulate society's functionality have also shaped contemporary space through the simplification and standardization of its components which, in ensemble with a powerfully constructed communications network, foster the development of the city in a number of specialized areas colored by large-scale operations' advantageous position in the production apparatus.

Instead of focusing on this pattern of uniformity in delimited fields, the book sets its focus on the transitions between different areas. These transitions are charged with urban architectonic potential. This is primarily because they are actually localized in the city, as regions. But also because they contain an openness which is a consequence of being situated on the periphery of the administrative and economic systems that manifest themselves. In other words, these transitions possess the capacity of being labile intervening spaces between firm spheres of interest. And finally, it is because they contain differences between the space that is on the one side and the space on the other which, when brought into a connection, can spawn a meaningful urban architectonic element, as we have seen in waterfront promenades between dense and open spaces in the city and in the hillside stairways that link diverse differences in height in the city's terrain.

Contemplating the transitions in the city's space, then, might just point the way toward a direct access to creating an architecture revolving around coherence.

The main contributions in the book come from recommendations put forth by nine architects, each of whom has prepared proposals that can be regarded as contributions toward the solution of a collective assignment. The theme of the assignment is transitions: the spaces that provide coherence in the present-day city and landscape areas; the spaces which inside the historical city scene had well-defined types and distinct forms. The harbor connected the sea with the city's area. The moat separated the city from the countryside. The avenues elongated the space of the manor out to the surroundings, and the city's streets provided a distinct spatial link between the citizens' private space and the space of the community. Nowadays, these images belong to the spheres of preservation and reminiscence. The spaces for working and for leisure, the landscapes for production and recreation, the spaces for traffic and for dwelling are today characterized by functional forms, machines and velocities that only permit mutual coherences among the parts in specially limited areas where the functional conflicts are brought under control. Put this together with the large-scale enterprise that so markedly influences how the landscape is being exploited and how the urban functions are spreading out, and we are headed for a situation where it is only with great difficulty that the space will be held together, cohesively, in a narrational picture containing other dimensions than the purely practical. This being the case, the intrinsic value which makes life worth living, which all practical dealings ought to serve, has now become invisible in the urban space. These are the questions that the assignment addresses: Can meanings be created in this thoroughly regulated space, meanings that address themselves to indivisible values? Where are the places in the city's space that can be re-adapted in such a way that the city's practical function and aesthetic content can sprout forth from one another? And finally, can such notions become a common target for the myriad of resolutions that are constantly developing and converting the urban space?

The assignment is ushered in with four articles, each of which illuminates from its very own point of view the relationship between the city's spaces and the culture in which these spaces play a role and, in doing so, the four articles speak about the dissociations and the coherences in the life that the city reflects.
In his article, "Of Other Spaces, Utopias and Heterotopias", Michel Foucault views the city as a historically determined order of spaces which organizes the society in relation to the prevalent outlook and disciplines the citizens so that they can operate in accordance with that rationality which gets the societal whole to function.

Within this order, which is constituted in the urban space by functionally allocated fields with a network of connections, Foucault directs the attention toward those fields like cemeteries, temporary markets and theaters which are positioned outside or which assume an exceptional position by virtue of being connected with all the other fields in the city. These fields, which he designates as heterotopias, are affiliated with the utopias' imaginative spaces but, in contradistinction, they are indeed real places in the city. By pointing out the heterotopias, Foucault emphasizes that fantasy's space has had its place in the city and that it will have to continue being a vital constituent in the city's order if the city is to avoid manifesting itself as a monitored labor camp.
For Louis Kahn, it is a given internal coherence between nature, the individual and society which establishes apriori the basis for the meaning of space. It is the proper task of architecture to articulate this connection and to respect it, both in the design of the buildings and in the design of the city. Basically, the city's space is a place for meetings: the meeting with the world as a given and the meeting with our fellow man as an ally in the open project of existence. It is this intuitively grasped connection with the world, which in the case of mankind turns into an aspiration, that creates society, the institutions, civilization and its material form. For Kahn, it is the dwelling that is the primary institution. Here, religion, technology, art and science are already at the beginning present in the forms as expression and implement for this aspiration which has today brought forth metropolises and explorations in outer space. "The Room, the Street and Human Agreement", as Kahn's piece is entitled, articulates this intimate connection - between the individual and the many, between the private and the public - which engenders the space's architectonic categories. In Kahn's perspective, these categories are institutions which architecture renders meaningful and vivid by actualizing the poetry of the beginning within them. In doing so, architecture renews the horizon of meaning, to which civilization addresses its exertions.
Jean Baudrillard's article, "The Evil Demon of Images",

treats of the effect that the media-picture has on the culture and on the relation to reality. He ascribes to architecture a visual property on a par with painting, inasmuch as it can get us to dream. All the way through the article, however, Baudrillard underscores how the media-picture models the perception of reality and how it disfigures and exhausts that same aspiration which Kahn holds up to the light. The technological pictures have superseded reality and have become what we aspire to, with the result that the longing for the space which is the very source of architecture has now been channeled into a charter-tour economy. Reality, the city, the landscape and the body are presented in the picture with a realism, a perfection and a repetitive effect which, in their intensity, surpass any other glance. The media-picture is emptied of references to anything that precedes the picture and at the same time it aestheticizes that banality which characterizes the urban space, which is no longer brought about by any spatially committed attentiveness.

It is in the media-picture's capacity to react to things, to multiply them and hollow them out into being pure images that the culture's transparency dwells. That which is supplanted in this transparency is the selective glance, the glance for which not everything is visible all at one time and from where the interplay of meanings arises.

In Vittorio Gregotti's article entitled "On Atopia", a decisive split between the building and the ground area upon which it is erected is described. This rupture takes its point of departure in the modern utopia which revolves around rationality and progress. Today, however, this utopia is realized in the forces of the market, which are bound in no way to considerations of solidarity. The dream about human equality has been reduced to a world-encompassing space of similarizing functions. Shaped according to a frictionless meeting between mass producers and mass consumers within which the locality's spatial and social characteristics and these entities' interplay are all being eradicated. All of the market's apparent incongruities are fundamentally coded by the same stringently reduced logic which, like a standardizing force, smoothes over the space and removes the foundation for authentic differences that give depth to cultures, regions and the space. Gregotti points out that, in recent years when it has been steadily intensifying in its effect, this development has been proceeding in direct opposition to the criteria of values that are simultaneously unifying what might be called the culture of architecture. It is in this discrepancy that Gregotti sees the urgent necessity for a dialogue, a communicative public action, which can, with all the experiences embodied by a culture, enlarge the narrow forms of logic which up until the present time seem to be enjoying such a free rein on shaping society's space in their own image.

The four articles cast a critical light on the city's recent developments and on its current condition. Where Foucault emphasizes fantasy's indispensable place in the city's pattern of localities is just where Baudrillard shows that fantasy and reality have been ousted to an equal degree in the canonized image of the surrounding world and indicates that this reacts to the architectonic space. Where Kahn points toward the intimate connection between people at a given place as an inalienable point of departure for architecture is right where Gregotti describes the globally effective forces that are decomposing these connections. What is inherent in the articles' critical perspectives is a profoundly potent reminiscence about value and meaning in the city's capacity to tie the many individual worlds together into one greater and inspiring whole.

That this perspective can and must be set into a continuing development and into an architectonic condensation, the city's space, constitutes the genuine ambition of this book.

In the introductory draft for the assignment, it is ascertained that it is a task of planning - and evidently, often a neglected one - to come up with the prerequisites necessary for being able, in a local building assignment, to take part in designing space that will engender coherence that runs across the proper limits of the individual task at hand: New street scenes, around which the functionally partitioned cities can orient themselves, will provide a content and a character. New contexts, which can surround the individual human being in such a way that one is not always referred into feeling sequestered, and always on the way somewhere else, somewhere that lies at some other desolate place, but renders it possible to be smack dab in the middle of the space, which is sufficiently encompassing and nuanced for being a "here".

In other words, the proposals in the book are not building on concrete, presently proposed assignment programs but rather on that potential that the architects are discovering in a number of existing localities where the projects formulate this: It would be possible to do this, right here; these considerations would be the right ones to implement, concerning this particular site's future. In this way, the projects can serve as studies for a planning effort, which will be imperative for guiding the interplay of public and private interests into a constructional perspective that can be more coherent than is often seen when the separate interests obtain their own controlled spheres.

In the introductory draft, the notion of transition is described both as a physical link and a mental, meaningful coherence which is procured by the space's design. This is correlated with a number of conflicting interests that make their mark on the urban space with an intensity that is often perceived as constituting reality's inevasible demand. Conflicting interests that manifest themselves in different ways and in a variety of compoundings on different levels of scale in the city. These levels of scale are designated in the assignment as typologies that can be denoted: The Collective Space, The Space's Middle Ground and The Edge of the Space. The collective space is the greatest scale. It is constituted by the large-scale space of mixed interests within which we live and work; it is no longer in possession of the public space's character effected through the representation of ideals upon which the community rests. The space's middle ground is the intermediate scale. It is the space that combines the private sphere with the city and which, to an ever increasing extent, is being emptied of functional coherence and social solidarity. The edge of the space is the smallest scale, in the sense that it is through the space's detail that referral is made to the common framework of understanding that constitutes today's horizon. Any period of time can be said to have a horizon of understanding which establishes a boundary, or an edge, within its space. This horizon of understanding can be experienced from within the space as all-encompassing, but it can also be seen as a threshold to something which lies outside, which has been crowded out from the current space of understanding, or to something which is even greater and even more encompassing.

The introductory draft for the assignment selects a number of transitional areas which in the near future might very conceivably be called in to the city's evolution and which contain the typologies' salient features. What we have here are typical situations, conceived as stimuli for the work and not as fixed frames, which mark out a singular individual assignment for each architect. This is why you'll find several different proposals for the same area, and some of the areas in question have not been dealt with at all, while other areas which were not selected from the outset are called into play. What is firmly fixed, however, in the disposition of the assignment is that for each typology, three architects have been chosen to work within the parameters of the pertinent scale. The nine resulting contributions thus group themselves in three parts, which are arranged accordingly, the one following the other.

OF OTHER SPACES: UTOPIAS AND HETEROTOPIAS

Michel Foucault

As is well known, the great and obsessive dread of the nineteenth century was history, with its themes of development and stagnation, crisis and cycle, the accumulation of the past, the surplus of the dead and the world threatened by cooling. The nineteenth century found the quintessence of its mythological resources in the second law of thermodynamics. Our own era, on the other hand, seems to be that of space. We are in the age of the simultaneous, of juxtaposition, the near and the far, the side by side and the scattered. A period in which, in my view, the world is putting itself to the test, not so much as a great way of life destined to grow in time but as a net that links points together and creates its own muddle. It might be said that certain ideological conflicts which underlie the controversies of our day take place between pious descendants of time and tenacious inhabitants of space. Structuralism – or at least what is lumped together under this rather too vague label – is the attempt to establish between elements that may have been split over the course of time, a set of relationships that juxtapose them, set them in opposition or link them together, so as to create a sort of shape. Actually it is not so much a question of denying time as of a certain way of dealing with what we call time and which goes by the name of history.

For one thing, the space which now looms on the horizon of our preoccupations, our theories and our systems, is not an innovation in Western history, having a history of its own. Nor is it possible to deny its fatal entanglement with time. To provide a very rough outline of its history, it could be said that there was a hierarchical system of places in the Middle Ages: places that were sacred and profane, protected and, on the contrary, open and undefended, urban places and rural places (for the real life of men anyhow). In cosmological theory, supercelestial places existed, in contrast to the celestial place, opposed in its turn to the terrestrial place; there were places where things could be found because they had been shifted there by violence and there were other places where, on the contrary, things found their natural position and rest. This hierarchy, contrast, and mingling of places made up that which might, very approximately, be called medieval space. That is to say, the space of localization.

This space of localization was opened up by Galileo, for the real scandal caused by Galileo's work was not the discovery, or rediscovery, of the earth's movement around the sun, but the assertion of an infinite and infinitely open space, in which the space of the Middle Ages was to some extent dissolved. The location of a thing, in fact, was no longer anything more than a point in its movement, its rest nothing but its movement slowed down infinitely. In other words, from Galileo onward, ever since the seventeenth century, localization was replaced by extension.

Nowadays arrangement has taken over from extension, which had once replaced localization. It is defined by relationships of neighborhood between points and elements, which can be described formally as series, trees, and networks.

On the other hand, we know very well the importance of the problems of arrangements in contemporary technology: storage of information or of the partial results of a calculation in the memory of a machine; circulation of discrete elements to random outlets (automobiles, for instance, or even sounds transmitted over telephone lines); location of labeled or coded elements within a randomly divided set, or one that is classified according to univocal or multiple systems, etc.

In a still more concrete manner, the problem of position is posed for men in demographic terms. The question of the arrangement of the earth's inhabitants is not just one of knowing whether there will be enough room for all of them – a problem that is in any case of the greatest importance – but also one of knowing what are the relations of vicinity, what kind of storage, circulation, reference, and classification of human elements should take preference in this or that situation, according to the objective that is being sought. In our era, space presents itself to us in the form of patterns of ordering.

In any case, I feel that current anxiety is fundamentally concerned with space, much more than with time: the latter, probably, merely appears to us as one of the many possible patterns of distribution between elements that are scattered over space.

Now, it may be that contemporary space has not yet lost those sacred characteristics (which time certainly lost in the nineteenth century), in spite of all the techniques that assail it and the web of knowledge that allows it to be defined and formalized. Of course, a theoretical desanctification of space, for which Galileo's work gave the signal, has already occurred: it remains to be seen whether we have achieved its desanctification in practice. It may be, in fact, that our lives are still ruled by a certain number of unrelenting opposites, which institution and practice have not dared to erode. I refer here to opposites that we take for granted, such as the contrast between public and private space, family and social space, cultural and utilitarian space, the space of pleasure and the space of work – all opposites that are still actuated by a veiled sacredness.

The (immense) work of Bachelard and the descriptions of the phenomenologists have taught us that we do not live in a homogeneous and empty space, but in a space that is saturated with qualities, and that may even be pervaded by a spectral aura. The space of our primary perception, of our dreams and of our passions, holds within itself almost intrinsic qualities: it is light, ethereal, transparent, or dark, uneven, cluttered. Again, it is a space of height, of peaks, or on the contrary, of the depths of mud; space that flows, like spring water, or fixed space, like stone or crystal.

In any case, these analyses, however fundamental for contemporary thought, are primarily concerned with inner space. But it is about external space that I would like to speak now. The space in which we live, from which we are drawn out of ourselves, just where the erosion of our lives, our time, our history takes place, this space that wears us down and consumes us, is in itself heterogeneous. In other words, we do not live in a sort of a vacuum, within which individuals and things can be located, or that may take on so many different fleeting colors, but in a set of relationships that define positions which cannot be equated or in any way superimposed.

Certainly, one could undertake the description of these different arrangements, looking for the set of relationships that defines them. For instance, by describing the set of relationships that defines arrangements of transition, roads, trains (and, with regard to the latter, think of the extraordinary bundle of relations represented by something through which one passes, by means of which we pass from one point to another, and which, in its turn, has the power of passing). Through the sets of relationships that define them, one could describe arrangements where one makes a temporary halt: cafes, cinemas, beaches. It would be equally possible to define, through its network of relations, the arrangements of rest, closed or partly open, that make up the house, the bedroom, the bed, etc.... However I am only interested in a few of these arrangements: to be precise, those which are endowed with the curious property of being in relation with all the others, but in such a way as to suspend, neutralize, or invert the set of relationships designed, reflected, or mirrored by themselves. These spaces, which are in rapport in some way with all the others, and yet contradict them, are of two general types.

First of all, the utopias. These are arrangements which have no real space. Arrangements which have a general relationship of direct or inverse analogy with the real space of society. They represent society itself brought to perfection, or its reverse, and in any case utopias are spaces that are by their very essence fundamentally unreal.

There also exist, and this is probably true for all cultures and all civilizations, real and effective spaces which are outlined in the very institution of society, but which constitute a sort of counterarrangement, of effectively realized utopia, in which all the real arrangements, all the other real arrangements that can be found within society, are at one and the same time represented, challenged, and overturned: a sort of place that lies outside all places and yet is actually localizable. In contrast to the utopias, these places which are absolutely *other* with respect to all the arrangements that they reflect and of which they speak might be described as heterotopias. Between these two, I would then set that sort of mixed experience which partakes of the qualities of both types of location, the mirror. It is, after all, a utopia, in that it is a place without a place. In it, I see myself where I am not, in an unreal space that opens up potentially beyond its surface; there I am down there where I am not, a sort of shadow that makes my appearance visible to myself, allowing me to look at myself where I do not exist: utopia of the mirror. At the same time, we are dealing with a heterotopia. The mirror really exists and has a kind of comeback effect on the place that I occupy: starting from it, in fact, I find myself absent from the place where I am, in that I see myself in there.

Starting from that gaze which to some extent is brought to bear on me, from the depths of that virtual space which is on the other side of the mirror, I turn back on myself, beginning to turn my eyes on myself and reconstitute myself where I am in reality. Hence the mirror functions as a heterotopia, since it makes the place that I occupy, whenever I look at myself in the glass, both absolutely real – it is in fact linked to all the surrounding space – and absolutely unreal, for in order to be perceived it has of necessity to pass that virtual point that is situated down there.

As for the heterotopias in the proper sense of the word, how can we describe them? What meaning do they have? We might postulate, not a science, a now overworked word, but a sort of systematic description. Given a particular society, this would have as its object the study, analysis, description, and "reading," as it is the fashion to call it nowadays, of those different spaces, those other places, in a kind of both mythical and real contestation of the space in which we live. Such a description might be called heterotopology. Its first principle is that there is probably not a single culture in the world that is not made up of heterotopias. It is a constant feature of all human groups. It is evident, though, that heterotopias assume a wide variety of forms, to the extent that a single, absolutely universal form may not exist. In any case, it is possible to classify them into two main types. In so-called primitive societies, there is a certain kind of heterotopia which I would describe as that of crisis; it comprises privileged or sacred or forbidden places that are reserved for the individual who finds himself in a state of crisis with respect to the society or the environment in which he lives: adolescents, women during the menstrual period or in labor, the old, etc.

In our own society, these heterotopias of crisis are steadily disappearing, even though some vestiges of them are bound to survive. For instance, the boarding school in its nineteenth-century form or military service for young men has played a role of this kind, so that the first manifestations of male sexuality could occur 'elsewhere," away from the family. For girls there was, up until the middle of this century, the tradition of the honeymoon, or "voyage de noces" as it is called in French, an ancestral theme. The girl's defloration could not take place "anywhere" and at that time, the train or the honeymoon hotel represented that place which was not located anywhere, a heterotopia without geographical coordinates.

Yet these heterotopias of crisis are vanishing today, only to be replaced, I believe, by others which could be described as heterotopias of deviance, occupied by individuals whose behavior deviates from the current average or standard. They are the rest homes, psychiatric clinics, and, let us be clear, prisons, in a list which must undoubtedly be extended to cover old-people's homes, in a way on the border between the heterotopia of crisis and that of deviance. This is because in a society like our own, where pleasure is the rule, the inactivity of old age constitutes not only a crisis but a deviation. The second element of my description: over the course of its history, a society may take an existing heterotopia, which has never vanished, and make it function in a very different way. Actually, each heterotopia has a precise and well-defined function within society and the same heterotopia can, in accordance with the synchroneity of the culture in which it is located, have a different function.

Let us take, for example, the curious heterotopia of the cemetery. This is certainly an "other" place with respect to ordinary cultural spaces, and yet it is connected with all the locations of the city, the society, the village, and so on, since every family has some relative there. In Western culture, one might say that it has always existed. And yet it has undergone important changes.

Up until the end of the eighteenth century, the cemetery was located in the very heart of the city, near the church. Within it, there existed a hierarchy of every possible type of tomb. There was an ossuary where the corpses lost their last traces of individuality, there were some individual tombs, and there were the graves inside the church, which conformed to two models, either a simple slab of marble, or a mausoleum with statues, etc. The cemetery, situated in the sacred space of the church, has taken on quite another character in modern civilization. It is curious to note that in an age which has been very roughly defined as "atheist, Western culture has inaugurated the so-called cult of the dead.

After all, it was very natural that, as long as people actually believed in the resurrection of the body and the immortality of the soul, not a great deal of importance was given to the mortal remains. On the contrary, from the moment when people were no longer so certain of survival after death, it became logical to take much more care with the remains of the dead, the only trace, in the end, of our existence in the world and in words.

In any case, it is from the nineteenth century onward that each of us has had the right to his own little box for his little personal decomposition, but it is only from the nineteenth century on that the cemetery began to be shifted to the outskirts of the city. In parallel to this individualization of death and the bourgeois appropriation of the cemetery, an obsession with death as "sickness" has emerged. It is supposed that the dead transmit sickness to the living and that their presence and proximity to the houses and church, almost in the middle of the street, spreads death. This great concern with the spread of sickness by contagion from cemeteries began to appear with insistence toward the end of the eighteenth century, but the cemeteries only moved out to the suburbs during the course of the nineteenth. From then on, they no longer constituted the sacred and immortal wind of the city, but the "other city," where each family possessed its gloomy dwelling.

Third principle. The heterotopia has the power of juxtaposing in a single real place different spaces and locations that are incompatible with each other. Thus on the rectangle of its stage, the theater alternates as a series of places that are alien to each other; thus the cinema appears as a very curious rectangular hall, at the back of which a three-dimensional space is projected onto a two-dimensional screen. Perhaps the oldest example of these heterotopias in the form of contradictory locations is the garden. Let us not forget that this astounding and age-old creation had very profound meanings in the East, and that these seemed to be superimposed. The traditional garden of the Persians was a sacred space that was supposed to unite four separate parts within its rectangle, representing the four parts of the world, as well as one space still more sacred than the others, a space that was like the navel, the center of the world brought into the garden (it was here that the basin and jet of water were located). All the vegetation was concentrated in this zone, as if in a sort of microcosm. As for carpets, they originally set out to reproduce gardens, since the garden was a carpet where the world in its entirety achieved symbolic perfection, and the carpet a sort of movable garden in space. The garden is the smallest fragment of the world and, at the same time, represents its totality, forming right from the remotest times a sort of felicitous and universal heterotopia (from which are derived our own zoological gardens).

Fourth principle. Heterotopias are linked for the most part to bits and pieces of time, i.e., they open up through what we might define as a pure symmetry of heterochronisms. The heterotopia enters fully into function when men find themselves in a sort of total breach of their traditional time. Then it is easy to see how the cemetery is a highly heterotopian place, in that it begins with that strange heterochronism that is, for a human being, the loss of life and of that quasi-eternity in which, however, he does not cease to dissolve and be erased.

Generally speaking, in a society like ours, heterotopia and heterochronism are organized and arranged in a relatively complex fashion. In the first place there are the heterotopias of time which accumulate *ad infinitum*, such as museums and libraries. These are heterotopias in which time does not cease to accumulate, perching, so to speak, on its own summit. Yet up until the end of the seventeenth century, these had still been the expression of an individual choice. The idea of accumulating everything, on the contrary, of creating a sort of universal archive, the desire to enclose all times, all eras, forms, and styles within a single place, the concept of making all times into one place, and yet a place that is outside time, inaccessible to the wear and tear of the years, according to a plan of almost perpetual and unlimited accumulation within an irremovable place, all this belongs entirely to our modern outlook. Museums and libraries are heterotopias typical of nineteenth-century Western culture.

Along with this type, bound up with the accumulation of time, there are other heterotopias linked to time in its more futile, transitory and precarious aspects, a time viewed as celebration. These then are heterotopias without a bias toward the eternal. They are absolutely time-bound. To this class belong the fairs, those marvelous empty zones outside the city limits, that fill up twice a year with booths, showcases, miscellaneous objects; wrestlers, snake-women, optimistic fortune-tellers, etc. Very recently, a new form of chronic heterotopia has been invented, that of the holiday village: a sort of Polynesian village which offers three short weeks of primitive and eternal nudity to city dwellers. It's easy to see, on the other hand, how the two types of heterotopia, that of the festival and that of the eternity of accumulating time, come together: the huts on the island of Jerba are relatives in a way of the libraries and museums. And in fact, by rediscovering Polynesian life, is not time abolished at the very moment in which it is found again? It is the whole story of humanity that dates right back to the origins, like a kind of great and immediate knowledge.

Fifth principle. Heterotopias always presuppose a system of opening and closing that isolates them and makes them penetrable at one and the same time. Usually, one does not get into a heterotopian location by one's own will. Either one is forced, as in the case of the barracks or the prison, or one must submit to rites of purification. One can only enter by special permission and after one has completed a certain number of gestures. Heterotopias also exist that are entirely devoted to practices of purification that are half religious, half hygienic (the Muslim "hammams"), or apparently solely hygienic (Scandinavian saunas).

Other heterotopias, on the contrary, have the appearance of pure and simple openings, although they usually conceal curious exclusions. Anyone can enter one of these heterotopian locations, but, in reality, they are nothing more than an illusion: one thinks one has entered and, by the sole fact of entering, one is excluded. I am reminded, for instance, of those famous rooms to be found on big farms in Brazil and throughout South America in general. The front door did not give onto the main part of the house, where the family lived, so that any person who happened to pass by, any traveler, had the right to push open that door, enter the room, and spend the night there. Now, the rooms were arranged in such a way that anyone who went in there could never reach to the heart of the family: more than ever a passing visitor, never a true guest. This type of heterotopia, which has now almost entirely vanished from our civilization, might perhaps be recognized in the American "motel" room, which one enters with ones own vehicle and lover and where illicit sex is totally protected and totally concealed at one and the same time, set apart and yet not under an open sky.

Finally, the last characteristic of heterotopias is that they have, in relation to the rest of space, a function that takes place between two opposite poles. On the one hand they perform the task of creating a space of illusion that reveals how all of real space is more illusory, all the locations within which life is fragmented. On the other, they have the function of forming another space, another real space, as perfect, meticulous, and well-arranged as ours is disordered, ill-conceived, and in a sketchy state. This heterotopia is not one of illusion but of compensation, and I wonder if it is not somewhat in this manner that certain colonies have functioned.

In a number of cases they have played, at the level of the general organization of terrestrial space, the genuine role of a heterotopia. An example of this, from the first wave of colonization in the seventeenth century, might be some of the Puritan colonies founded by the English in America, which were absolutely perfect places.

Or those extraordinary Jesuit colonies, set up in South America: wonderful, totally regulated colonies, inwhich human perfection was actually reached. The Jesuits of Paraguay had established settlements in which existence was regulated point by point. The village was laid out according to a strict pattern around a rectangular square at one end of which stood the church; on one side, the college, on the other the cemetery, while, facing the church, there was a street which met another at a right angle. Each family's hut lay on one of these two axes, reproducing exactly the symbol of Christ. Thus Christianity made its fundamental mark on the space and geography of the American world. The daily life of individuals was regulated not by the whistle, but by the bell: the same hour of awakening laid down for all, with meals at midday and five o'clock. Afterward people went to bed and, at midnight, came what was known as the conjugal awakening: at this sound of the monastery's bell, each of them did his and her duty.

Brothels and colonies, here are two extreme types of heterotopia. Think of the ship: it is a floating part of space, a placeless place, that lives by itself, closed in on itself and at the same time poised in the infinite ocean, and yet, from port to port, tack by tack, from brothel to brothel, it goes as far as the colonies, looking for the most precious things hidden in their gardens. Then you will understand why it has been not only and obviously the main means of economic growth (which I do not intend to go into here), but at the same time the greatest reserve of imagination for our civilization from the sixteenth century down to the present day. The ship is the heterotopia par *excellence*, in civilizations where it is lacking, dreams dry up, adventure is replaced by espionage, and privateers by the police.

(Published in "Architecture Culture 1943-1968, Joan Ockman (ed.), Columbia University, Graduate School of Architecture, Planning and Preservation. New York. Translation: Jay Miskowiec.
Published originally as "Des Espaces Autres" in Architecture Mouvement Continuité 5 (October 1984, pp.46-49)
© 1993, The Trustees of columbia University in the City of New York and Rizzoli International Publications, inc.)

THE ROOM, THE STREET AND HUMAN AGREEMENT

Louis I. Kahn

I have some thoughts about the spirit of architecture. I have chosen to talk about the room, the street, and human agreement.

The room is the beginning of architecture.

It is the place of the mind.

You in the room with its dimensions, its structure, its light respond to its character, its spiritual aura, recognizing that whatever the human proposes and makes becomes a life.

The structure of a room must be evident in the room itself. Structure I believe is the giver of light. A square room asks for its own light to read the square. It would expect the light either from above or from its four sides as windows or entrances.

Sensitive is the Pantheon. This non-directional room dedicated to all religions has its light only from the oculus above, placed to invest the room with inspired ritual without favoritism. The entrance door is its only impurity.

So powerful was this realization of appropriate space that even now the room seems to ask for its release to its original freedom.

Of the elements of a room the window is the most marvelous. The great American poet, Wallace Stevens, prodded the architect, "What slice of the sun does your building have?"

To paraphrase: what slice of the sun enters your room. What a range of mood does the light offer from morning to night, from day to day, from season to season and all through the years.

Gratifying and unpredictable are the permissions the architect has given to the chosen opening on which patches of sunlight play on the jamb and sill that enter, move, and disappear.

Stevens seemed to tell us that the sun was not aware of its wonder until it struck the side of a building.

Enter your room and know how personal, how much you feel its life. In a small room with just another person what you say you may never have said before.

It is different when there is more than just another person. Then in this little room the singularity of each is so sensitive that the vectors do not resolve. The meeting becomes a performance instead of an event, everyone saying their lines, saying what they said many times before.

Still in a large room the event is of commonalty. Rapport would take the place of thought.

This room we are in is big without distinction. The walls are far away yet I know if I were to address myself to a chosen person whose smile would tell me of appreciation I believe the walls of the room would come together and the room would become intimate.

If I were now reading, the concern would be diction. If this room were the Baptistery of Florence, however, its image would have inspired thoughts in the same way as person to person, architect to architect.

So sensitive is a room.

The plan is a society of rooms.

The rooms relate to each other to strengthen their own unique nature. The auditorium wants to be a violin. Its lobby is the violin case.

The society of rooms is the place where it is good to learn, good to live, good to work.

Open before us is the architect's plan. Next to it is a sheet of music.

The architect fleetingly reads his composition as a structure of elements and spaces in their light.

The musician reads, with the same overallness, his composition as a structure of inseparable elements and spaces in sound.

A great musical composition is of such entity that when played conveys the feeling that all that was heard was assembled in a cloud over us. Nothing is gone as though time and sound have become a single image.

The corridor has no position except as a private passage. In a school the boy walks across a hall as in his own classroom where he is his own teacher observing others as others do. The hall asks for equal position with the library.

The society of rooms is knit together with the elements of connection which have their own characteristics.

The stair is the same for the child, the adult and the old. It is thought of as precise in its measures particularly for the young boy who aspires to do the floors in no time flat both up and down. It is good also to consider its landing as a place to sit, near a window with possibly a shelf for a few books. The old man ascending with the young boy can stop here, showing his interest in a certain book and avoid the explanations of infirmity.

The landing wants to be a room.

The bay window can be the private room within a room.

A closet with a window becomes a room ready to be rearranged.

The lightless corridor, never a room, aspires to the hall overlooking the garden.

The library, the work court, the rooms of study, the place of meeting want to group themselves in a composition that evokes Architecture.

The libraries of all university schools sit well in a court entrance available to all its students as a place of invitation.

The entrance courts and their libraries and the gardens and paths knitting them together form an architecture of connection.

The book is an offering of the mind.

The work court of a school of architecture is an inner space encircled by workshops available to construct building experiments. The rooms of study and criticism are of a variety of dimension and spaces in their light, small for the intimate talk and work and large for the making of full size drawings and group work.

Rooms must suggest their use without name.

For an architect a school of architecture would be the most honored commission.

The Street is a room of agreement.

The street is dedicated by each house owner to the city in exchange for common services.

Dead-end streets in cities today still retain this room character. Thru streets, since the advent of the automobile, have entirely lost their room quality. I believe city planning can start with realization of this loss by directing the drive to reinstate the street where people live, learn, shop and work as the room out of commonalty.

Today we can begin by planting trees on all existing residential streets, by redefining the order of movement which would give these streets back to more intimate use, which in turn would stimulate the feelings of well being, and inspire unique street expression.

The street is a community room.

The meeting house is a community room under a roof. It seems as though one came naturally out of the other.

A long street is a succession of rooms given their distinction, room for room, by their meeting of crossing streets. The intersecting street brings the remote from afar; it infiltrates any opening it meets. One block in a stream of blocks can be more preferred because of its particular life. One realizes the deadliness of uninterested movement through our streets, which erases all delicacy of character and blots out its sensitive nature given to it of human agreement.

Human Agreement is a sense of rapport, of commonness, all bells ringing in unison — not needing to be understood by example but felt as an undeniable inner demand for a presence. It is an inspiration with the promise of the possible.

Dissension does not stem from need but from the mad outburst of frustration. From the mad outburst of frustration. From the hopelessness of the farawayness of human agreement.

Desire, not need, the forerunner of the new need, out of the yet not said and yet not made, seems to be the roots of hope in dissension.

How inspiring would be the time when the sense of human agreement is felt as the force which brings new images. Such images reflecting inspirations and put into being by inspired technology.

Basing our challenges on present day programming and existing technologies can only bring new facets of old work.

The city from a simple settlement became the place of the assembled institutions. The settlement was the first institution. The talents found their places. The carpenter directed building. The thoughtful man became the teacher. The strong one the leader.

When one thinks of simple beginnings which inspired our present institutions, it is evident that some drastic changes must be made which will inspire the re-creation of the meaning, City, as primarily an assembly of those places vested with the care to uphold the sense of a way of life.

Human agreement has always been and will always be. It does not belong to measurable qualities and is therefore eternal. The opportunities which present its nature depend on circumstances and events from which human nature realizes itself.

A city is measured by the character of its institutions. The street is one of its first institutions. Today these institutions are on trial. I believe it is so because they have lost the inspirations of their beginning. The institutions of learning must stem from the undeniable feeling in all of us of a desire to learn. I have often thought this feeling came from the way we were made, that nature records in everything it makes how it was made. This record is also in man and it is this within us that urges us to seek its story involving the laws of the universe, the source of all material and means, and the psyche the source of all expression, Art.

The desire to learn made the first school room. It was of human agreement. The institution became the modus operandi. Agreement has the immediacy of rapport, the inspiring force which recognizes its commonalty and that it must be part of the human way of life supported by all people.

The institution will die when its inspirations are no longer felt and operate as a matter of course. Human agreement, however, once it presents itself as a realization is indestructible. For the same reason that a man is unable to work below his level of comprehension.

To explain inspiration I like to believe that it is the moment of possibility when what to do meets the means of doing it.

City planning must begin to be cognizant of the strength and character of our present institutions and be sensitive to the pulse of human relations, which senses the new inspirations which would bring about new and meaningful institutions. Traffic systems, sociological speculations, new materials, new technologies are servants to the pulse of human rapport which promises revelations yet not felt but in the very core of human desires.

New spaces will come only from a new sense of human agreement which will affirm a promise of a way of life and will reveal new availabilities and point to human support for their establishment.

In India and Pakistan I realized that a great majority of the people are without ambition because there is no way in which they are able to elevate themselves beyond living from hand to mouth and what is worse, talents have no outlet. To express is the reason for living. The institution of learning, of work, of health, or recreation should be made available to all people. All realms of expression will be opened. Each singularity will express in his way.

Availabilities to all can be the source of a tremendous release of the values locked within the unmeasurable in living, the art of living.

One city can distinguish itself from the other by just the inspirational qualities that exist in sensing natural agreement as the only true source of new realizations.

In that sense the spaces where it is good to learn, where it is good to live and work may remain unexpressed if their nature is not redefined.

It is not enough just to solve the problem. To imbue the spaces with newfound self-quality is a different question entirely. Solution is a 'how' design problem, the realization of 'what' precedes it.

About Inspired Technology.

The wall that enclosed us for a long time until the man behind it, feeling a new freedom, wanted to look out. He hammered away to make an opening. The wall cried, "I have protected you." And the man said, "I appreciate your faithfulness, but I feel time has brought change".

The wall was sad, man realized something good. He visualized the opening as gracefully arched, glorifying the wall. The wall was terribly pleased with its arch and carefully made jamb. The opening became part of the order of the wall.

The world with its many people, each one a singularity, each group of different experiences revealing the nature of the human in varied aspects is full of the possibility of more richly sensing human agreement from which new architecture will come. The world cannot be expected to come from the exercise of present technology alone to find the realms of new expression. I believe that technology should be inspired. A good plan demands it.

A word about silence and light.

A building being built is not yet in servitude. It is so anxious to be that no grass can grow under its feet, so high is the spirit of wanting to be. When it is in service and finished, the building wants to say, "Look, I want to tell you about the way I was made." Nobody listens. Everybody is busy going from room to room.

But when the building is a ruin and free of servitude, the spirit emerges telling of the marvel that a building was made.

When we think of the great buildings of the past that had no precedent, we always refer to the Parthenon.

We say it is the building that grew out of the wall with opening. We can say, in the Parthenon, light is the space between the columns; a rhythm of light, no-light, light, no-light which tells the tremendous story of light in architecture that came from the wall.

We are simply extending what happened long ago; the beginning may be considered the most marvelous; without precedent yet its making was as sure as life.

Light is material life. The mountains, the streams, the atmosphere is spent light.

Material, non-conscious, moving to desire; desire to express, conscious, moving to light all meet at an aura threshold where the will senses the possible.

The first feeling was of Beauty, the first sense of harmony, of man undefinable, unmeasurable and measurable material, the maker.

At the threshold, the crossing of silence and light, lies the sanctuary of Art, the only language of man. It is the treasury of the shadows. Whatever is made of light casts a shadow. Our work is of shadow. It belongs to light.

When the astronauts went through space, the earth presented itself as a marvelous ball, blue and rose, in space. Since I followed it and saw it that way, all knowledge left me as being unimportant. Truly, knowledge is an incomplete book outside of us. You take from it to know something, but knowing cannot be imparted to the next man. Knowing is private. It gives singularity the means for self-expression.

I believe that the greatest work of man is that part which does not belong to him alone. If he discovers a principle, only his design way of interpreting belongs to him alone. The discovery of oxygen does not belong to the discoverer.

I invented a story about Mozart. Somebody dropped a dish in his kitchen, and it made a hell of a noise. The servants jumped, and Mozart said, "Ah! Dissonance." And immediately dissonance belonged to music, and the way he wrote interpreting it belonged to him.

Architects must not accept the commercial divisions of their profession into urban design, city planning and architecture as though they were three different professions.

The architect can turn from the smallest house to the greatest complex, or the city. Specializing ruins the essence of the revelation of Form with its inseparable parts realized only as an entity.

A word about Beauty.

Beauty is an all-prevailing sense of harmony, giving rise to wonder, from it, revelations.

Poetry. Is it in beauty? Is it in wonder? Is it in the revelation?

It is in the beginning, in first thought, in the first sense of the means of expression.

A poet is deeply in thought of beauty and existence. Yet a poem is only an offering which to the poet is less.

A work of architecture is but an offering to the spirit of Architecture and its poetic beginning.

(Printed in *A+U*, Vol.3. no.1, 1973)

EXCERPTS FROM "THE EVIL DEMON OF IMAGES"

Jean Baudrillard

Summary: In the dialectical relationship between the real and the image it is, as far as we are concerned, the image that has triumphed. It has imposed its own inherent, short-lived and amoral logic, a logic of the eradication of its own reference and a logic where meaning implodes as the message vanishes from the medium. The image is not a carrier of meaning; in a manner of speaking, it revolts against that usefulness which we naïvely attribute to it. The image assumes the place of reality.

Apropos the cinema and images in general (media images, technological images), I would like to conjure up the perversity of the relation between the image and its referent, the supposed real; the virtual and irreversible confusion of the sphere of images and the sphere of a reality whose nature we are less and less able to grasp. There are many modalities of this absorption, this confusion, this diabolical seduction of images. Above all, it is the reference principle of images which must be doubted, this strategy by means of which they always appear to refer to a real world, to real objects, and to reproduce something which is logically and chronologically anterior to themselves. None of this is true. As simulacra, images precede the real to the extent that they invert the causal and logical order of the real and its reproduction. Benjamin, in his essay 'The Work of Art in the Age of Mechanical Reproduction', already pointed out strongly this modern revolution in the order of production (of reality, of meaning) by the precession, the anticipation of its reproduction.

It is precisely when it appears most truthful, most faithful and most in conformity to reality that the image is most diabolical – and our technical images, whether they be from photography, cinema or television, are in the overwhelming majority much more 'figurative', 'realist', than all the images from past cultures. It is in its resemblance, not only analogical but technological, that the image is most immoral and most perverse.

The appearance of the mirror already introduced into the world of perception an ironical effect of *trompe-l'oeil*, and we know what malefice was attached to the appearance of doubles. But this is also true of all the images which surround us: in general, they are analyzed according to their value as representations, as media of presence and meaning. The immense majority of present day photographic, cinematic and television images are thought to bear witness to the world with a naive resemblance and a touching fidelity. We have spontaneous confidence in their realism. We are wrong. They only seem to resemble things, to resemble reality, events, faces. Or rather, they really do conform, but their conformity itself is diabolical.

We can find a sociological, historical and political equivalent to this diabolical conformity, to this evil demon of conformity, in the modern behavior of the masses who are also very good at complying with the models offered to them, who are very good at reflecting the objectives imposed on them, thereby absorbing and annihilating them. There is in this conformity a force of seduction in the literal sense of the word, a force of diversion, distortion, capture and ironic fascination. There is a kind of fatal strategy of conformity. A recent example may be found in Woody Allen's film, *Zelig* (...)

More generally, the image is interesting not only in its role as reflection, mirror, representation of, or counterpart to, the real, but also when it begins to contaminate reality and to model it, when it only conforms to reality the better to distort it, or better still: when it appropriates reality for its own ends, when it anticipates it to the point that the real no longer has time to be produced as such.

For some time now, in the dialectical relation between reality and images (that is, the relation that we wish to believe dialectical, readable from the real to the image and vice versa), the image has taken over and imposed its own immanent, ephemeral logic; an immoral logic without depth, beyond good and evil, beyond truth and falsity; a logic of the extermination of its own referent, a logic of the implosion of meaning in which the message disappears on the horizon of the medium. In this regard, we all remain incredibly naive: we always look for a good usage of the image, that is to say a moral, meaningful, pedagogic or informational usage, without seeing that the image in a sense revolts against this good usage, that it is the conductor neither of meaning nor good intentions, but on the contrary of an implosion, a denegation of meaning (of events, history, memory, etc.). I am reminded of *Holocaust,* the television series on the concentration camps...(...)

For all these reasons I do not believe in a pedagogy of images, nor of cinema, nor *a fortiori* in one of television. I do not believe in a dialectic between image and reality, nor therefore, in respect of images, in a pedagogy of message and meaning. The secret of the image (we are still speaking of contemporary, technical images) must not be sought in its differentiation from reality, and hence in its representative value (aesthetic, critical or dialectical), but on the contrary in its 'telescoping' into reality, its short-circuit with reality, and finally, in the implosion of image and reality. For us there is an increasingly definitive lack of differentiation between image and reality which no longer leaves room for representation as such.

This collusion between images and life, between the screen and daily life, can be experienced everyday in the most ordinary manner. Especially in America, not the least charm of which is that even outside the cinemas the whole country is cinematographic. You cross the desert as if in a western; the metropolis is a continual screen of signs and formulae. Life is a travelling shot, a kinetic, cinematic, cinematographic sweep. There is as much pleasure in this as in those Dutch or Italian towns where, upon leaving the museum, you rediscover a town in the very image of the paintings, as if it had stepped out of them. It is a kind of miracle which, even in a banal American way, gives rise to a sort of aesthetic form, to an ideal confusion which transfigures life, as in a dream. Here, cinema does not take on the exceptional form of a work of art, even a brilliant one, but invests the whole of life with a mythical ambience. Here it becomes truly exciting. This is why the idolatry of stars, the cult of Hollywood idols, is not a media pathology but a glorious form of the cinema, its mythical transfiguration, perhaps the last great myth of our modernity. Precisely to the extent that the idol no longer represents anything but reveals itself as a pure, impassioned, contagious image which effaces the difference between the real being and its assumption into the imaginary.(...)

The movie stars do not constitute a subsidy for infatuation; they stand as an ideal which is actualized in a forcible manner. It is often said that they get us to dream. But dreaming is something different than being fascinated by certain images. The screen idols are, however, immanent in relation to the life that transpires in images. They constitute a system of luxurious pre-fabrication, radiant syntheses of life's and love's stereotypes. *They personify but one sole passion:* the image's and the desire's residence in the image. Certainly, they get us to dream; they *are* the dream. And they possess all its characteristic traits: they bring about an intense effect of condensation (like a crystallization), an effect of presence (which is directly contagious) and most of all, they possess a character of immediate visual materialization (illustration) of desire, a characteristic also indigenous to the dream. Accordingly, they do not implicate any romantic or sexual fantasizing; they constitute immediate visibility, immediate reproduction, material amalgamation, desire's ruining itself in the image. The fetishes and the fetish objects have nothing with the fantasy of procuring, but everything to do *with the image's material fiction. (...)*

All these considerations are a bit wild, but that is because they correspond to the unrestrained film buff that I am and have always wished to remain – that is in a sense uncultured and fascinated. There is a kind of primal pleasure, of anthropological joy in images, a kind of brute fascination unencumbered by aesthetic, moral, social or political judgements. It is because of this that I suggest they are immoral, and that their fundamental power lies in this immorality.

This brute fascination for images, above and beyond all moral or social determination, is also not that of dreaming or the imaginary, understood in the traditional sense. Other images, such as those in painting, drawing, theatre or architecture, have been better able to make us dream or imagine; other modes of expression as well (undoubtedly language makes us dream better than the image). So there is something more than that which is peculiar to our modern media images: if they fascinate us so much it is not because they are sites of the production of meaning and representation – this would not be new – it is on the contrary because they are sites of the *disappearance* of meaning and representation, sites in which we are caught quite apart from any judgement of reality, thus sites of a fatal strategy of denegation of the real and of the reality principle.

We have arrived at a paradox regarding the image, our images, those which unfurl upon and invade our daily life – images whose proliferation, it should be noted, is potentially infinite, whereas the extension of meaning is always limited precisely by its end, by its finality: from the fact that images ultimately have no finality and proceed by total contiguity, infinitely multiplying themselves according to an irresistible epidemic process which no one today can control, our world has become truly infinite, or rather exponential by means of images. It is caught up in a mad pursuit of images, in an ever-greater fascination which is only accentuated by video and digital images. We have thus come to the paradox that these images describe the equal impossibility of the real and of the imaginary.

For us the medium, the image medium, has imposed itself between the real and the imaginary, upsetting the balance between the two, with a kind of fatality which has its own logic. I call this a fatal process in the sense that there is a definitive immanence of the image, without any possible transcendent meaning, without any possible dialectic of history – fatal also in the sense not merely of an exponential, linear unfolding of images and messages but of an exponential enfolding of the medium around itself. The fatality lies in this endless enwrapping of images (literally: without end, without destination) which leaves images no other destiny than images. The same thing happens everywhere today, when production has no destiny apart from production – overdetermination of production by itself – when sex has no destiny other than sex – sexual overdetermination of sexuality. This process may be found everywhere today, for better and for worse. In the absence of rules of the game, things become caught up in their own game: images become more real than the real; cinema itself becomes more cinema than cinema, in a kind of vertigo in which (to return to our initial problem, that of resemblance) it does no more than resemble itself and escape in its own logic, in the very perfection of its own model. (...)

In my opinion, the particularly erotic dimension about our present-day image world emanates from this. In many cases, this erotic and pornographic picture factory – the whole advertising industry's armament of breasts, buttocks and genitals, the display of the naked body and of the sexual body – has no other meaning than this; it is not the awakening of some kind of desire but rather the representation of the thing's purposeless objectivity (whereas seduction constitutes a *challenge* to the thing's purposeless objectivity). The sexual and the nudity – whether it appears in the advertisement or elsewhere – no longer serves as anything other than special effect, as credibility effect, a broken-hearted attempt at underscoring the existence of something or other. *The sexual is no longer anything else but a transparency ritual.* That which formerly ought to be concealed now serves only to mask, paradoxically enough, how little truth there is and how little there is of reality. And of course, it also takes part in this incorporeal passion. From where does our fascination with these erotic or pornographic pictures stem? Certainly not from seduction. We don't even get a good look at them in the proper sense. In order for there to be a gaze, an object has to cover and then disclose itself. It has to be vanishing at every moment. That's why there's a kind of quivering which is present in the gaze. These images of nudity, on the other hand, are not captured by any interplay between emergence and vanishing. The body is already right there, just like the other objects, without the vestige of any possible absence, in the condition of radical illusionless-ness that constitutes the pure presence. In a real image, some parts are visible and other parts are not. Insofar as the visible parts render the others invisible, what crops up is a kind of rhythm of emergence and secrecy, a line upon which fantasy can stream forth. But here in the nude picture, everything is visible in an even manner, and everything plays its part inside the same depthless space. And this is exactly where the fascination stems from: from this bodilessness. This is the aesthetics of bodilessness, of which Octavio Paz has spoken. The fascination, it is this incorporeal passion surrounding a gaze with no object, surrounding a gaze with no image. It has been a long time since all our media theatrics – including that of the body and including all that with the sexual – has transgressed the wall of amazement. The consternation about the body's indignation behind the glass, about the sexual's indignation behind the glass, about the empty stage where nothing goes on anymore and which fills up the gaze anyway. It is not only the stage of the sexual, it is also the stage of enlightenment and of politics: it's not happening anymore, and nonetheless we are satiated by it.

Do we wish for this fascination? Do we crave this form of pure presence; do we crave the world's *pornographic objectivity?* How are we to know? Without any doubt, there is a collective dizziness surrounding the flight forward into the obscenity which issues from a pure and empty form and where we, at the same time, see ourselves playing through the sexual immoderacy and its forfeiture of quality, the visible's immoderacy and its decline. For this fascination, which constitutes a kind of magical disappearing act, can be found in the pornographic pictures as well as in all of modern art, whose purpose and compulsive idea, literally speaking, consists in no longer being visible, but in enjoining any and every seduction of the gaze, nonetheless. The modern art is not at all an art of seduction anymore and nor is the modern sexuality.

On the other hand, this obscenity and the indifference that characterizes it do not necessarily lead to a dead point. Possibly, they can again become collective values – or they can become certain expedient values. What can be seen, moreover, is that certain new rituals are reconstituted around them; these are the rituals of transparency. Thirdly, what we find ourselves doing, undoubtedly, is nothing else than playing out obscenity's comedy and sexuality's comedy, in much the same way that other societies play out ideology's comedy for its own sake. For example, the Italian society is playing out confusion and terrorism's comedy. – In advertising, it is the comedy of the disrobed and "prostituted" female body that plays itself out, right there (from this, the naïveté around the imputations against this "prostitution" of the female body and the naïveté about any virtuous lawmaking). Sexual liberation, the omnipresent pornography, including that of the enlightenment, that of the participant and that of free expression: if all this were really true, it would be insufferable. Were all this really true, we would really find ourselves situated in the obscenity, which means to say, in the naked and primary truth, without spuriousness, but not without exigency: the things' insane demand on expressing their truth. Fortunately, we have not come this far, for as the things culminate, in that instant when they must be corroborated, they always turn around, and this reversibility protects their secrecy.

No one can really say whether the sexual has been liberated or not - no one can really say whether the index-figure for sexual gratification has risen or not. In sexuality, as in art, the notion of progress is absurd. On the other hand, obscenity, like transparency, belongs to the order of progress. And it moves inevitably forward for obscenity, precisely because it does not belong to the order of sexual desire but rather to the order of picture-frenzy. The preoccupation with and the ferocious hunger for images grow and grow in every way. *It has become our true sexual object,* our desire's sole object. And it is in this inversion, in this conflation between the desire and its equivalent, materialized in the image (and this pertains not only to the sexual desire but also to the conflation between the desire to know and its equivalent, materialized in "information", between the desire for the dream and its equivalent, materialized in the whole world's Disney-lands, between the desire for space and its equivalent, programmed as charter trips, between the desire for the play and its equivalent, programmed as telematics in all its forms), it is right in the midst of the promiscuity, in the image's omnipresence and in the image's virus-like defilement of the things, that our culture's transparency and obscenity consists.

There are no limits for our controls over this, for in contradistinction to the gendered species of animals who are monitored by a kind of internal biological regulation, the images are in no way protected against an unrestricted pollution, inasmuch as they do not arise via sexual pathways and inasmuch as they know nothing about either sex or death. Undoubtedly, this is why they absorb our interest in such an obsessional way, in that period of recession for the sexual and for death, whose place they usurp. Through them, we are undoubtedly dreaming about the amorality that reigned among the one-celled animals, who formed themselves interminably through contact and knew only of asexual connections.

(translated, in part, by Dan A. Marmorstein from Carsten Juhl's Danish translation of Baudrillard's text, from Cahiers Internationaux de Sociologie, Vol.LXXXIII, 1987 (printed in *Billedets onde ånd,* Det Kgl. Danske Kunstakademi, Copenhagen, 1990) and, in part, by Paul Patton and Paul Foss in "The Evil Demon of Images", published by The Power Institute of Fine Arts, University of Sydney, Australia, 1988).

ON ATOPI

Vittorio Gregotti

The theme of internationalism proposed by the avant-gardes had at least two inspiring motives, on which it is useful to reflect in order to compare them with the present meaning of the word. In the first place, internationalism contributed to a polemic against nationalisms in the name of art as an absolute, non-imitative expression that took the form of geometric abstraction and analytical reason. Second, the internationalism of the avant-gardes was based on the idea of novelty and utopia as values, and on the construction, in the name of technique and progress, of a language for a classless society where the essence of a problem was the basis for its expression.

The "return to order" of the mid-twenties revolted against such ideas. This continued in the thirties with the late nationalisms of regime architectures, with the *Heimatstile*, and later with neo-regionalistic tendencies, defense of local building traditions, and the theme of *mediterraneità*. Each of these positions, in turn, had its own driving motives and foundations. But although these contained many contrasts in political and ideological character, their results in the field of architecture were quite convergent.

Internationalism then reappeared in the architecture of the fifties as the reign of new procedural techniques based on concepts such as productivity, formalization of procedures in project execution, and organization of tasks, which were all thrust into the world of the project through the division of labor and specialization of production. But they also represented the value of objectivity of technique and formalization of thought as opposed to the reduction of functional rationality to mere politics and economics.

The foundations and reasons of this second neo-technical and neo-positivist internationalism, which was particularly dominated by North American thought, also converged with respect to society's development in the postwar period.

The internationalism that we experience today is different. As is often stated, it represents an internationalism of nonmaterial financial currents, of scientific and technical information, and of mass communication, with their respective laws of behavior and consumption. Some argue that this system has become so rambling, widespread, and mobile that it avoids any possibility of centralized control, and this may be good. But it also avoids any possibility of democratic control, any perspective on the common good, even any rational planning, and this is certainly very bad.

This process, whose idea of infinite possibilities excludes rules or ideologies, has created obvious difficulties regarding the foundation of any authentic difference. Subjectivity as a source of differentiation has itself weakened, with problematic consequences for forging an artistic practice of architecture.

Even the higher quality found in the interesting objects produced in the artistic field, which has its own forms of measured diversity, seems like an obstacle to the foundation of any authentic difference, since such production follows the homogenization of a market unified by mass communication, which requires continuous, indifferent inventions.

Still, we cannot effectively address this difficulty by locking ourselves within the convent of the spirit, or by pursuing a return to localisms or the fragmentation of dialects. Even less can we turn to new nationalisms, although that is the phenomenon we have right before our eyes. This is true not only for the claims for regional independence sweeping through many parts of Europe and the Soviet Union, but also for the attempt to address the great complexity of interdependencies by seeking a place of discontinuity to isolate and resolve problems while trying to define their limits and characteristics.

In the specific case of our discipline, moreover, recent years have been marked by a strong interest in context in all its various aspects: natural, historical, monumental, conservational, and reconstructional. In short, this interest has sought to open a dialogue with what exists, which is seen to possess the depth and stratification from which the site derives its specific identity, and which must be the foundation for any modification of the site.

The culture of architecture has adopted and elaborated this concern, and has substantially altered its scale of values by placing at the center of its own actions a conception of the project as a thoughtful way to maintain a critical distance while engaging the context. But we still have to conclude that the growth of cities and transformation of territories is, in the large majority of cases, headed in the opposite direction.

Indifferent to place and to historical patterns of settlement, which they constantly violate even when the rules are completely obvious, new buildings are formed and arranged according to principles derived from the forms of internationalism I described. In an ambiguous identification of progress and consumption, they model themselves on types and behaviors presented by mass communication as forms of reassurance, and signs of the advanced state of a social body.

Above all, this portrait describes the laws of formation that unite the urban peripheries of European cities. But the consolidated historical centers are also under continuous attack from such principles, which we might call principles of oriented atopia: that is, principles of settlement based on something other than the idea of place.

In urban peripheries, we often see homogeneous residential neighborhoods that lack internal hierarchies and that, because they look elsewhere, gradually lose any reference to the identity of their own existing urban centers, whose fabric and layout once served as a model for the gradual consolidation of those peripheries.

Following a severing of the ties that once linked production and service establishments to their sites through the use of local materials, energy, and labor, such peripheral establishments seem to wish to be deliberately atopical. They close themselves within their own programmatic nature, creating a scattered global system of similar functions, which are completely independent of their specific condition of settlement and which focus on repeating a behavioral as well as a functional paradigm. To be sure, this is often a mere matter of dispersion of localization, due to banal reasons such as hand costs and ease of access. However, we must realize that a decisive split has occurred between land and building. This is what has corrupted entire regions and landscapes, extreme peripheries of urban centers whose presence has now, at least in Italy, come to characterize the great roads of travel and, in general, the intersections that offer the greatest advertising opportunities.

From a tradition that once located a large factory in the countryside, near its sources of energy, or at the urban periphery, close to its sources of labor, such building-objects have either completely lost their power of spatial and social aggregation or, at their worst, completely turned these characteristics inside out.

At times, this shift involves recently formed typologies, whose immaturity regarding settlement often takes the form of a shapeless system of aggregations, with large built spaces and vast service-related terrains, which is connected to the great highway infrastructure and which remains partly hidden in those undefined spaces of conurbation that open themselves, with illogical leaps in scale, into the historical-natural landscape, squandering it completely.

We are speaking of landscapes, if we can still call them that, that are rapidly spreading. Often built according to extraEuropean models, they reject all integration or even any interaction with the tightly woven historical fabric of our territories.

Many years ago, toward the end of the fifties, British scholars such as Ian Nairn and Gordon Cullen attempted to offer a general interpretation of the exploding phenomenon of settlements, particularly in that undefined area between countryside and urban periphery. The phenomenon of atopia was not as evident in those years, and the fragmentation sprang more from domestic concerns. There was an attempt to understand the phenomenon in terms of its distinct novelty, by resorting to categories such as collage cities and urban surrealism. In other words, one attempted to view the phenomenon, even with all its degenerations, as part of the general process of settlement formation, observed at an incomplete phase.

But today I believe we must conclude that this is no longer the case. The phenomenon of atopia has clearly assumed an intention that places it on a totally different plane.

Supermarkets, parking lots, highway service stations, airports and their parking areas, transfer points between various means of transport, showroom centers along urban exit roads are all part of these atopical typologies. To them we must add the residual spaces, shipping container yards, used car dealerships, auto graveyards, the odd spaces between highway interchanges, unused "green spaces," junkyards, and abandoned farmlands. Unlike the great markets of antiquity, these atopical typologies offer none of the spontaneous and temporary gathering that used to characterize those spaces *extra muros.* They are, on the contrary, regulated by relentless internal laws of distribution and equally relentless laws of investment and profit. But such laws are in no way rooted to the site. In terms of morphology and resources, they have no need for the site, because their selling point involves offering the user the momentary illusion of belonging to a different, more advanced, and more reassuring world than the one encountered in everyday life. Atopical buildings take on the features of industrial manufacture, which uses laws of consistent performance and recognizability to guarantee the quality of the product and the safety of its handling by the user. In other words, atopical buildings have extended the rules for designing industrial products into architecture, for which they are improper.

In some ways, the social fabric that encompasses solidarity, contrasts, and a sense of belonging no longer exists for such non-places. Rather, a great universal void opens between the individual and the market, where the product's system of reference is completely abstract and nonspatial.

This judgment might of course result from a distortion of historical perspective on our part; one might imagine that these fragments of buildings will, in time, and against their own volition, assume a specific character and identity: specific, at least, to a historical moment and its concept of space.

Such an interpretation might be supported by the quality of settlement assumed by certain great monuments of the past that have been recontextualized with the passage of time, or that have themselves constructed new principles of settlement after the original reasons for their location had been lost. Or again, it might draw on the great systems of territorial transformation carried out by colonization, which transfers organizational models elaborated in totally extraneous sites, ranging from the Roman system of land division to the religious colonization of South America, to mention only two examples.

We could also cite the highly expressive ways that modern atopical typologies have been interpreted by the cinema (for example in a film like *Paris Texas),* or by Allen Ginsberg's prophetic poetry, or by much of contemporary painting, and thus imagine, as some argue, that we can also find authenticity in such typologies from an architectural point of view. From that perspective, it would be interesting to discuss what kinds of compatibilities are possible (and if they are possible) between the principles of identity and belonging, which architects discuss so much these days, and the principles of atopia. Whether it is possible to establish any form of interconnection between them, or how one might directly articulate the material offered by specific atopical features in terms of urban design, has at times been attempted in the past twenty years.

Perhaps the unease we feel regarding the formal organizations of these atopical typologies comes mainly because they are insufficiently radical. They do not seem able to draw significant morphological materials from their own existence outside of context, or from their own nature as celibate machines. Nor do they seem to use their extraneous state as a dialectical element with regard to their context.

Certain great products of modern engineering, for example, present (we do not know how consciously) a poetic quality based on a strong internal coherence and on a dialectic with their context.

The most obvious defect of these atopical typologies seems to be their inability to regulate the vast open spaces that functionally accompany them; or rather their inability to design such spaces so that they mediate with the surroundings and with the land (an inevitable source of support and confrontation), with its geographic and technical nature, as well as with (or consciously against) the historical depth that it encompasses.

In any case, there is no doubt that atopicality might be interpreted as a sign of an inevitable mechanism of international interdependence that is cultural as well as political and economic in structure — a sign that has yet to find a significant form of spatial organization in the territory of architecture.

Such interdependence still often takes the form of control and domination, opposing attempts by existing communities to secure the largest possible scope for their own traditions within the process of unification. Or perhaps such atopicality still facilitates the brutal exploitation of varying economic conditions among the peoples of the world.

Could it move instead toward solidarity, toward that "communicative public action" of which some philosophers speak? This is perhaps a naively positive interpretation, but one that is dictated by an intimate need and that can, at least as a hypothesis, shift the destructive impetus of atopia into architecture's own territory, transforming it into a dialogue of solidarity, even with the context.

(Published in "Inside Architecture" by Vittorio Gregotti, Peter Wong (Translator), Francesca Zaccheo (Translator) Kenneth Frampton. The MIT Press, Cambridge, Mass., 1996. © The MIT Press.)

PROJECT THEME: TRANSITIONS, THE INTRODUCTORY DRAFT FOR THE ASSIGNMENT

Carsten Juel-Christiansen

The interest in the phenomenon of 'transitions' is symptomatic of changes in the perception of wholeness.
The spatial, social and architectonic coherence within a given locality which was positioned inside a meaningful universe has been dissolved over the course of a long period. The whole's restoration within an international perspective as a modern utopia has been sapped by the forces of development which were accepted as being utopia's preconditions. The experiences of reality's complexity have fostered an understanding that the multitude of essential details and patterns in the different contemporary descriptions of reality has become so wide-ranging that no one whole can be secured in a single picture that is easy to see.
The interest in transitions in the architectonic space signals partly that there is no articulated notion of wholeness for shaping coherence in the space and partly that the existing connections between the parts cannot be apprehended as architectonic forms. The pragmatic contemporary space consists predominantly of separate and juxtaposed elements. In this organization, it is a planning assignment in itself to create a foundation for architectonic transitions which can be worked up both as physical passages and as membranes between spaces of different character.
Our current reality is characterized by three conditions which represent crucial changes in connection with the modern space: globalization, individualization and simulation. In these changes, certain relations which were previously in possession of a well-established coherence are being put into play. These are the relation between body and place, the relation between individual and community and the relation between repetition and difference. The tendencies here are for the place to be dissolved in the communication landscape. The community is obliterated into a sum of individuals. The many differences reproduce a constant repetition of the same. The repercussions are perceived as loss of meaning, which corresponds to possible self-realization; loss of public space, which corresponds to a media-permeated reality; loss of body, which corresponds to communication's network.
Architectonic transitions as a theme must be seen in the light of these sweeping changes in order to be able to identify the conceptual complexes surrounding dissociations within which the treatment of the spatial transitions can be inserted. The proposed point of departure is seated in three distinct 'typologies' that are seen here as architectonic reactions to the course of development as we have observed it. Each one of the typologies refers to its own scalar level and each to its own complex of differences.

The Collective Space:
Reaction (especially) to the globalization of the forces that dominate the space's development. With their super-national scale and narrowly defined interests, they encroach upon the local space and weaken its capacity for representing common values and open meanings in the form of a public space. The collective space designates a space of admixture. It is articulated in a dense integration of differently scaled elements representing international and local interests within a given locality.
The vectors in the collective space are:

accessible

private   public

inaccessible

The Space's Middle Ground:
Reaction to the individualization of the society.
By and large, it is typical of the economic, technological, social and sign-related development that the middle ground is being forfeited as a mediating transition and symbol for the connection between near and far, or between 'the innermost and the outermost'. Subjectivity's innermost autonomy and the community-instituting outermost are being pressed deeper in and farther away. The middle ground vanishes in the ever expanding space which opens itself up and which is structured by culture's pragmatic partitions. At the same time, the political and democratic regulation is subject to a fundamental interest in reproducing the circumstances for the very same development that has brought about the loss. The articulation of the space's middle ground is an organization of the locality's place as a bodily space which renders the individual world a part of the others' world. The vectors in the space's middle ground are:

                    collective
  local   global
                    individual

The Edge of the Space:
Reaction to the pragmatic space's transparency and to reality's simulations in the media's reduplication.
No longer does space extend outward in an emancipatory movement. Instead, it branches out in reduplications, simulations and virtualities which bring forth a hyper-reality. In this situation, the space is simultaneously totally revealed and infinitely reproduced. The articulation of the edge of the space is a covering over of a part of space in order to elucidate the space's depth and invisibility. Articulating the edge is tantamount to making place for differences - making place for that which has no place. The vectors at the edge of the space are:

                    non-place
  the blind angle   developmental perspective
                    place

As analytic constructs, these three typologies themselves actually represent a form of transition. They offer an attempt to encircle possibilities in the contemporary reality's space, where local architectonic transgressions of the space's pragmatically simplified frames can give rise to notions about more comprehensive coherences. [1]
The strategies for the local transitions, physical passages and spatial membranes within the aforementioned typologies can, by way of introduction, be sketched out as an interplay between damming and flooding in the form of:
Double-exploitation of the surface
Fusion between the space's stratifications
Displacement of the horizon.

1. See also: *Monument og Niche*, Carsten Juel-Christiansen, Rhodos, Copenhagen, 1985.

THE SITES

The Collective Space
1. Vestskoven
2. The Amager Commons
3. Bispeengen
4. Dybbølsbro

The Space's Middle Ground
5. The Northern Harbor
6. Vesterbro

The edge of the Space
7. Ishøj
8. Nørreport

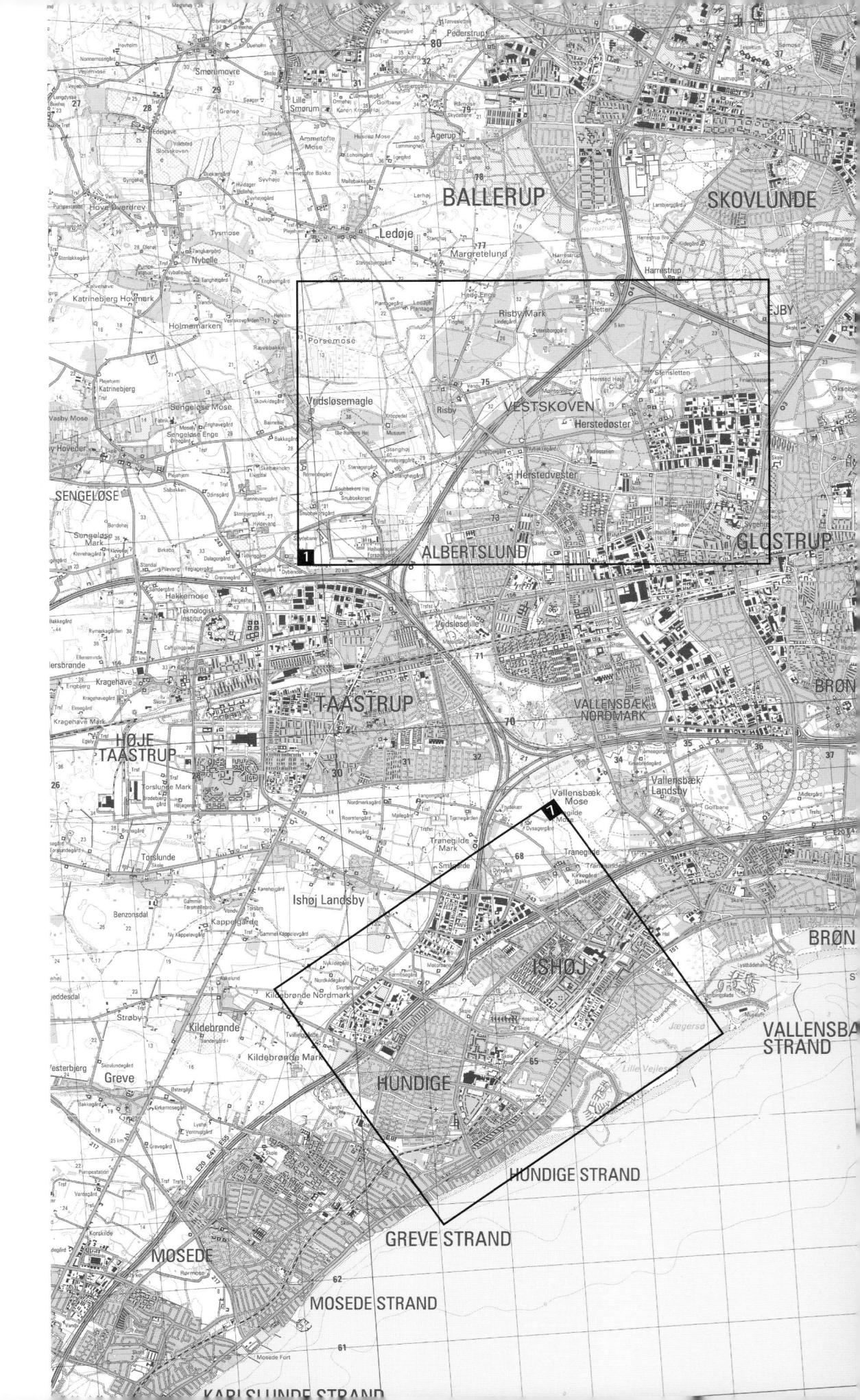

Copyright Kort & Matrikelstyrelsen (A.87-00)

HELLERUP
KØBENHAVN
SØBORG
EMDRUP
MØRKHØJ
BISPEBJERG
UTTERSLEV
Utterslev Mose
HUSUM
BRØNSHØJ
Bellahøj
VANLØSE
FREDERIKSBERG
RØDOVRE
VALBY
VIGERSLEV
HVIDOVRE
KONGENS ENGHAVE
VEDØRE
AVEDØRE HOLME
Vester Sandhage
Skrædderholm
KALVEBODERNE
Nordre Klapper
KALVEBOD FÆLLED
Koklapperne
Svenskeholm
Vildtreservat
Kongelunden
Sydvestpynten
AMAGER FÆLLED
SUNDBYVESTER
SUNDBYØSTER
Bella Center
TÅRNBY
KASTRUP
KØBENHAVNS LUFTHAVN
Tømmerup
Skelgårde
Viberup
Ullerup
Store Magleby
DRAGØR
Sydstranden
Søvang
CHRISTIANSHAVN
Kløvermarken
Christiansborg
Amalienborg
Rosenborg Slot
Kastellet
Langelinie
Refshalen
Nordhavnen
Stubben
RENDEN
MIDDELGRUND
KONGEDYBET
HOLLÆNDERDYBET
Middelgrunds Fort
Prøvesten
Østerhavnen
Amagerværket
Fælledparken
SVÆLGET
E20
2
3
4
5
6
8

STEEN HØYER

Introduction – on architecture's second nature.

The manifestation of culture must today be regarded as an element in the aggregate conception of nature. An interplay that is often designated the *second nature*, as opposed to the polarization of building vs. landscape and nature.
The state of affairs that culture is contained *within* the conception of nature expresses the cognition that the conception of knowledge today cannot be described in terms of some aggregate structure – as has been the ideal from the Renaissance to modernism, in central, parallel or organic models. Knowledge has to be perceived instead in the form of large, overlapping and yet delimited fields in a vertical construction – as opposed to being an endless horizontal structure.
The body as architectonic element that holds on to the world in interplay with the horizon and the liquidity can be an emblem of the aforementioned. It is around the formation of the local premises that all this work revolves – as concentrated expression, as mirror of the surroundings or as condensed knowledge. Everything that - within the scope of reality - can be understood only with the eyes.
These spaces are being regarded as a second-nature conception: architectonic elements of earth, trees, water, gravel, concrete, glass or steel – and combinations thereof.

Elements that form part of that space which today serves as the city's characteristic common denominator. A space which, in the beginning, was a result of flexibility and effective transportation. But the open landscape-like space is central, since resources, balance and development have become common goals in the society. And yet without any corresponding unequivocal method or idea – which the society symbolized previously through the city's spatial structure and through its distinctive building arrangement.
In this more complex pattern – which refers once again to the new conception of knowledge and to the second nature – the landscape elements become images of time, resistance, process and balance – the slow and steady – in contrast to the fleeting and dynamically technological world.
Therefore, the relationship between the organic and the inorganic in architecture will inevitably become something different than what it is today. For example, it is easy to envision that a more independent use of plant material will become an active element in the city's landscape, whether this comes about in the large urban scale or on the avenue, the grove or the water, as an architectonic element regarded with the same value as the building structures. To put it simply, the task before us consists in creating a solution that will conjoin the horizon with the body, through an interpretation of the space in the given locality.

Assumption and tools
1) The conception of knowledge and its architectonic consequence.
2) The space, the light and the climate as monumentality.
3) The relativity of the horizons – the topography's and the sea's horizons.
4) The liquidity – water, sediments, plates, foldings, shrinkages and growth.

The method
The program, the space, the topography and the accessibility in the project, which create faults or the "black holes".

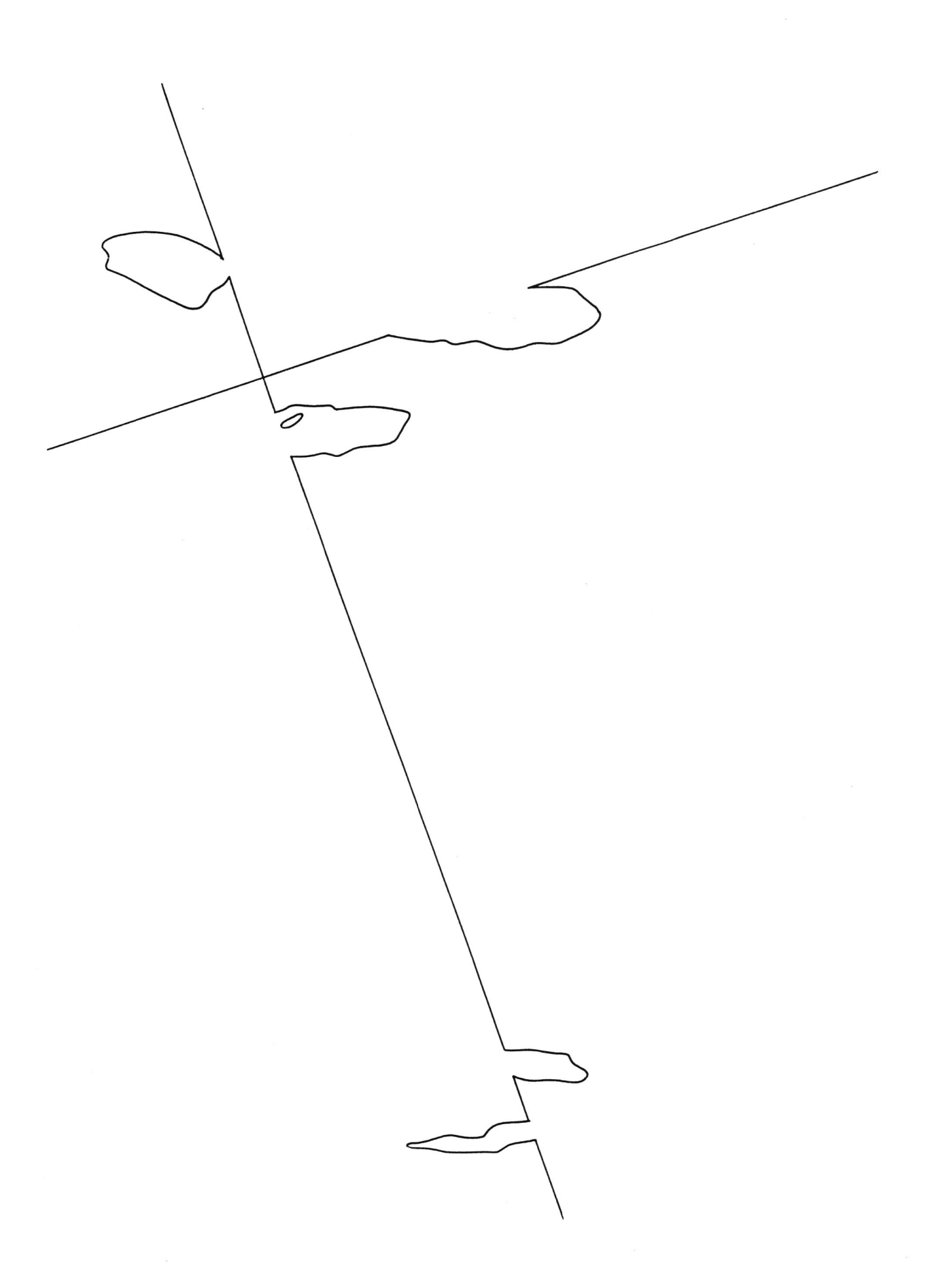

VESTSKOVEN - I
Glostrup Industrial Park.
Today, the area is situated as a pocket in Vestskoven [the Western Forest], if we go by the map and by the eye's penchant for fashioning graspable entities.
This proposal is based on making the area accessible, and consequently a section of the surrounding area, by removing fences and by homogenizing the surface coverings. What arises as a result is an open and narrative landscape, which manifests itself spatially as a surface with "container boxes" – positioned in an immense clearing in the woods.

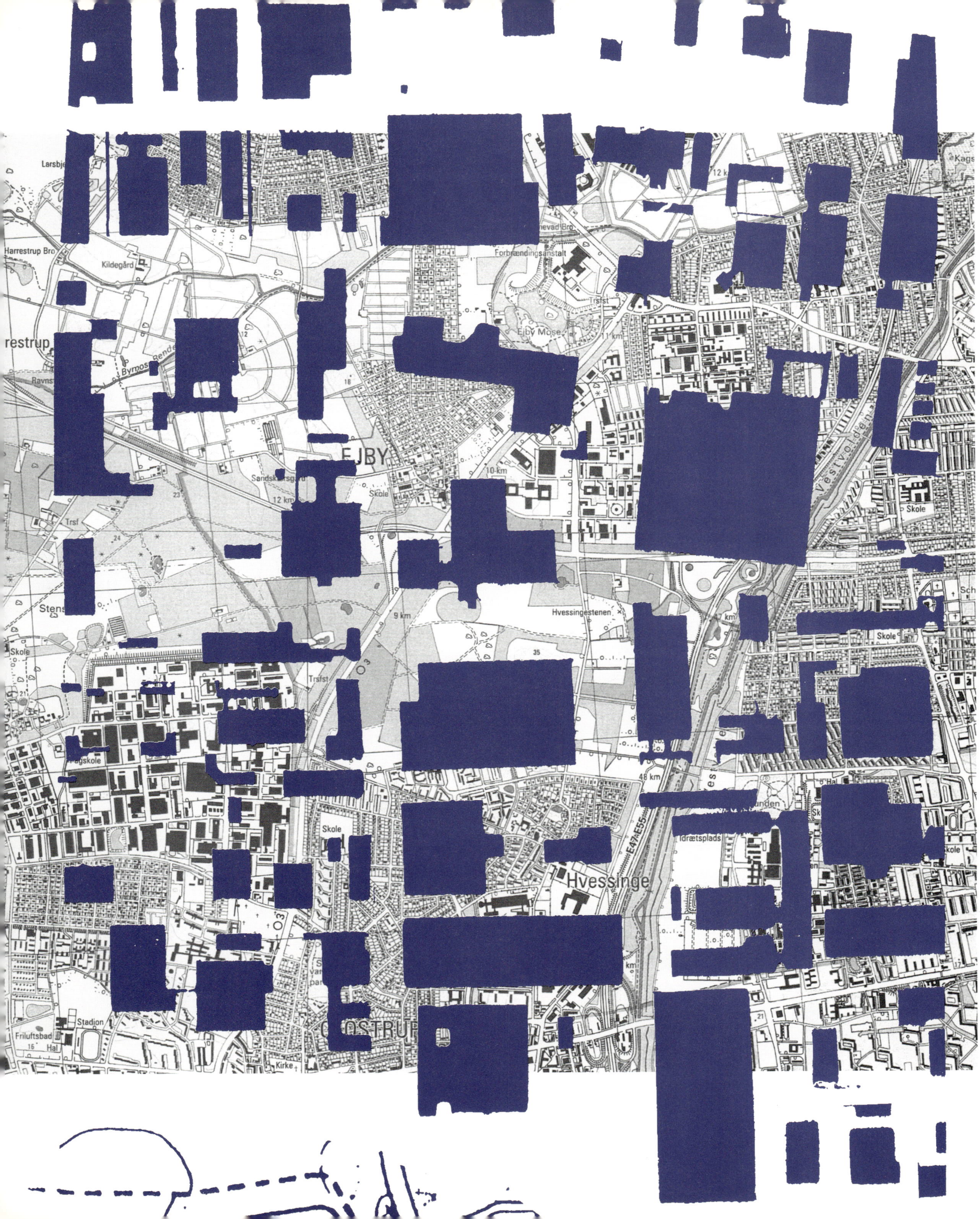
Harrestrup Bro
Kildegård
Forbrændingsanstalt
Trsfst
Ejby Mose
11 km
EJBY
12 km
Skole
10 km
Vestvolden
Skole
Trsf
9 km
Hvessingestenen
Skole
Trsfst
48 km
Idrætsplads
Hvessinge
E47/E55
Skole
Stadion
Friluftsbad
Hal
Kirke

VESTSKOVEN – II
Glostrup Industrial Park.
The development takes its point of departure in "VESTSKOVEN – I" with the cleared surface – along with the notion about a duplicity in the mutual relation between the organic and the inorganic space.

"THE INTERPLAY"
1. This way of thinking is exploited here in a process which immediately presupposes a supplementary planting in the free areas.
2. As the firms move away, they will eventually be taken over by a system of forest plantations. At a certain time, the entire region will be converted to a part of the existing Western Forest – even though we are regarding the entire industrial park, from the moment the plan comes into force, as a natural park.

The plantations can consist, broadly speaking, of all species, from larch, birch and aspen to linden, chestnut, thuja, spruce and cherry – but there should only be one type in each plantation.

The strategy is based on creating a unity between industry, park and forest, as seen at any time whatsoever – as well as on engendering a development that is not a one-dimensional linear development but rather one that subsumes process and balance, and one which constantly forms new wholenesses going through transformation – again and again.

When service and industry have left the area and the plantations come to merge completely with the domain of the forest, the mixed forest will come into being, with the growth of maples and birches, for example – after which the forestry will determine the expression.

41

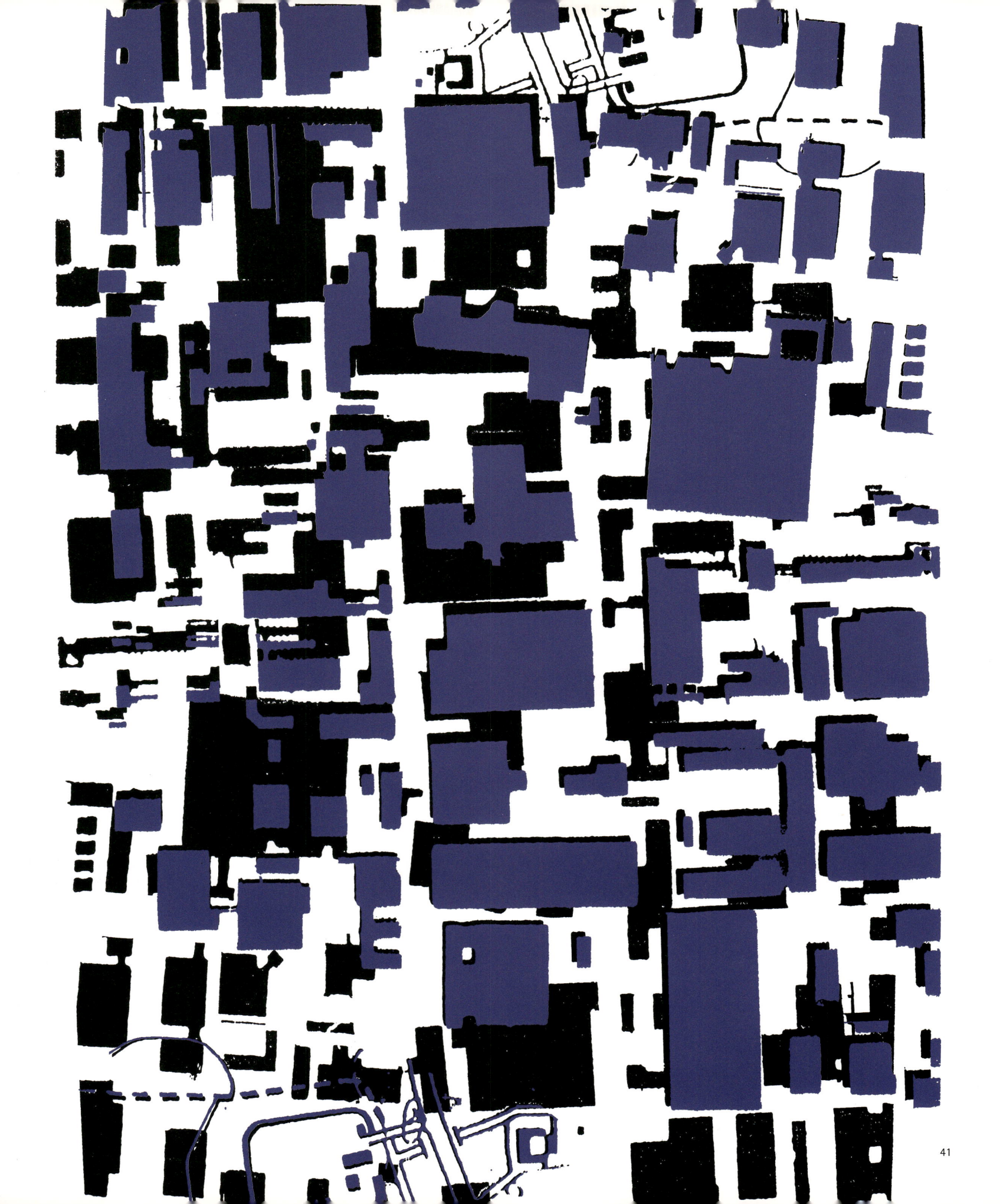

THE LANDSCAPE and the fluid layer

The Danish landscape consists of an atmosphere with a high humidity and concomitantly a soft light with many intermediate nuances – because we have a mild climate and the island's many nearby aqueous surfaces reflect and refract the light.
The atmospheric layer of light, water particles and cloud formations fashion the vast heavenly vault above this membrane, which consists of the culturally created landscapes. The delicately undulating surface, which again reflects its genesis and its age-old subterreanean layers of deposited sediments in foldings.
The surface of the cultural landscape has traces leading all the way back to the Bronze Age, but it has predominantly fashioned its image after the scattering of farms in the eighteenth century, with distinct units and precise boundaries. This type of cultural landscape was again radically altered in the twentieth century, when the city's open expansion and vast communication lines have come to stamp the expression.
All these traces, elements and open surfaces are situated in a richly varied relief, bearing the marks of the most recent Ice Age, which took place about 15,000 years ago. Glacial masses brought along sediments and deposited them when the ice melted, and the resulting volumes of water formed moraines in composite hill formations, systems of valleys and gulleys and plains of glacial melt. This process has repeated itself over the past two million years, in the course of the six known Ice Ages. It is a process that has folded, pushed, scraped and deposited sediments of clay, sand, gravel and stone in layers measuring 50 – 200 meters in thickness – bearing strong traces of the previously existing surface relief of the cretaceous- and tertiary-eras and subsequently marked by the climatic erosion of wind and water.
In certain periods, the ocean covered the land; upheavals of the land and risings in the water level have been alternating steadily ever since water was brought to earth by a falling meteor. Through the times, however, the ocean's sedimentary deposits have formed layer upon layer upon layer. From chalk- and limestone-layers to plastic types of clay and layers of volcanic ash. The ice, the melted water and the rain have formed the earlier eras' ocean deposits for more than 200 million years.
It therefore seems reasonable to characterize the landscape as a water landscape, consisting of layers and plates of different material under constant change, in an ongoing process, and within which human activity actually plays a very small part, albeit a very visible one. Light, time, water, layer and process become some of the key words for the understanding of the landscape, and thus they become an essential part of the architectonic content. The contents are not fashioned by an established aesthetics, but rather by an attitude wherein the landscape is considered to be a dignified workplace, and where the mark is taken in the production areas' logistics. An architectonic plan has never been determined by an aesthetic restriction, but has always had its roots planted in a practical development – and as a norm, it can become generative of values. It does demand, however, that there is somebody who points – and this demands a lot of time for achieving a general understanding of different kinds of experiential pictures.
The monumental Denmark dwells in this vast landscape coherence – in the light's and the weather's meeting with the land's age-old developmental history – in the drama that arises when millions of years of history and the future are amalgamated in the presence of one single moment. These are the conditions that Martin A. Hansen describes, with such impact, in relation to the essence of art in the book, "Dansk vejr" (The Danish Weather), from 1953.
But how we will be able to sustain and develop this tradition when the country is generally perceived in three categories: 1) the scenically beautiful reservations; 2) the building monuments and 3) all the unimportant stuff that's left over in the everyday and the workaday landscape?
If we take a look at twentieth century's space through the nineteenth century's aesthetic landscape's spectacles, we arrive spontaneously inside the dilemma that is sketched right into the aforementioned trichotemy. The landscape is perceived as a static and framed picture, which from the museum, from the screen and the Toyota's windshield, is supposed to safeguard our historic identity. This can, in itself, be said to be reasonable enough – but only if everyday life – the present day one as well as the future one – is the object of the same degree of interest and enthusiasm. The landscape must be perceived as a workplace – and not be treated merely as scenery.
The problem is seated in how we are developing that urban expansion which has been taking place since the sixties and up until today, with its open suburbs and immense communication lines, in relation to the unsteady development going on in the agricultural sector; this development has rendered energy- and communications-facilities architectonically unparalleled in the twentieth century. The question is, how can we broadly define qualities inside this new space and incorporate them into the planning?
The traditional cultural landscape has lost its symbolic value, as a direct result of the loss of the whole's structure. What remains is the surface's meeting with the water, the light and the wind, transpiring transversely to the urban – where we will have to develop a respect for life and for the balance between stable and slow accretion and dynamic and speedy construction. Viewed as a life story with an ambivalence in the conception of time as the result of culture's existence on nature's terms. But this becomes a long and difficult process, because it calls for a change of attitude: from contemplating the surroundings as an incidental random resource to the open consideration of these surroundings as equal and dignified life, containing unexploited possibilities.
Today, interest has gathered around the cultural-historical monuments, whether these be of a building-related or a landscape

nature. On the other hand, the nearby – everyday work-landscapes abide in trivial unimportance. Iconographic architecture's interest, then, also continues to gather itself around the idyllic, the pastoral or the great classic landscape drama.

The question is whether the Danish landscape, with it never ending history – from chalk to spring barley – stretching from coast to coast – ought to be allocated a new starring role. The task is to distil the simple and solitary landscape-related locution – and build this great scale into the place and into the given assignment program. A processual way of thinking that must take the culture's dynamics as nature into consideration – a way of thinking where flexibility is afforded a higher proiority than steering and control – along with a knowledge about nature in the landscape which subsumes time in development, elements, space, structure, light and colors. A method for phasing out modernism's functional zone plans – and much of the static, anonymous installation that has been described above.

The task has always been to find a good functional and aesthetic placement for one's facility and thereafter, to design it into the area, with the salient features that time's emblem of the world marks out, on one occasion. There is nothing new in this way of thinking – and throughout the course of history, we can discover this approach in the best facilities of building- and landscape-types and landscape gardening. What it is that is "new" really consists in focusing only on contemporary times, on the history and on architecture's fundamental breadth.

Every place is unique. Unique in the sense that it contains a particular expression. The space of the landscape's surface and the landscape's topography always forms a special and singular expression – and consists of fragments of layers, ranging from the bedrock, the lime and the plastic clay deposits to the Ice Age's sedimentary water-deposits of stones and gravel under climatic and cultural-technological influences. From the beginning of time, across the byways of the water landscape, through the villages and the forests, to the industrialization's communications network and energy streams. A cubit-long table of contents, with an endless combinatorics, from which the essential must be derived – and what is most essential does not always dwell in that which is immediately visible. The limestone horst in the Hanstholm moraine hills' distinct island-form could serve as an essential inspiration for the site's layout.

Every area is unique – and what is special is registered as the distillate of substance, light, space or structure. That which identifies the place and which can provide a take-off point and generate space in new layouts. Both climatic and light conditions fluctuate to a significant extent, even within the relatively small area constituted by Denmark. The direction and the intensity of the wind vary around 20 % and the amount of precipitation can vary as much 100 %. The climate, the soil and the culturally conditioned influences change the vegetation, from the dune grasses to the oak trees, and even many of the most traditional Danish species reveal themselves to have been imported with some certain purpose in mind. Is there anything more Danish than Hans Christian Andersen and the hollow road-side poplar of the "The Tinder-Box"', which was actually imported from Canada? Is there anything more Danish than the summer beach's rose hips, which was brought back home in the middle of the nineteenth century from temperate Japan in order to stop the sand from drifting? The change in the landscape that has been the most dramatic, however, has transpired through land draining. The cities, and also the greater part of all of the cultivated areas, including the forests, have been drained – that means to say almost 80 % of the total land area. The landscape, then, has radically changed in character in the course of a little more than a hundred years – since the day that the brewer Jacobsen and the co-operative movement laid the foundation for the large-scale crop of barley – comprising 25 % of Denmark's total area.

The place's light is unique, The Danish light is not only special by virtue of its Nordic character; it also changes as we move through the different parts of the country. The small island nation, with what is always a trifling distance to the shoreline and the humid climate, not only emanates a soft light with many intermediate nuances. It also gives off an especially high light, which is experienced most distinctly on spits and peninsulas, where the light's reflection from two bodies of water is refracted in the atmosphere's water particles. An experience that feels overwhelmingly monumental in the open, somewhat cloudy landscape, as can be experienced, for example, on West Amager or at Asnæs. The light there, which is modulated by the drifting cloud formations – which are regenerated with an average lifetime of only ten minutes.

There is a need for creating out from what exists, and out from simple programs – without recourse to the past's stylized reference-images. A direct projection of the place into the program, and vice versa. What remains standing from the tradition are the architectonic effects and the need for that which provides identity for the human. If the architectonic experiences are taken too much at face value – and if we do not focus on their historic significance – a whole arsenal of effects turns up. From dense and closed to sparse and open – from forests of peristyles to massive walls and plazas, to avenues, plantations, crevices and mirror. If you just consider, for example, Piranesi's drawings, you have before you the richest architectonic tale that has even been created.

The surface as the bearer of the element still has to be central. Where the element and its space have been crystallized by the place – and where plant material and building material support one another and form part of a unity. This has been seen before, in the villages from around the turn of the (nineteenth to the twentieth) century, and in the country manor layouts with their adjoining lands – it certainly seems possible that it would crop up again. The scale is greater today and the organization is something new. The images come, perhaps, from the place's underground, its light and its history, drawn together into layouts, constructions and materials. However, the elementary human needs are the same, and so are the individual architectonic effects. The building's thickness, the horizon, the secure state of mind and the cherry-tree grove's June-snowfall continue to be equally important as anchoring in time and space. But the climate, the light and the horizon constitute the monumental, as has been mentioned, and liquidity, sediment, layers, traces, rupture and gliding create a starting point for the aesthetic implements that are to be employed in the program of the given task.

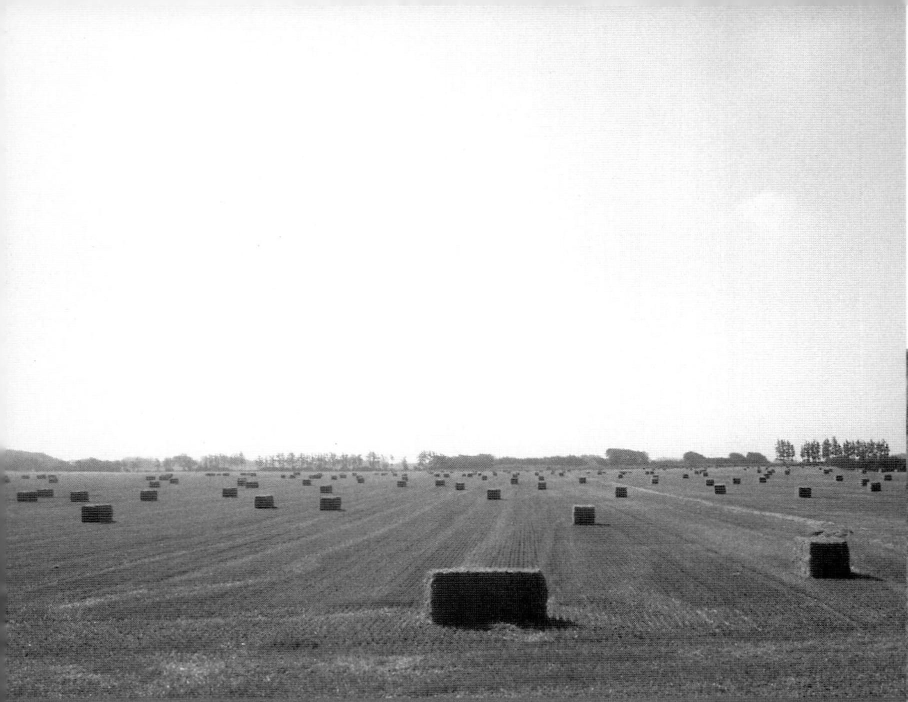
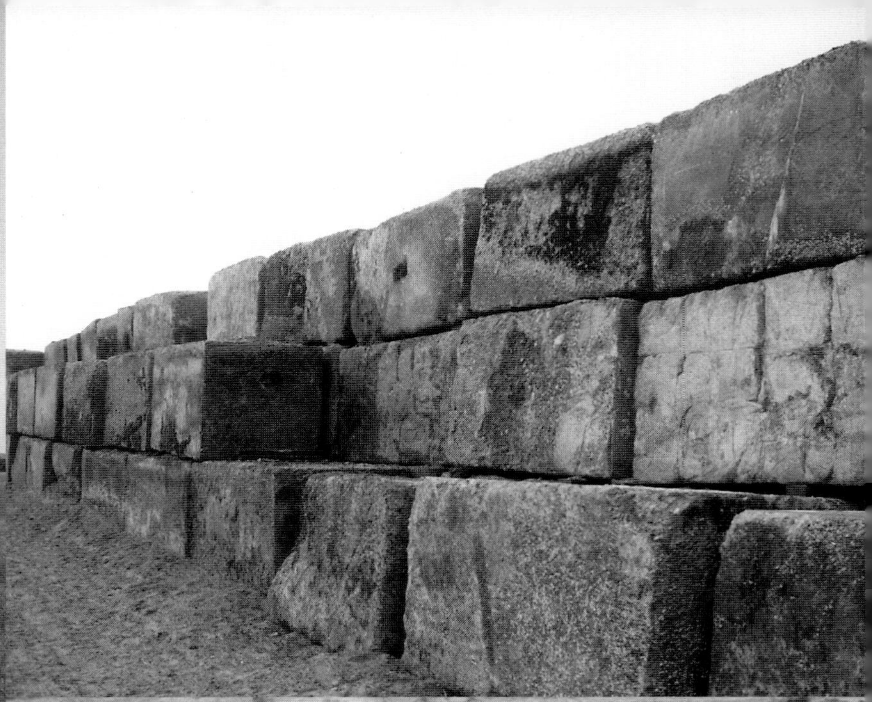
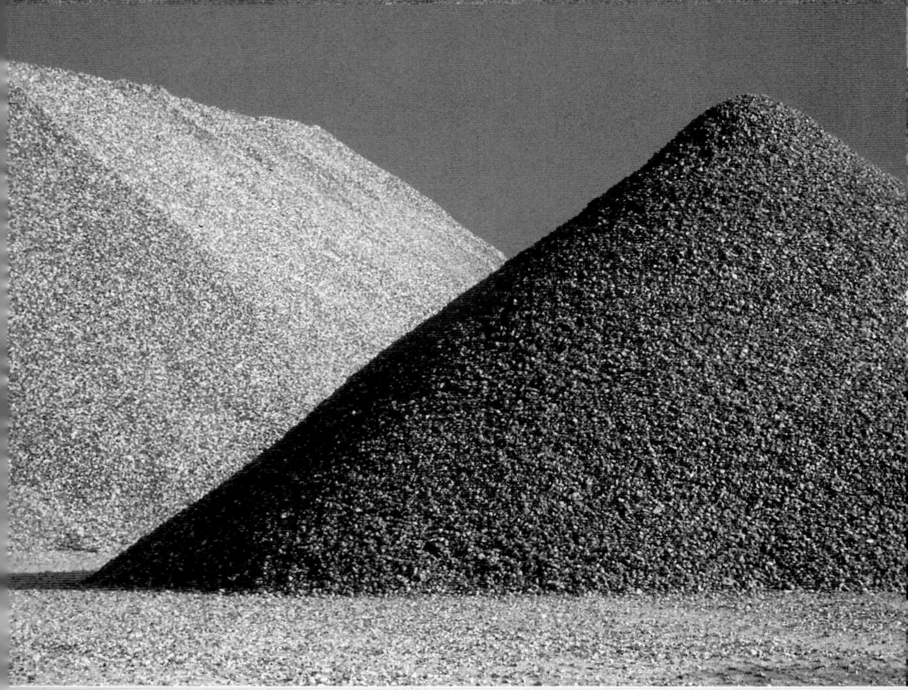
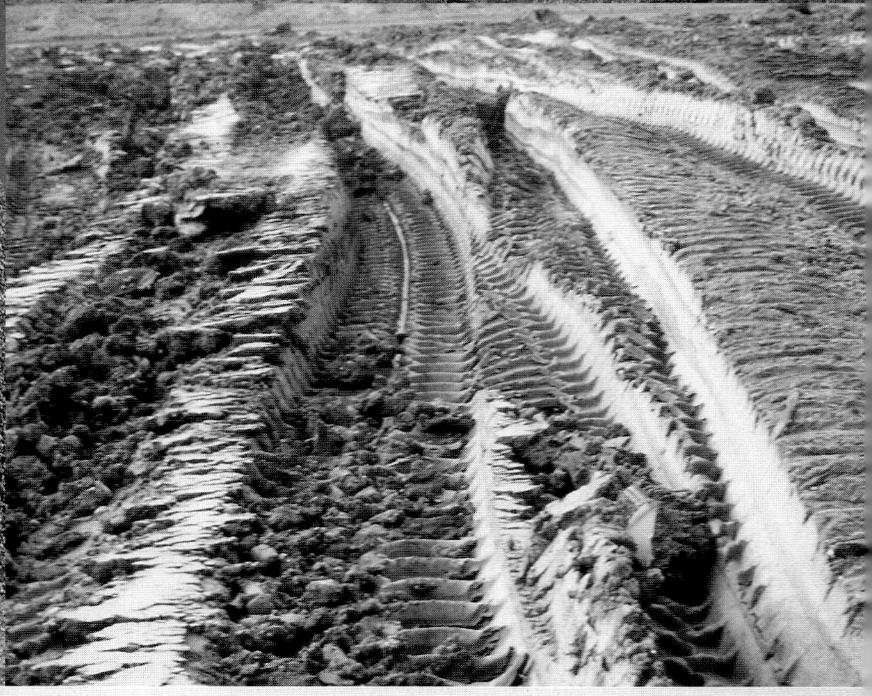

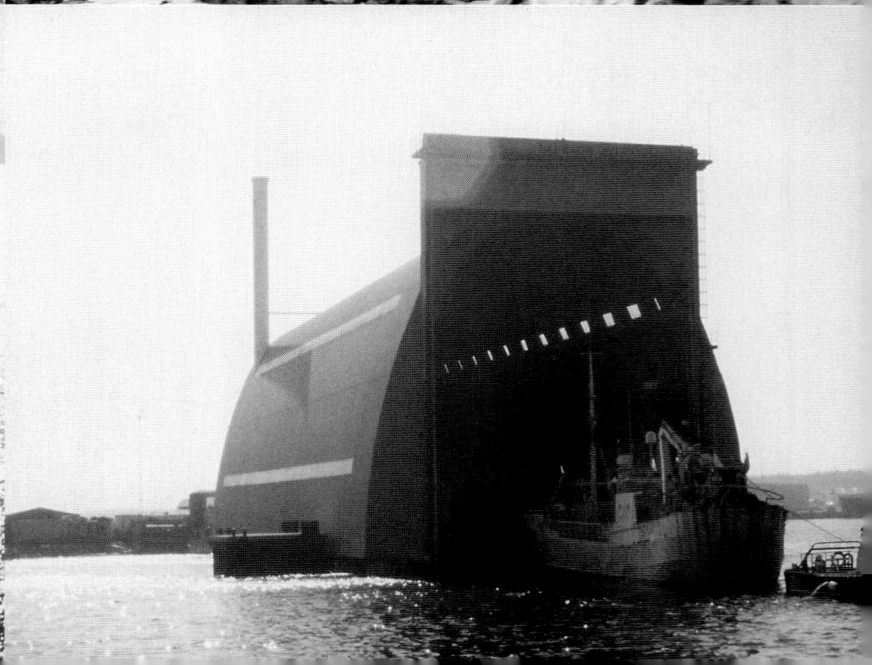

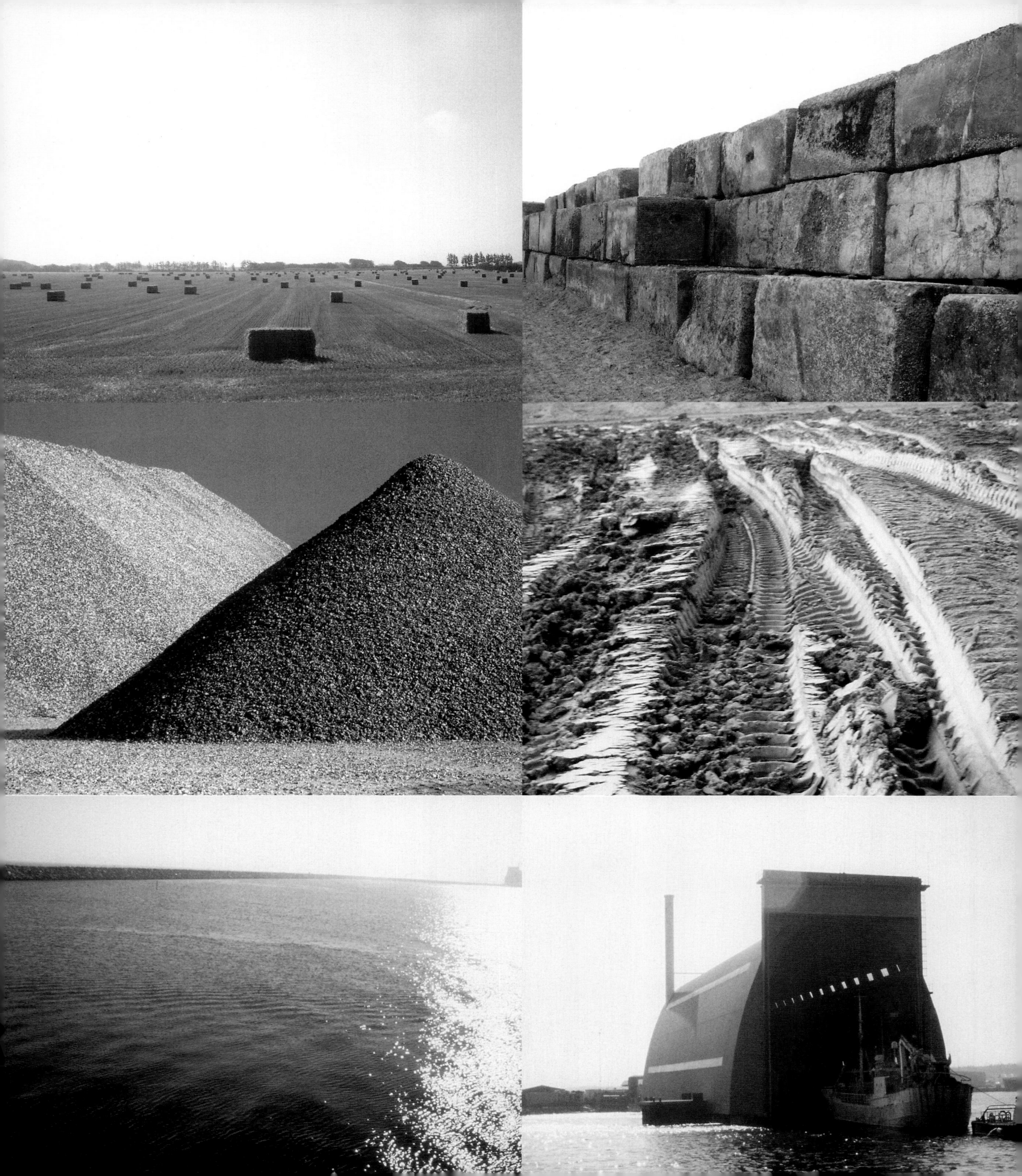

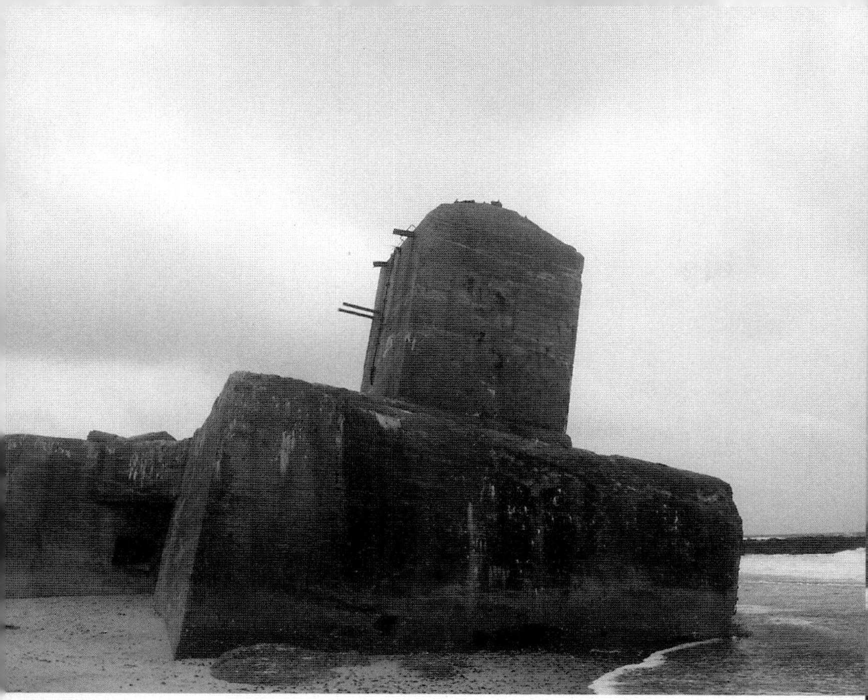
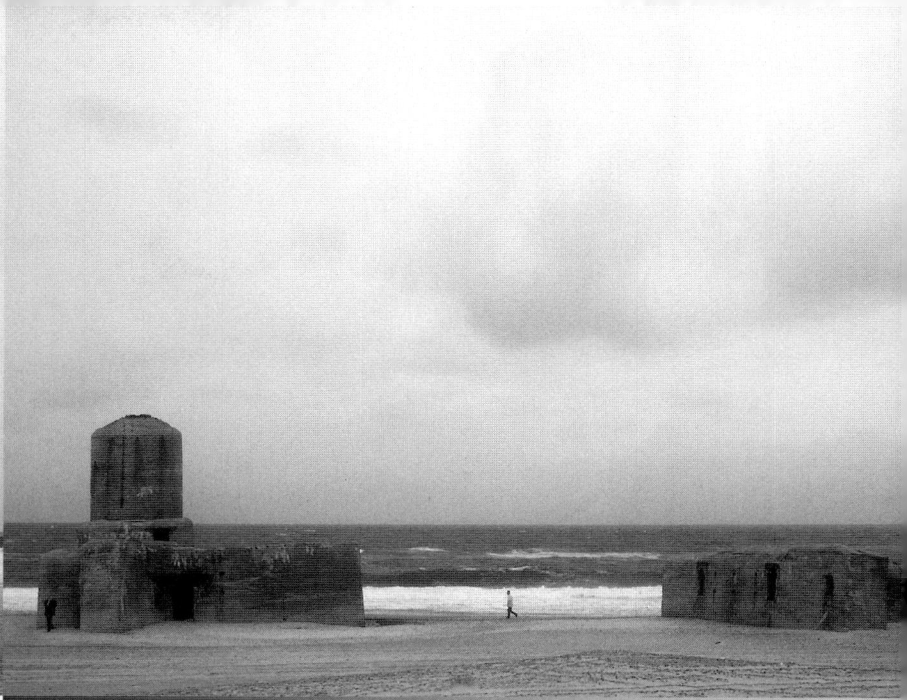
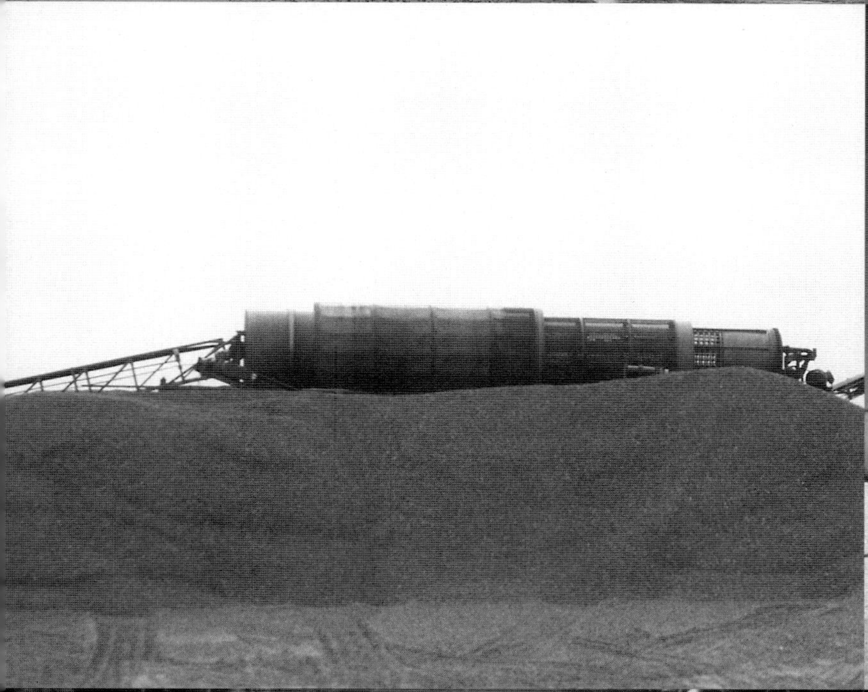
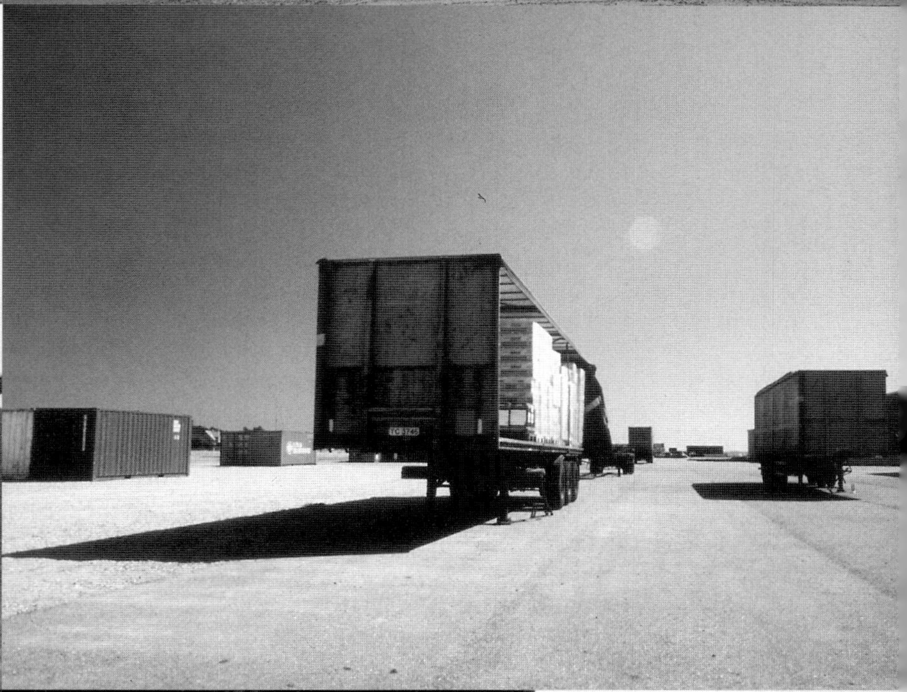
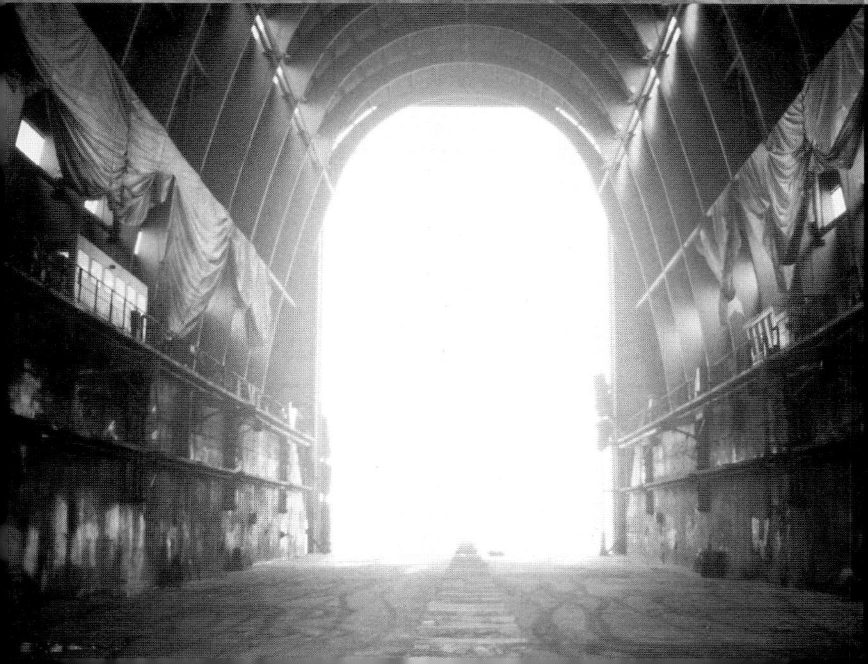
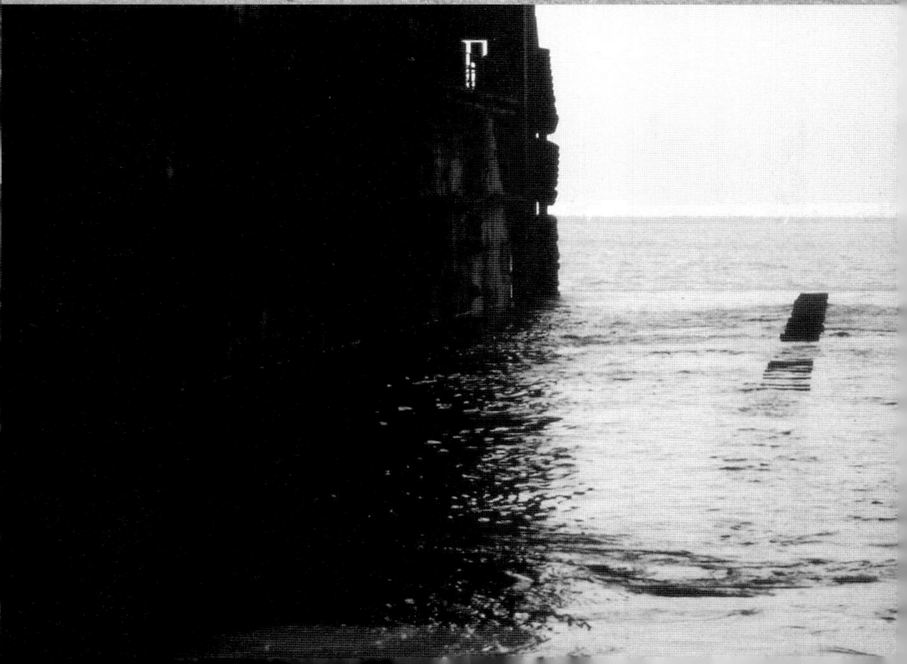

DEPOSIT LANDSCAPE ON LOLLAND
The place and the fundamental idea

THE LANDSCAPE
The landscape of South Lolland is an open and evenly smooth low-lying terrain, consisting of young moraine and marine foreland. The entire area in the vicinity of Rødby was formed by upheavals after the most recent Ice Age and reclaimings dating from the beginning of the twentieth century, which have gradually been transformed into water meadows and fields.

In this open landscape, the heavenly vault and the soft light both play a predominant role, together with the moisture and the water. The landscape articulates that which is especially Danish through the light's meeting with the surface and the water. The elements on the surface become secondary: forests and terrain movements do not form spaces as they do in other parts of the country, but groves and farmyards are spread out over the large agricultural surface.

The highway from Maribo to Rødbyhavn (Rødby harbor) is also situated "upon" the landscape's surface and not as a part of the landscape's space, as in other highways running through Sjælland, Funen and Jutland, which were laid down after this one. The highway running through Lolland does so in relatively long straight segments on low embankments and with few, albeit effective, bends in the road. The road's rhythm is primarily established by the road's own elements: embankments, bridges and ramps, which all are planted with trees in order to intensify and render visible their expression – each element has its own variety of tree. It is these artificial elements – and not some predominating external landscape – which create the spatial experience. The garden architect, Professor C. Th. Sørensen, at the end of the nineteen-forties, created this characteristic composition of earthwork elements on the surface.

SKETCH PROJECT'S MOTIVES
The project's idiom has been developed through a drawing together of the area's special expressions – historic, substantial, spatial and climatic. The light and the elements' relative connection to the surface and the floating landscape, which is further amplified through dredging. The chief motives are the formation of the landscape and the relative water level, the cultural landscape's surface, the elements and the vast light-space. Or to put this another way – place and history – substance and reflection - buoyancy and time – wind and light.
Motive 1: the formation of the landscape – and the relative terrain.
Motive 2: buoyancy/liquidity and time – in the slow process.
Motive 3: the surface, the elements and the direction.
What has been carried out from the chief motives is a drawing together of images, carrying this forth all the way to what could be called a grammar of drawing.

The program-related fixations are thereafter incorporated spatially into the aggregate picture. The intention in this method of working is to attain certain distinct motives and points in the very fluid developmental situation which constitutes the terms of the reclamation.

THE PROJECT'S ELEMENTS
The soil formations have been laid out for a horizontally elevated plan. The new horizontal plan establishes a landscape collage of lake- and water-landscapes, as parts of an existing past, present and future. In order to bring the new landscape plan into relief, the slopes are concave – with a soft transition between the lower grounds (3) and the upper grounds (2). The horizontal plan ought to lie in level +15. Moreover, the precise directions, in interplay with the soft and flexible earth elements, establish a mirror of the overall image of the Danish cultural landscape. In every direction – from regions with modestly hilly moraine landscapes - to vast level reclamation areas – layer upon layer of cultural landscapes' forms are elaborated – in an interplay of soft organic movements and precise geometric lines.

THE LAKES AND THE WATER-LANDSCAPE
The placement of water surfaces on plateaus seems to be a mistake, at first glance. But the encounter with this mirror of the sky and the alder trees and the water lilies' proximate sensual scale constitutes a conscious interpretation and a relativization of the place's and the area's special origins and singular character, which via upheavals and reclamations carry Lolland's precise meeting with the sea out of focus. It is the region's connection with the water and the sea, over the course of time, which we have transposed further into this raised water surface in order to elucidate the salient features in the area – along with the large new surfaces of lake in the excavated fields. Relative water levels in visible and near contact.

An elucidation which might not be evident at first glance, but which will clearly leave behind a recollection in the images of the flourishing heavenly mirror's placement above the horizon, framed in by trees, and the mirror edge's razor sharp meeting with the excavation's lake mirror, images of the landscape's skyline and of the embankment- and sea-landscape.

EPILOGUE
One composition comprised of three motives from the water, the light and the earthwork elements in the relative and fluid landscape – as described above.

This has transpired through the working method and the motive sketching, the chain of events in relation to the road experience – along with the new collage-landscape level, with the contrast posed by the water surfaces and the water-lily lake to the lake's reflecting images and the sky's horizon.

The task has been to establish a recreational landscape, as a comprehensible mirroring of an urban, infrastructural cultural landscape, and at the same time, to integrate and propagate the special Danish aesthetic values within a plan that both encompasses the immediate, proximal sensory impressions and the emblems established by the elucidation of the sky's and the horizon's space in simple distinct images. In other words, the task has been to create *something special* – to engender a project that will fashion new images in the aggregate picture of Denmark.

The new landscape plane, surface in level X

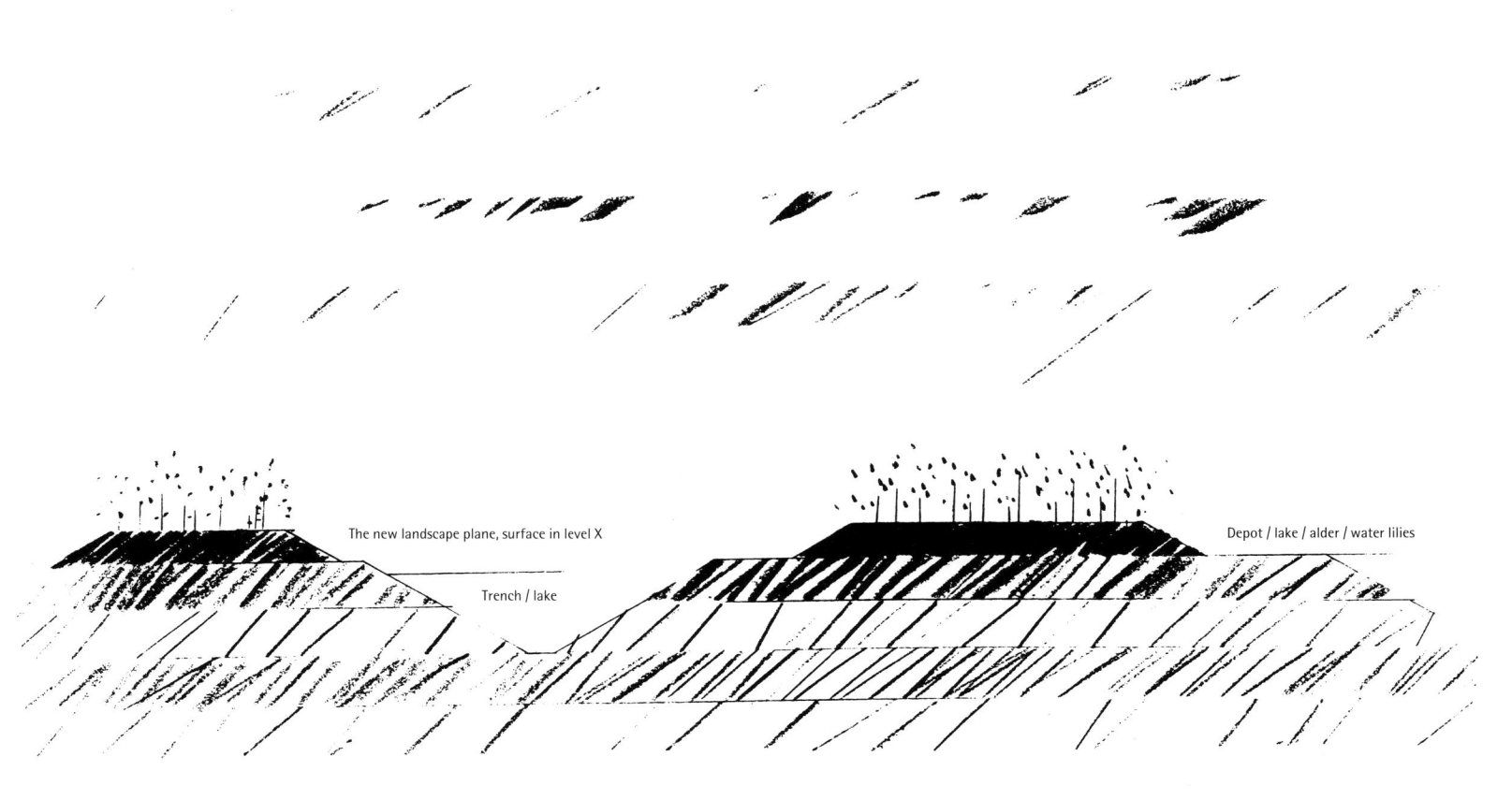

Trench / lake

Depot / lake / alder / water lilies

Layers & the relative horizon. Sectional view in the new landscape.

50

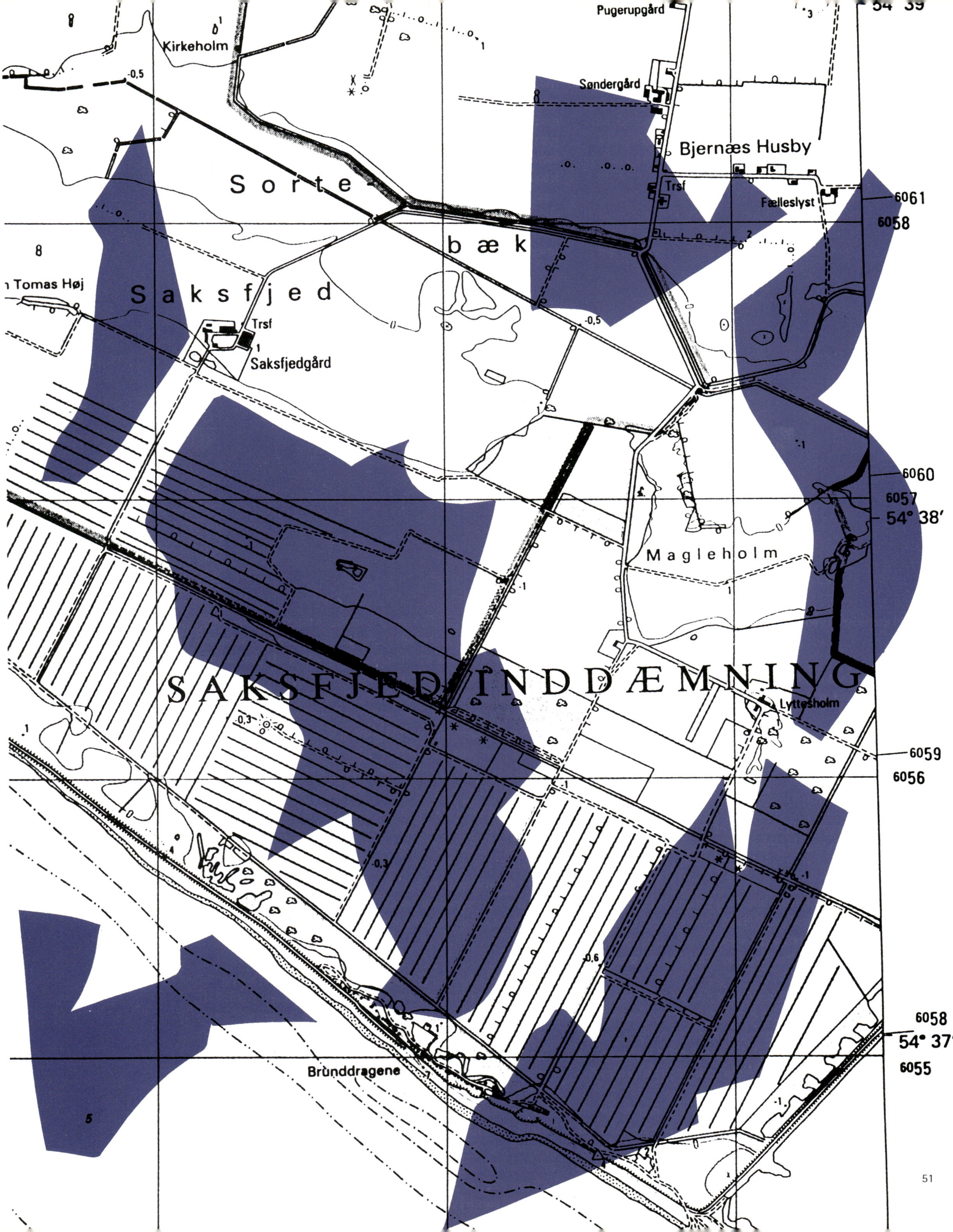
Pugerupgård
54° 39'
Kirkeholm
Søndergård
Bjernæs Husby
Trsf
Fælleslyst
6061
6058
Sorte-
bæk
Tomas Høj
Saksfjed
Trsf
Saksfjedgård
6060
6057
54° 38'
Magleholm
SAKSFJED INDDÆMNING
Lyttesholm
6059
6056
6058
54° 37'
6055
Brùnddragene

WEST AMAGER

From the Sjælland's Bridge to the Køge Bay. The great regional wedge cuts its way almost all the way into the heart of the city and by this means, it is unique.

The notion is to unify this green wedge with an energy landscape of windmills and energy forests, in order to clear the city – in such a way – in a dual sense, inasmuch as the windmill park is capable of producing more than half of Copenhagen's electric power. At the same time, Denmark is displaying an overall and clear signal, extending from the place out toward the horizon – since the windmill park is 12 kilometers long – and creating a symbol right at the point where the new Øresund bridge-connection will be meeting the road's first interchange, where the exit sign indicates: Denmark, turn right – Europe, straight ahead. (There's only one sign analogous to this one. It's just north of Kolding, and there it indicates: "Copenhagen, to the right, Hamburg, straight ahead." Strangely enough, it seems you've always got to turn off the road to get to Denmark.)

To point the wedge clearly out toward the horizon, into the landscape that is about to take root in an area around the Sjælland's bridge and in doing so, to define all of Amager as an island in relation to road-, air- and sea-traffic.

Along with this, bringing together production and recreation, on the basis of the same fundamental idea as in the proposals for the Western Forest, which point toward the place, the process and the global communications landscape.

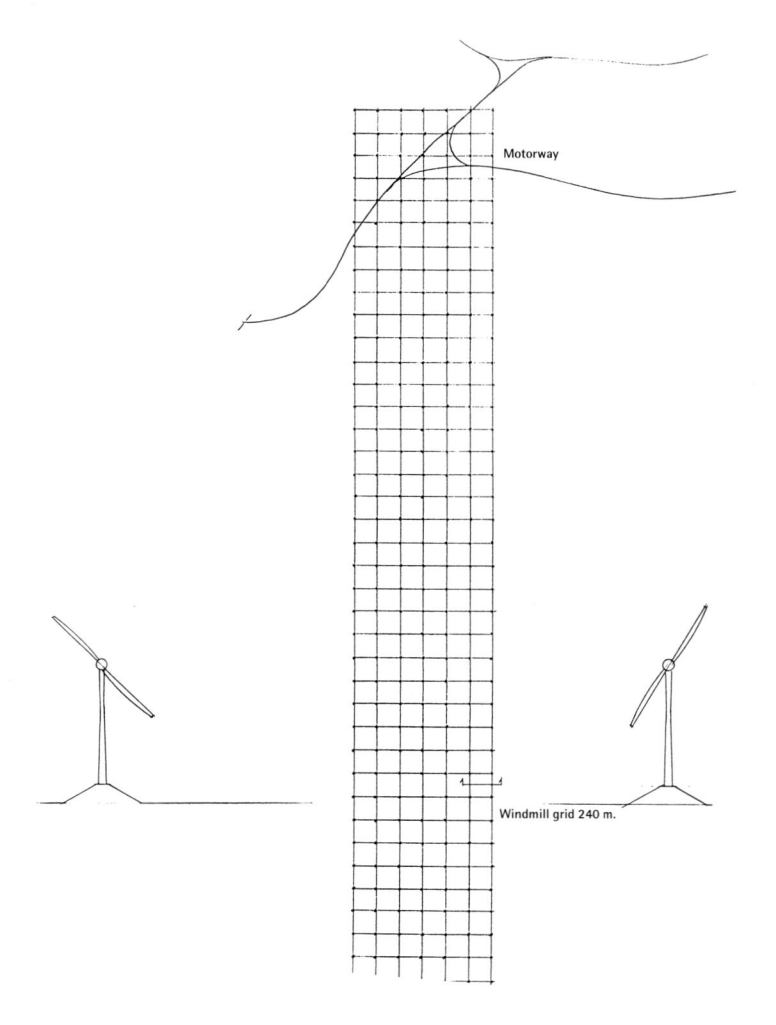

Motorway

Windmill grid 240 m.

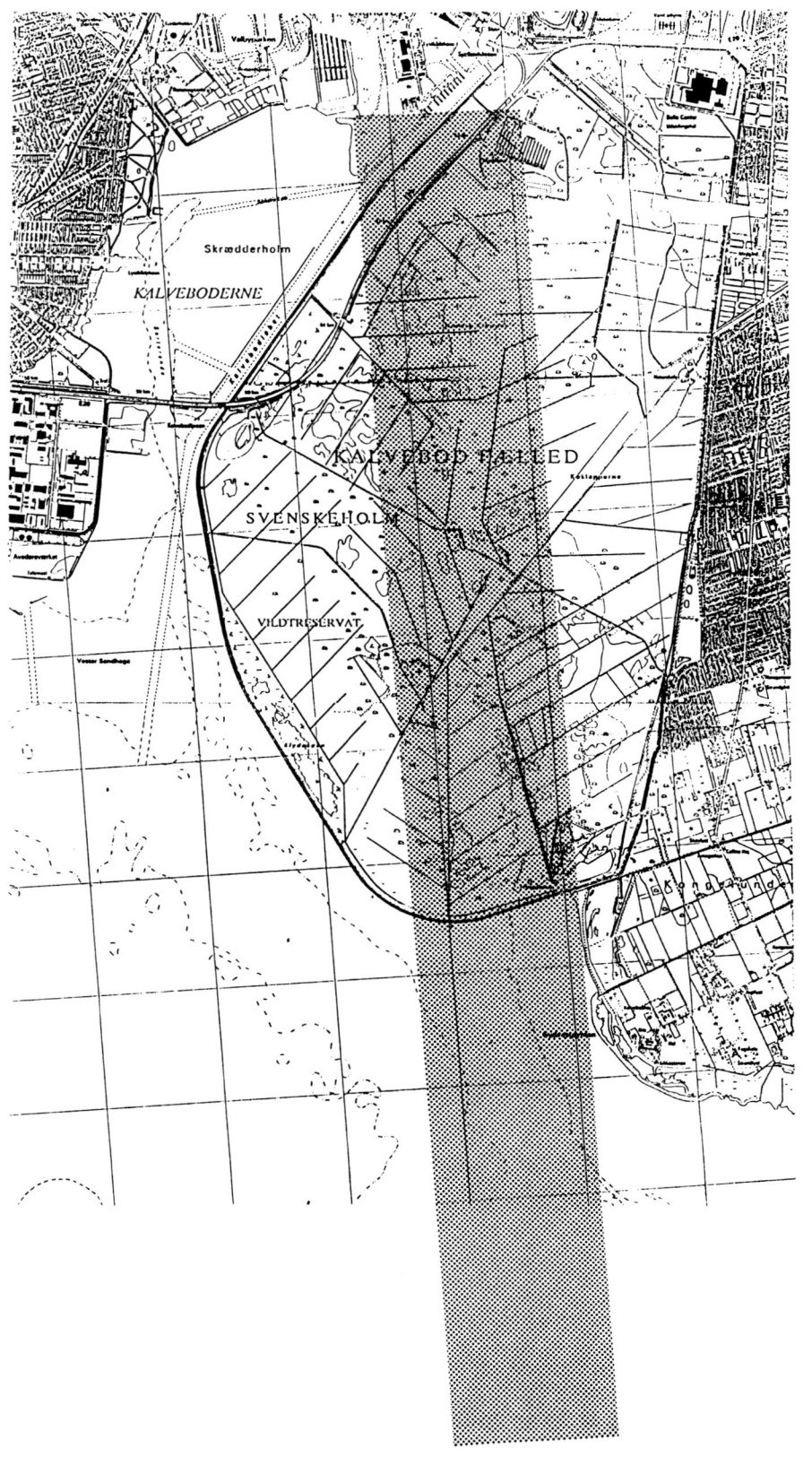

Windmill park, 1,5 x 12 km.

THE AVEDØRE POWER PLANT

Avedøre Holme (Avedøre Islet) can be characterized as a monument to energy and transportation, a bounded, closed island (like a citadel). A gigantic service area whose sole purpose is to transform energy. The energy plays a role by virtue of the Avedøre power plant's situation on its own reclaimed plateau, as the termination of the bay. Discharge/ projection - charging - emptiness - etc.

This elevated plateau, with its energy and purifying plants, constitutes a monumental surface in relation to the reclaimed container-service-area, the Køge Bay and Copenhagen's skyline, insofar as the whole narrative about modern society can be read in one rounded horizon.

The placement and the scale are, in themselves, qualities that will appear most intensely when the surface is opened up and made accessible. And it is also contrasted by the self-created scale that will supervene when the area is set free for non-permanent construction, and when the spontaneously growing vegetation is allowed to remain there. After fifty years, the situation ought to be reviewed.

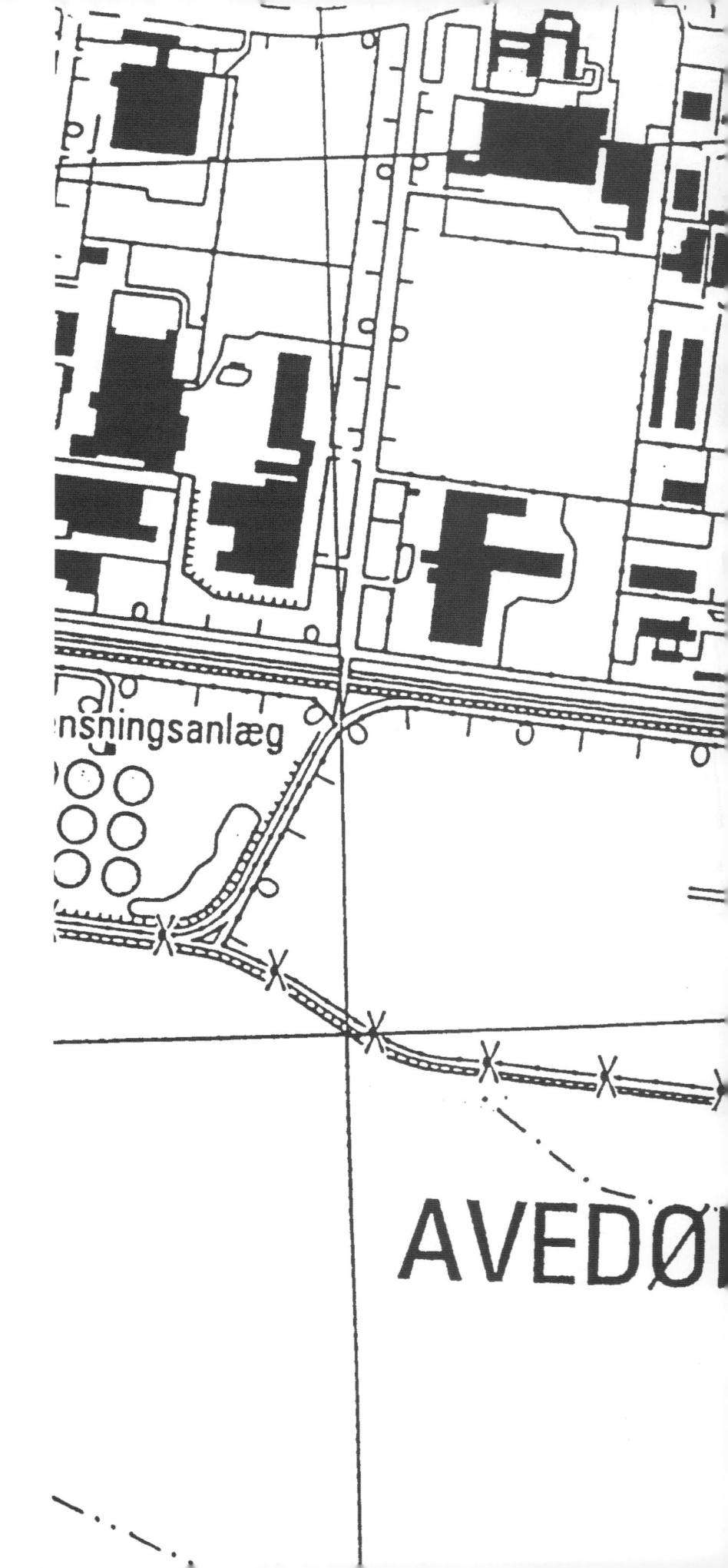

Trsf

Pumpestation

Avedøreværket

Telemast

HOLME

3

THE MEETING OF THE STOREBÆLTSBRO
WITH SPROGØ

Considered as a whole, the new Storebælt (The Great Belt) bridge connection has proved to be a most successful project. Like a ribbon, it hovers over the surface of the water inside a space that possesses all the monumentality of the climate and the light.

Due to the entire layout's dimensions, its central position and its symbolic meaning, all the links in the project have been exceedingly important.

However, Sprogø, which has been so carefully restored, lies there today left behind like a world that has lost its connection with time and space. Now, Sprogø can only preserve its identity as a museum reservation, but what it gets is a mega-island slab in tow. And, against its will, it finds itself bickering with the new radar-control tower. All in all, it is becoming all too easy to compare Sprogø with some forgotten Christmas decoration at a January closeout sale. Just a few hundred meters distance over the surface of the water has, to be sure, only got the island to sail in its own sea, leaving it to its own devices. But the thought that the consequence of the permanent connection might become an utterly new abstract landscape – a world that might have lifted the project out over the competent and solidly conceived ... such a thought lies far off in a time that has a more positive attitude to the past than to the future.

The guiding idea in the proposal is that all of the new island can be dispensed with simply by cutting a slit, as it were, or a fissure in the water's surface and letting the cars drive down into a roadway submerged beneath the water level. The iron sheet pilings tightly lining the sides of the roadway would meet one another in the middle of the sunken road section, in a narrow crevice of light. The train's tunnel ramp is conceived in an analogous way. A little bit closer up, what can be perceived is that the water's surface opens itself up in a narrow slit. The road's declivity provides a shorter, grotto-like contrast to the bridge expanse's vast free horizon space. The sunken parts could be thought of as being utilized for service functions and as rest areas, as well as for positioning security apparatus. Today, the present surface of the new island is a security zone, which could just as well be positioned in a low-water area, and possibly even secured with a sheet piling concealed beneath the surface of the water. The solution entails that Sprogø would regain its obvious right to the belt. Viewed from a distance, the East Bridge's ramp plunges directly down into the surface of the water, and Sprogø exists as the island in the Storebælt. The light, the fissure and the sentence are retold in a geological time-space.

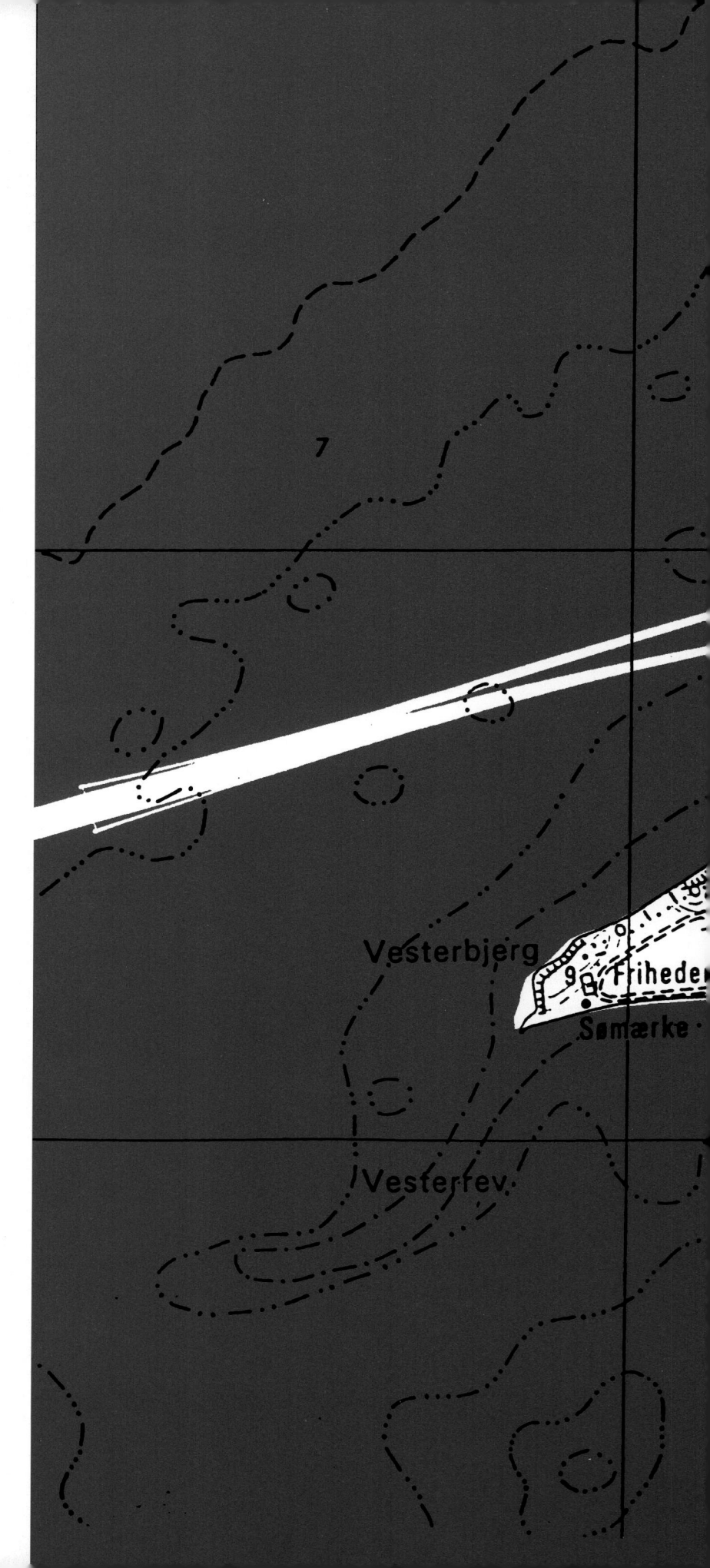

Sprogø

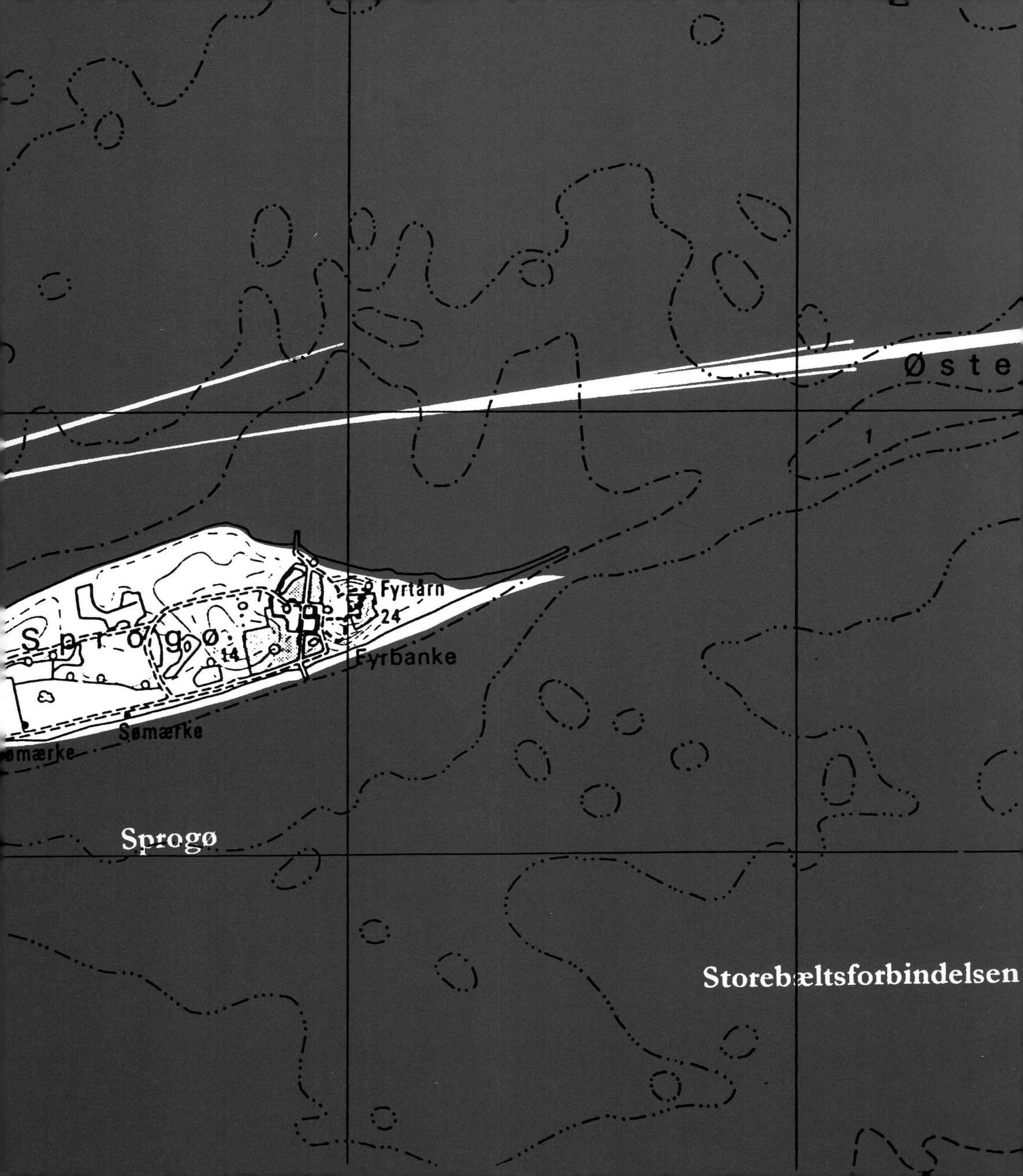

Storebæltsforbindelsen

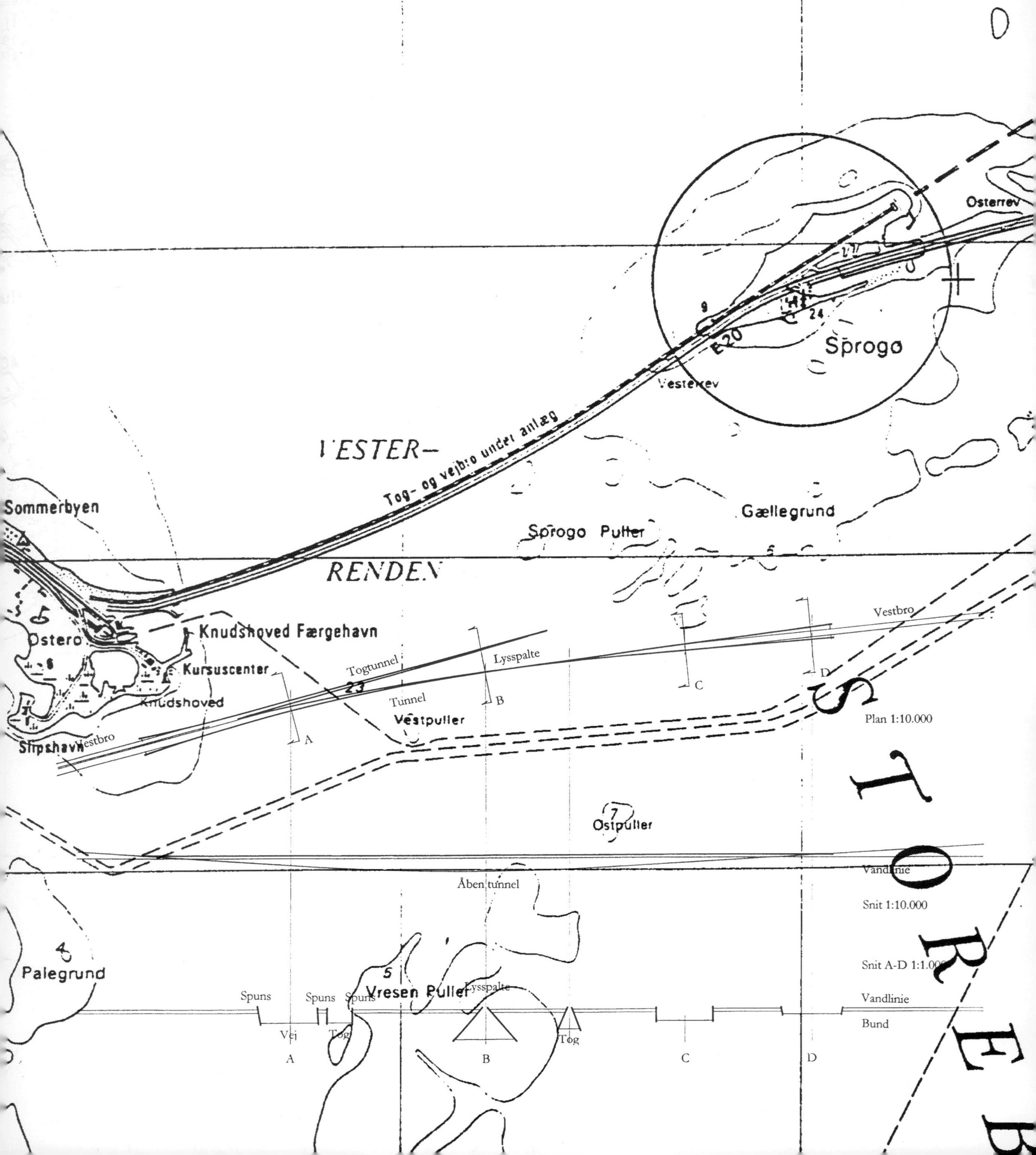
Østerrev
Sprogø
E20
Vesterrev
VESTER-
RENDEN
Tog- og vejbro under anlæg
Sommerbyen
Gællegrund
Sprogø Puller
Knudshoved Færgehavn
Østerø
Kursuscenter
Knudshoved
Slipshavn
Vestbro
Togtunnel
23
Tunnel
Lysspalte
Vestpuller
A
B
C
D
Plan 1:10.000
Østpuller
Vandlinie
Åben tunnel
Snit 1:10.000
Snit A-D 1:1.000
Palegrund
Vresen Puller
Spuns
Vej
Tog
Bund
STOREB

Map showing the Storebælt (Great Belt) fixed link area with Korsør, Halsskov, Svenstrup and Sprogø.

Labels visible on the map:
- E20
- Højbjerg, 105 km
- Krusesminde, Svenstrup, Halseby, Tårnborg K
- Vagtbanke, Go-kartbane, Tårnbjerg
- Tunnel under anlæg, Projekteret
- Halsskov Færgehavn, Tårnborg, Tårnholm
- Halsskov Rev, Vandrerhjem, Marsk Stigs Rev
- Halsskov, Magleø, Korsør Nor
- STER-ENDEN
- 71
- Sygehus, 105 km, 265, 150
- KORSØR, Korsør Skov, Bonderup Huse
- Restr., Bonderup
- Klarskov 29, Lille E.
- Kursuscenter, Klarskov
- Eskilstrup Overdr.
- 33
- Togtunnel
- service, 39
- A, Motorvej, Østbro
- P-service, Gangtunnel
- Tog
- Vestbro
- Sprogø
- Egholm Flak
- Storebæltsforbindelsen
- Rasteplads
- Plan & snit 1:1.000
- Tog, Motorvej, Service, Ø, Vandflade, Ærhoved
- Dæk
- A — A
- Egholm
- 42

HIGHWAY MONUMENT in Vejleådalen

Vejleådalen (the Vejle River Valley) is one of the green wedges that the 1947 urban plan of Greater Copenhagen mapped out as a recreational area. A grandiose stroke in the new urban formations, which was meant to ensure easy accessibility to open-air areas and simultaneously secure a central structure in how the city was to be built up. Considered as a whole, the areas are open, with a relatively low requirement on being constantly looked after. The direct outcome of this is that we, in this small and well-ordered country, easily perceive the area as nature. But, in fact, the wedge – down to the smallest blade of grass – is a result of the special Danish management of Western European interests after World War II.
The most significant element in this planning is the highway. The highway that lies on the edge of the wedge and fills it with an incessant whizzing, sounded in the memory of the dream about freedom, which is the road's very idea! The idea about – or the symbol of – happiness and paradise, which always consists in one form or another – and which, in our world, is retrieved inside the airport and on the highway.
The wedge is pierced by Denmark's very first railway line, running from Copenhagen to Roskilde, braided by the highway, and it contains the largest monuments created in our time.
The monuments are those spaces that turn up in the vast, gentle intertwinements – and which the soft lines of the light fittings do so carefully delineate. A gigantic spatial symbol about an epoch which moreover embodies the dream about the natural nature in shielded plantings. A symbiosis of function and dream, as the societal expression of the idea about the transition into the new millennium. A space whose meaning corresponds to the cathedrals of earlier times. It is here that my project takes its mark – in the emblem that is the road's rapid, linear and transient precision – combined with the larch plantings' sober-minded and diffuse presence.

Tueholmsøen

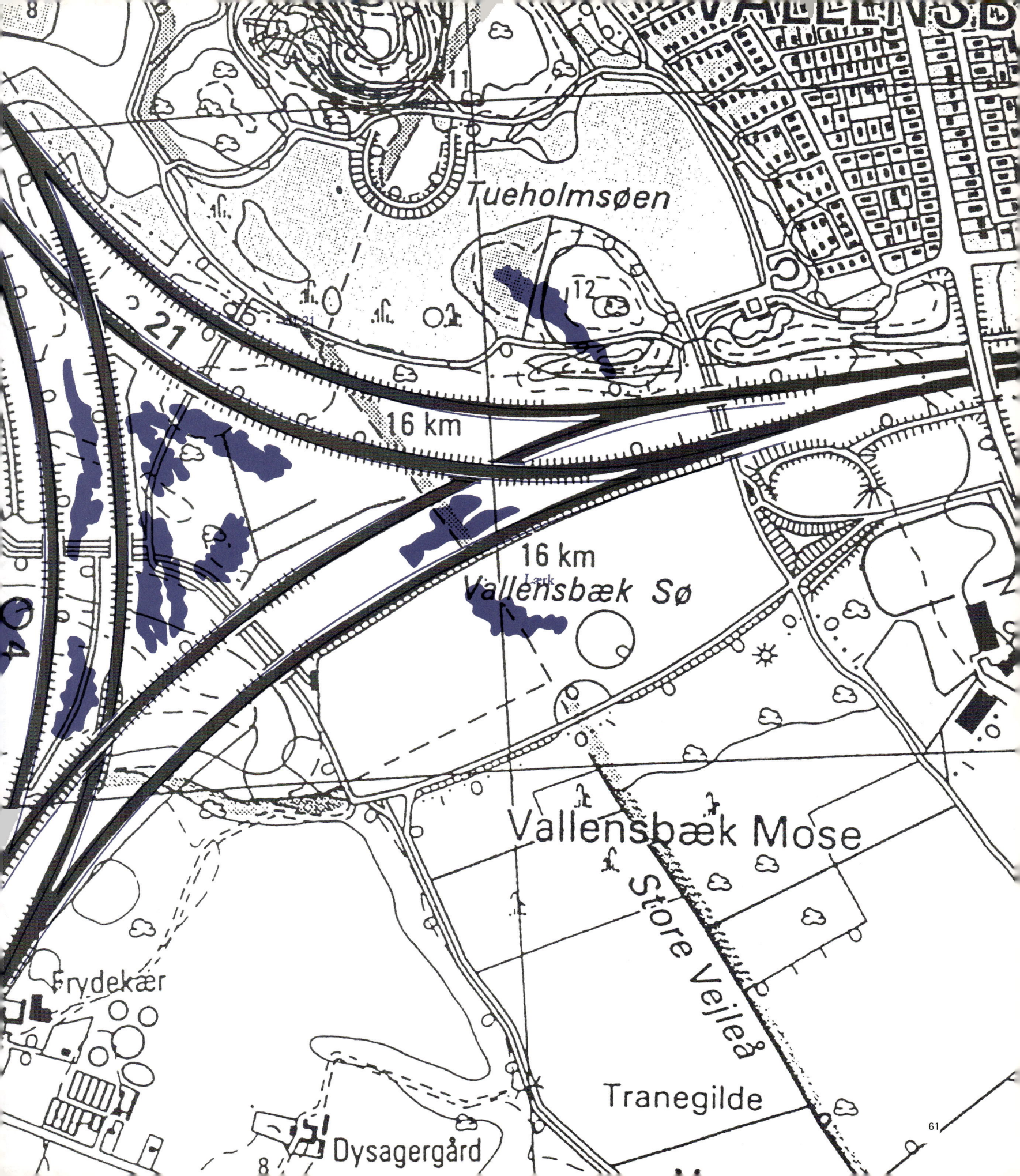

16 km

16 km
Lærk
Vallensbæk Sø

Vallensbæk Mose

Store Vejleå

Frydekær

Tranegilde

Dysagergård

KONGENS NYTORV

The open square at Kongens Nytorv (the King's new market place) is the city's central and collective space – currently as well as historically. This large area was laid out in 1670. Subsequently, it was spatially maintained by Charlottenborg (now an exhibition hall and the home of the Royal Danish Academy of Art), the line of Nyhavn - moving out toward the harbor and the Sound, and it is also secured by the equestrian statue positioned in Charlottenborg's baroque axis.

The plaza's irregular form is fashioned by an analogous number of building facilities of swinging quality. An oval of pruned elm trees and a smaller grove of free-growing elms in the middle have functioned for a few hundred years as a space-creating rotary element and as a veiling filter for the somewhat less successful architecture.

The working idea here is that the thinking behind this urban architectonic construction is turned the wrong way around – because the plantings have primarily been put into use as apologetic intermediary links. "If it is the frame that has something wrong with it, then you have to repair the frame, and not try to replace the painting or change the wall." In the best instance, only a good emergency solution can issue from this mentality.

Bassiner   Elletræer

PROPOSAL

The proposal proceeds to clear the open square with all the assurance that Charlottenborg and the plaza's axes and lines can manage to stand there all on their own. In drawing out the water's buoyancy, a sequence of shallow pools is formed. Besides serving as its own motif, this series will primarily double the room vertically, through reflection. It is this verticality that will secure the new space via the new irregular, atmospheric columnar space. The climatic and aqueous space as Denmark's monumental main motive is secured, and stylized, in this central position. The drawing forth of these pools constitutes a variation on the 1st proposal. What has been added is a light veil of alder trees in the water surfaces. The alder trees, which can be formed as multi-stemmed alder trunks, will grow as high as 6-10 meters. In the large space of the open square, they will appear like dispersed grasses – closer up, they appear as veils, and they will officiate in facilitating the pause taken here.

The equestrian statue will remain on his place and regain his freedom, on his way to an eternally diffluent ambiguity, secured by history.

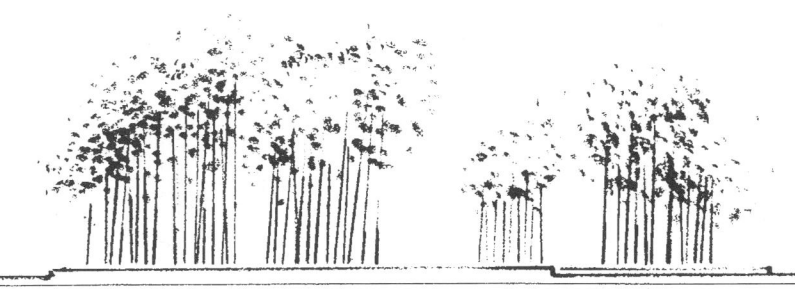

Bassiner   Elletræer

Charlottenborg

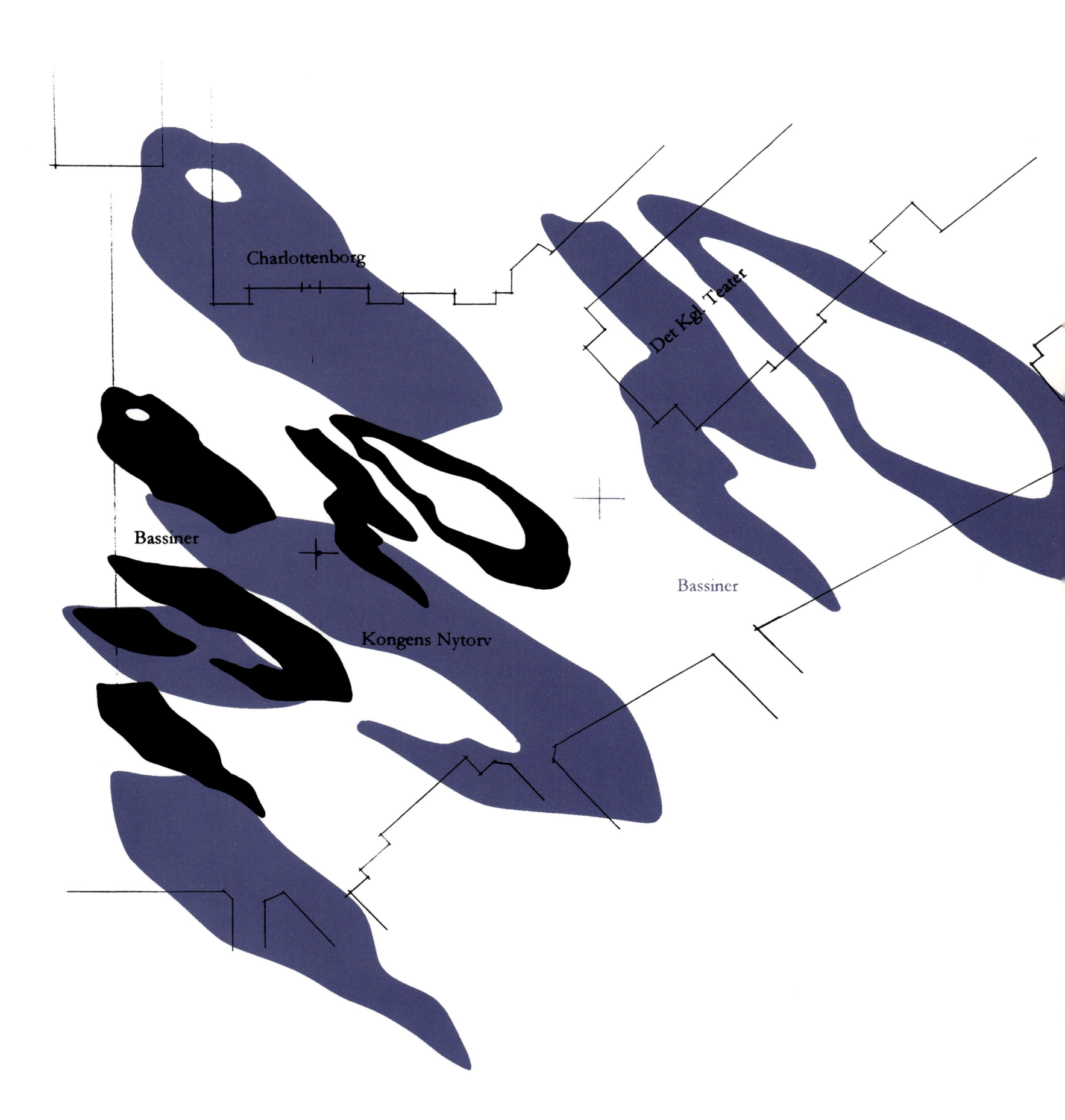

Det Kgl. Teater

Bassiner

Bassiner

Kongens Nytorv

63

JENS KVORNING

Approach
The notion of transition – linked up with the city and with architecture – makes its appearance both conceptually and concretely as a polysemantic phenomenon. If the most essential property and quality is the non-single-valued and non-definable, then it would seem most fruitful to undertake a series of *circumscriptions* of the phenomenon – both in the form of analytical approaches and through experimentation and annexations. Annexation as a form of provocation of the four designated case-study areas ought to reveal what properties the change makes visible or probable.
The act is equated with the observing analysis and considered part of a project which has the purpose of fostering a greater consciousness about the character of transition and about its role, its significance and its possibilities of being articulated in the present-day urban landscape.

Transition
Philosophy, physics and ethnography all link up the concept of transition with some form of transformation, a fundamental change. Change in existence, change in life conditions and change in form of consciousness. Change in state. Transition from one stage along life's way to the next.
In history, the concept is employed as the designation for the transition between two periods, each of which is consistent in itself.

The transition, in this connection, is often a hybrid form, unstable, difficult to characterize with the aid of the conceptions and with that way of understanding which is the predominant one. This is precisely why the understanding of how one form is going through dissolution while a new one is assuming form often becomes a controversial matter. In the history of architecture, mannerism, perceived as being an attempt to wrest itself free from the Renaissance's grammar, has constituted such a much-debated question. In everyday speech, the conception makes its appearance both in an entirely concrete sense – to cross over something, to be lifted free from something. The pedestrian crossing. The railroad crossing. The bridge as a transition. But everyday speech also links up the conception with the unstable intermediate period – 'a transition presented itself in such a way' – understood as something provisional or unstable. The journey through the transition thereby also turns into something uncertain, a provisional position between two certain worlds.
The conception makes its appearance in the theory of composition as an element or a piece that is inserted between two larger or more significant compositional elements. Independent, yet existing nonetheless merely by virtue of the more significant elements between which it is inserted.
Transition is separation *and* unification. Transition is change – but it has been brought into a new situation by carrying out the transition. When you get involved with transitions, you are being brought into an unstable position yourself. The dialectics between unification and separation, between change and stabilization, secure the essential nature of transition.

The urban transition
In the plain of ruins, the fields between the extant buildings make their appearance as transitions established by zones or territories that have lost their original meaning. Only the archaeologist's investigations and redrafts can evoke the original order in the zones, whose significance has faded, and insert what is extant into the context of its original meaning.
But these transitional zones immediately take on a new role by rendering the extant observable in a new way. The front side and back side are rendered one and the same. Directions are annulled and fragmented, or else they overlap and are collocated. The original separation between private and public is dissolved, and the two territory-types glide over into one another. The staging in the symmetry and the perspective are superseded by edge, point and line fragments. The front colonnade that originally flanked a street now stands there – observed from one position as the termination of a vast foreland - observed from another position as a detached monument. New polysemantic and overlapping spatial forms turn up in between couplings and overlappings that are formed as you – set free from the original staging of movement – move around freely in this landscape. This faint significance stages or elicits the full charge of meaning once again. This space for new staging and for otherness attracted the romantic painters, who created a large number of interpretations of the evidently faintly significant intermediate terrain, which was thereby installed into a new image- and symbolic-universe.
The landscape garden appropriated and aestheticized this way of staging, with its hidden axes between suddenly appearing monuments. That which gave a convincing representation of nature was rendered measurable and taken into possession through the placement of the monuments. But the nature-like was, with this, also being collocated with the monuments.
In its ideal project, modernism replaced the romantic garden's monuments with the modern city's detached buildings. The pathway became a road. The natural terrain assumed the role of the faintly significant middle ground, which was evoked and allocated a certain significance through the building of the new city's monuments – the detached buildings as housing or offices, monuments or some other form of collectivity.
But the city is composed of other forces than the aesthetic. The city has arisen, historically, as the place for connection and exchange. The economic exchange in the form of commodity trading and financial transactions. The scientific exchange as the merging and exchange of different qualifications, the knowledge about the world market, the knowledge of changes, the knowledge about knowledge. The cultural exchange, as the reflection and clarification of the material.
The place for urban formation was designated through its accessibility. The density increased the possibility of exchange.
The modern city replaced this density with the effectivization of the city's communications. The city opened itself up physically and created a new landscape. But this was not the landscape that modernism's ideal project had put forth. Instead, the city assumed the form of a dispersion of all its components. All that had bestowed meaning upon the city up until now was afforded equal status. An urban landscape opened itself up to, and assumed the form of, the market's assessment of the individual activities' and the buildings' economic significance. To an ever-increasing degree, the urban realm became an economically homogenized space. Only the market could single out the unique. In spite of vast differences in the appearance of the individual elements, they were immediately swallowed up by the new city's penchant for generalizing and for juxtaposing. The street – the social space – became the road, specializing in effective transportation. The plaza and the park became the open area – the uncoded place, where anything could occur, or where maybe nothing at all was happening. The pre-industrial city certainly remained inherent within this new urban landscape, with its symbol-laden buildings and plazas, but it was becoming more and more weakened in its capacity to communicate with modern urban existence through the agency of the previous periods' monuments and meanings. Internationalization and sharpened specialization have tended to displace the independence of communications from the city and

67

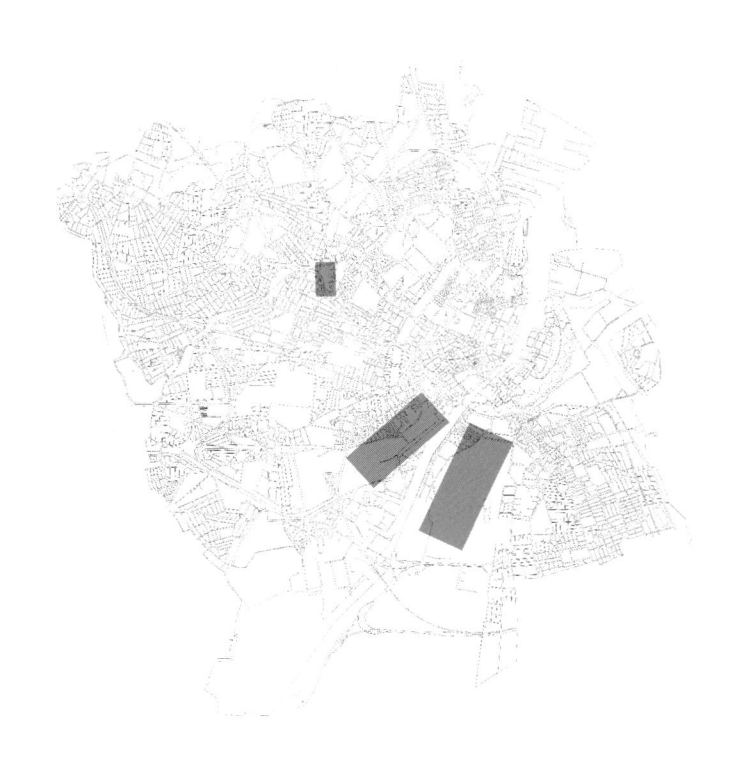

the regional territory to the regional and the international. The interchange is bound up to a lesser degree with the place and to a greater degree with the communications network. In the new landscape of dispersion, various functions spread themselves freely out over the landscape; they are connected with the most accessible points and emancipated – by virtue of their high speeds – from the necessity of physical connections. A number of functions implement a kind of strategic withdrawal to a position, from where it is possible to communicate in many directions all at once without being bound to the structure in any one particular region.

However, the city of the information society, in its actual existence, is split between two courses of development. The physical speeds and the orientation toward an ever-increasingly international market propel one part of the urban formation toward the total dispersion of elements in a combined landscape without any form of subordinate or overall arrangement of the individual elements. Without any possibility of telling whether the natural landscape or the built-up landscape is the predominant one. Without clear differentiations between the collective and the private space. With juxtaposition and generalization of the individual elements, no matter how great the exertions they make in order to stand forth as something special.

But at the same time, other equally radical courses of development set their focus on the potentials of the historic city, which is in demand as the recollection-space for an exponentially growing international tourism, and responsive to a sharpened general interest in the culture as the bearer of identity and provider of explanations. Collocated with the modern city, with respect to its accessibility via the electronic networks, the classical city constitutes an equally potentialized space of innovation for the information industry as the open city.

The spatial coincidence of economic, scientific and cultural exchange, which originally characterized the city, has now become dissolved, with the result that in the current situation, different parts of the city correspond to different aspects of the exchange. The dense city's public space is carried back to something ostensibly authentic and is staged in new ways which, without mirroring any kind of everyday life, are nonetheless expected to be capable of establishing images of coherence and historic continuity, and therewith of being able to fulfill the need for identity and the requirement with respect to the perception of the new global middle class. At the same time, these newly staged, history-laden urban spaces are subject to a vehement pressure for control and for privatization and, by this means, they distance themselves from the traditional definition of the collective space. The approach to the city's dissolution, which can be seen manifest in many occidental urban regions through the placement of diverse urban fragments along the immense communications arteries, has been perceived as a manifestation of the city's dissolution, and regarded as a documentation of the fact that the high speeds of communication are moving in the direction of dissolving the city and of rendering it into a global dispersion. However, this accumulation of fragments along the immense communication arteries can also be seen as the manifestation of a society that has not yet managed to get its actual urban regions to function effectively, and this allows any public investment in high-capacity communications channels to erode, as a direct result of the competition around attaining the best placement. Thereby, this dispersion along the immense communication arteries can just as well be regarded as the manifestation of something backward instead of being the image of what is to come.

In a most grotesque way, the plain of ruins that the modern war created points – with the famous picture of Hamburg after the bombings – toward the current landscape. That which has been built up has forfeited its original structure and significance and has slipped back into a form of heterogeneous landscape. The streets, which originally obtained their significance through their relation to what was built up there, have survived and have now become the place, as such, for the new city. The resulting urban landscape constitutes a dispersion of detached fragments of the classical city combined with the city, which attempts to conquer the best possible placement in connection with the communications networks by superimposing itself directly over them – and thereby eradicating them in their capacity as communications networks. Random volumes, which do not manifest anything collective, assume the role of monuments or dominants, and accordingly render this conception into a purely visual phenomenon. A transitional landscape.

That city within which the information society is evolving – and which it is simultaneously creating – consists both of the historic center and the open city which modernism placed on the agenda and which, in terms of its extension, dominates the modern landscape. Both types are transformed and allotted new roles; they are supplied with new significance that is subject to the current processes of transformation. The historic center appears, structurally and visually, as an island of *otherness* in what is otherwise a homogeneous field. The restoration of the otherness is being sought, but precisely through this process, it becomes worn down and tends toward becoming equivalent to the leisure parks built up on the edge of many great occidental cities. What is happening is an ongoing homogenization of the city.

The collective space must be discovered inside this situation and it must be understood in a new way. The public space has come to be defined as the site of a social praxis, as a place where somebody spends time. The public space is going through a transformation; it is itself in the midst of a transition. To an increasing extent, it is becoming shaped by an economic praxis instead of a social praxis. The public space is defined quantitatively as a place where there are many people present and not according to considerations about why they are present or what they are doing there. In this respect, it is the parking lot at the mega-shopping

center that qualifies as one of the most public places.
But at the same time, the pre-industrial city's public space is being re-staged as the cultural and historical space of recollection. And in this new staging, it supposedly establishes the framework for a social praxis. But this is a praxis with no connection, or at best with only faint connections, to the everyday life grounded in the site. And because of this, the space's traditional cultural meaning is being worn down, and it yields to the general homogenization of the city's space. This supervenes, in the final end, with the same function as the screen image – you can zap between the different urban-related programs.

Strøget, Copenhagen's centrally situated pedestrian street, has now become almost analogous, with respect to its contents, with the large shopping centers found in the suburbs. The very same chain stores and the very same chain restaurants are now found in all the large shopping centers. The retail turnover in Lyngby is of the same magnitude as that in downtown Copenhagen. It is only the presence of a number of traditional cultural institutions that turns the center of Copenhagen into a different kind of downtown area. There is something here that offers *resistance*. The traditional city center can therefore be perceived as a transitional landscape. In the current day's urban reality, there is a particular sequence inserted between homogeneous and predominating forms. And the downtown area is also a transitional landscape in the sense that one only stays there while passing through – as a regional tourist on the weekend's staged shopping trips or the evening's amusement raids – or one stays there as an international tourist. The foreland and the suburbs are no longer dominated by the historical center; they hold sway over the center or they exist alongside of it, without appearing in any simple or fixed relation.

If public life has anything to do with being open to exchange and open to the meeting with what is foreign, then it can rightly be said that people tend to be more extroverted at home in front of the TV set and the on-line computer than they are inside the traditional space of the city. As part of this general tendency, however, new types of collective space continue to come into existence. These are linked up with different sub-cultures, which reinterpret existing codes, conquering and re-staging hitherto disregarded spaces in the city. Which intervene in the transitional zones. Or in the spaces that are going through a transitional phase.

Program

Insofar as homogenization and generalization are the prevailing tendencies, it is imperative that otherness be installed as a counter-strategy. Seeing that the social praxes that have traditionally availed themselves of the public space and that have engendered this space *as* public space can no longer resist the homogenization, it is imperative that other forms of praxis-space relationships be scanned and examined. Since the densification and the condensation that have traditionally characterized the public space can no longer resist the homogenization, it is imperative that the counter-strategy be to investigate emptiness, slowness and the uncoded or differently coded space.

Case-study areas

What the four selected sites – Bispeengsbuen [Bispeeng Overpass], Dybbølsbro/ railway terrain, Amager Fælled [the Amager Commons] and Vestskoven [the Western Forest] – possess in common are precisely this uncoded or differently coded, the non-condensing – and in certain respects, the void.

They fashion transitional spaces within the urban structure by virtue of this otherness. All the selected sites display an otherness, perceived as structural and spatial types that you would not expect to encounter at the sites in question. They also constitute transitional spaces, in a contrary sense, insofar as they are unaffected or only mildly influenced by the processes of transformation that the city is subject to. They manifest themselves as expressions for a slowness or constancy, which serve both to distinguish them from and conversely to link them up with the problem posed by transformation. One aspect of the transition is the transformation – a person has become something else by undergoing the transition, and the transition itself is frequently an unstable or labile zone. However, the case-study areas both differentiate themselves from and become urban transitions precisely by *not* taking part in the ordinary processes of transformation. They become different. They become an intermediate station, experienced as something uncertain that you just have to go through, precisely on account of their constancy.

Moreover, they contain a number of conjunctions in their ways of posing the problems - and in their mutual references. They all encompass the phenomenon – of moving over and across without coming into contact with – and the parallel phenomenon – the confrontation between the local and the regional without these two spheres establishing direct connections with one another. This disintegration and disjunction are characteristic of the modern city, fostered by a manner of thinking and a set of categories that wills the separation. Three of the case-study areas, however, are not parts of the modern city. They have been artificially implanted into the dense city, or else they constitute artificial landscapes which, on account of this artificiality, have rendered the integration into the city's ordinary structure impossible. Taking their location into account, one would otherwise have expected that such integration would be forthcoming.

To a certain extent, the areas refer to one another in terms of direction or movement: Dybbølsbro [the Dybbølsbro bridge and the adjacent area] points over toward Amager Fælled, and standing on the bridge you are borne aloft sufficiently to catch a glimpse of the vast commons behind the buildings on Islands Brygge. The very same metro-train that you look down over as you walk across the Dybbølsbro bridge passes over your head as you walk below Bispeengsbuen or when you drive over its expanse. The

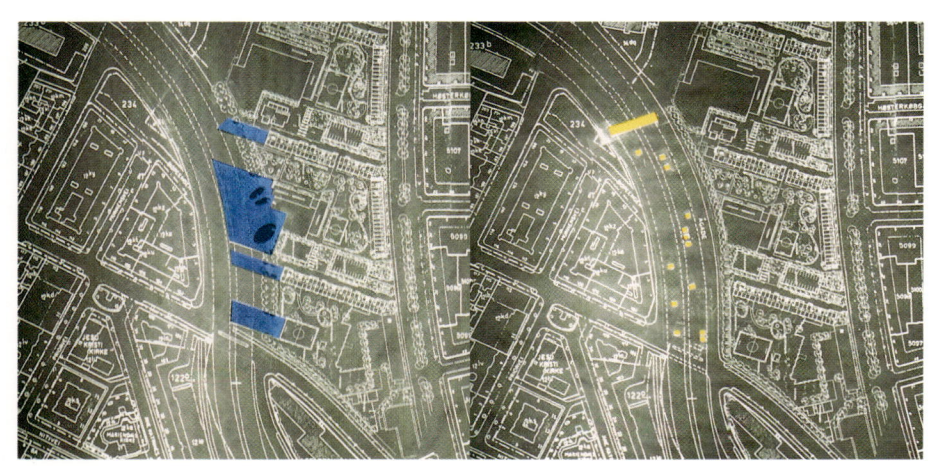

Bispeegnsbuen

highway traffic that passes over you as you walk under the overpass at Bispeengsbuen meets you once again on the Amager Fælled and in the Western Forest. As separation, as sound. At the same time, as energy and destruction.

With this, another theme is introduced, which is exposed within, and which conjoins, the case-study areas. The accessibility that has served as the prerequisite basis for the city has developed such high-voltage communications arteries that the city now has a hard time getting in contact with them. It is only through one form of transformer or another that the city can link itself up with these rapid and specialized communications currents. Historically, it was precisely right there in the surface boundary between the street's movement, as manifestation of the accessibility, and the house, as the framework around the specialized enterprise, that the city's potential was realized. This classical interface has been superseded by a specialization of the city's space and by specialized connecting links to the communications arteries. The spaces that are spontaneously placed in the category of transition are, to a certain degree, bound up with this phenomenon. This high-energy zone, engendered by the especially rapid movement, establishes around itself an emptiness or a zero-energy. A common feature of the three centrally placed case-study areas thus becomes the dialectics between the attraction and the destruction of the communications energies.

Bispeengsbuen

Bispeengsbuen [the overpass at Bispeeng] lifts the regional traffic free from the local. But under the overpass, a kind of vacuum arises, there where the two very different worlds found on either side of the overpass do not manage to infiltrate their way into one another and do not even succeed in getting in contact with one another. Nor does the local life manage to penetrate in any other way and take possession of the space through its activities or to utilize the space under and around the bridge. The space remains an imprint of the road, which has been raised, a mute or quiet imprint, a trace, or a fissure, which does not get filled in. The skin, with the wide road, has been lifted free, but the wound has not healed; no new active surface membrane has been established. The surrounding city's changes seem only in a very restricted sense to have made any impact and to have instigated change at this site. At the very same time that the city's currents attain their maximum in intensity up above, the place below remains stagnant, faint in significance – it does not emerge as a place. The space beneath the bridge is fixed. There are no elements inside the space that articulate time, through the seasons or through growth. The surface has been paved with the most everlasting material, granite. The bridge stands there in raw concrete. The illumination changes only a trifle in the course of the day. The two sides have entrenched themselves in toward the space

The Amager Commons

beneath the bridge. The high-rise building establishes distance and delineates the boundary with a continuous hedge and a line of trees. On the other side, a belt of greenery has been laid out between the neighborhood of courtyard blocks and the space beneath the bridge. The unimpeded connection, which the upheaval of the intense, regional traffic ought to entail, is effectively impeded through this disposition of the two building complexes.
The boundaries of the surrounding building complexes are marked in such a way that the elevated road is reiterated. It is not the intersecting movements between the two sides for which room is being made. What the stage is being set for is rather a meaningless movement, like that which transpires up above, with the flow of the regional traffic. Pedestrians who wish to cross over here are compelled to undertake this movement in spite of the space's partitions and boundaries. The transverse movement arouses suspicion. The space's otherness penetrates the viewer. By being inside a space that has not been implicated into the everyday life of the area, one who comes to a stop and remains in the space becomes a suspect – the observations one makes from this spatial and mental position become distorted. Others who hang out there or pass through the space are regarded as being potentially dangerous or deviant. One's movements become more and more affected, affectedly normal, affectedly innocent.
In its referrals to the surrounding city, the space exists in a mirroring opposition to the city's directions and meanings. As the windows in the apartment block mirror the cars' movements down upon those who might have gone astray beneath the bridge, the two flanking buildings reflect the place where you came from – and do not refer to where you are going.
Any testing out and provocation of the space must fundamentally square its accounts with the meaningless repetition of the highway up above. This can transpire by (A) accepting the absence of life in the space beneath the bridge and by dividing the terrain between the two buildings. Or it can transpire by (B) making an attempt to install the space into a larger urban and comprehensible coherence.
A: Activation / re-defining / opening / distorting the boundary. If the boundary toward the High-rise buildings is executed as a water surface, then the territory of the high-rise complex will be drawn in under the bridge. But the boundary, without being space establishing, will remain a boundary for most of the year. The boundary will take on breadth. It will be opened. It will take on expression. It will begin to speak through mirrorings and reflections of the weather – while nonetheless remaining a boundary. As you come into contact with it from the high-rise complex on Lundtoftegade, the water surface will be experienced as a park element, while from the other side, it will make its appearance as an architectonic element belonging to both the street and the plaza.

Through its segmentation, the water surface will guide the transverse movement across Lundtoftegade and Borups Allé. The upheaval of the boundary will occur in the freezing weather of winter. Instead of distance and emptiness, the boundary will become a skating rink, and thus it will become active, gathering and inviting. The same thing will happen on a warm summer day.
B: Producing the place.
The space beneath the bridge is empty of meaning. By allocating it a meaning which does not issue from the immediately observable everyday life in the area but links this space up with a more general way of posing the problem and with a larger comprehensible space, perhaps it can become - in a new way - a place inside consciousness; it can become produced *as a place* – and thus it can gradually attract new forms of life and activity.
Inside the traditional city, the city's center is the place for the exchange of information. Today, information is accessible in other ways and is consequently not bound up with the city's centrality. The space beneath Bispeengsbuen stands in a situational connection with the telephone building, which is one of the largest junctions for the exchange and transport of information. In accordance with the logic of modern communications, this junction does not articulate itself in any perceivable way inside the city. As a reference to this point and as a commentary on the information currents' disintegration with the urban structure, a glass box is mounted into place. The box contains 256 monitors, which will continuously put any viewer into contact with the whole world. In the pavement, a number of monitors will also be set into the pavement. The empty place thus becomes one of the places that is most saturated with information. Perhaps this new situation will gradually produce the site with a new meaning. In this way, it can become a place for new activities and win a new urban role for itself. Perhaps it will merely remain a commentary on a current phenomenon. In any event, the glass box itself will serve the local purposes by indicating the pathway between the two buildings. And it will document the information currents' disintegration with the urban structure and the localized cultures.

Amager Fælled
The roads which transverse the Amager Commons, and thereby bring us into the Commons, cross over them, in a certain sense. In everyday speech, it's even said that one
drives "over" the Commons. The road leading from the Sjaelland's Bridge is perceived as being "façade-less". And the new highway moves, in a very real sense, over the Commons, for a long stretch. And therewith, as is the case with any highway, it is defined by steady and continuous movement, without any contact with that which is passing through. The regional, then, has no points of connection with the Commons.
The surrounding local worlds, however, also have a difficult time penetrating the commons. This vast area is protected, and may only to a limited extent take on new facilities that are linked with the surroundings. But the surroundings have also fashioned an edge up against the Commons in the understanding that this was supposed to be a closed area. It is only by infiltrating narrow and very private suburban streets on the Sundby side, or through the belt of institutions or businesses on the Islands Brygge side, that you can gain access to the Commons. The Commons is therefore, both in the regional and the local coherence, a transitional zone, exposed through its inaccessibility.
Once you have entered the Commons, you find yourself immediately swallowed up and cut off from the world from whence you came. The vegetation closes up around you straightaway. The transition between the two worlds is not slow and gradual, but rather abrupt and definitive.
The Commons contain an almost aggressive transformational force. The woods have caught hold and are advancing into all the places where they can thrive. But there are places that remain nearly empty. Only with different growths of grasses. They offer a testimony about the artificial, about waste and about the ground's poisoning. And you become further attentive to the danger heralded by the signs warning of the presence of warheads. Nature is not idyll. The nature is not nature. The open space is dangerous. But the open space is also a prodigious potential of otherness.
The new urban development, Ørestaden, will swallow up a part of the Commons. But if the Commons' wildness is *not* tamed, it will retain its power to fashion a world in itself that will be able to surround and engulf the visitor as soon as he/she has left the city's safe territory. The Commons will remain a resistance to the homogenization of the urban landscape.
The proposal for articulation addresses itself toward elucidating the Commons in the context of the surroundings and elucidating its power, and securing it as resistance in the urban structure. Especially on the Islands Brygge side, the Commons has been regarded as an area that can be enlisted according to need, which has given rise to a number of institutions and small businesses being placed as an edge zone, which weakens the experience of the Commons.
On the Islands Brygge side, the Commons' forest growth is carried as far as Artillerivej, and a sequence of precisely formed corridors and transitional spaces is established, which opens up the forest primeval and renders it penetrable. The institutions that will remain situated on Artillerivej will have access via these corridors. The access corridor is fashioned over the theme of bridge and door – conjoining and separating. Two equally wide sheets of Corten-steel or concrete placed, respectively, vertically – half buried, as wall - and horizontally, as bridge. In a symbolic way, they hold back the forest primeval and pave the way into the forest and into the Commons. With its materials and its proportions (1:1:2), the access space establishes a formal resistance against the organic and guides that which is formal, considered as the city's order, into the forest primeval. But via its materials, which refer to the dumping ground – and to the city from whence this dumping

ground came – a bridge to earlier layers in the area's history, running transverse to this history, is also being constructed.

Vestskoven

Driving through the Western Forest or on the Ring Highway is like driving though a moorland plantation in Jutland. There are no exits, because there is no need for exits – one only need to make it through here, further, onward!

As you are driving through, however, you notice that there are pathways that lead under the road, between the plantations on either side – and there are creatures that move along these paths, even if you don't engage in any contact with them. The theme of the two worlds, which are in spatial contact but nonetheless constitute separate spaces, in the mental dimension and in the senses of movement and activity, is played through once again here, but in a different scale than at the Bispeengsbue and the railway terrain.

If we compare the Western Forest with Dyrehaven [wildlife park north of Copenhagen] the difference which becomes apparent is the way in which the former links itself up with its surroundings. If we may call the coupling with the surrounding neighborhoods the coupling to the local and the coupling via the greater roads the coupling to the regional – it can be said that Dyrehaven embodies a mingling between these two types of couplings. In the Western Forest, one has to render himself local, you might say, in order to come into the area. The regional roads drive right through, right over, right on past. The forms of communication in the new city, of which the Western Forest is a part, have become specialized and organized according to a hierarchy. One specific layout belongs on the one level or on the other – not on several different levels.

At the same time that the Western Forest, through its scale, becomes a part of the regional coherence, it accordingly remains local and thus an obstacle or a transition, when considered in its urban and scale-related context. A neutralizing and transformational landscape between the Roskilde finger's and the Frederikssund finger's urban communities.

It is the ultimate plantation. Systematic plantings. Monocultures. Its almost aggressive will toward becoming forest in a hurry rubs off on its use. The use is dominated by the purposive. By the trip one takes by bicycle. By the jogging route. The sauntering that we know in Dyrehaven is rarely seen here. The Western Forest is inscribed into a different kind of world. Into another kind of life rhythm. It belongs to the modern city's logic of extraordinary spaces and purposiveness – with distinct borders and no overlappings. The provocation could consist of placing the automobile culture's ultimate facilities – the service station and the rest stop – as the stopping place and the access to the forest, and consequently opening the forest up to the regional, within which it inscribes itself by virtue of its scale.

A new kind of rest stop, for the Sunday excursion, where the energy of the great highway is ensnared and transformed, so that it

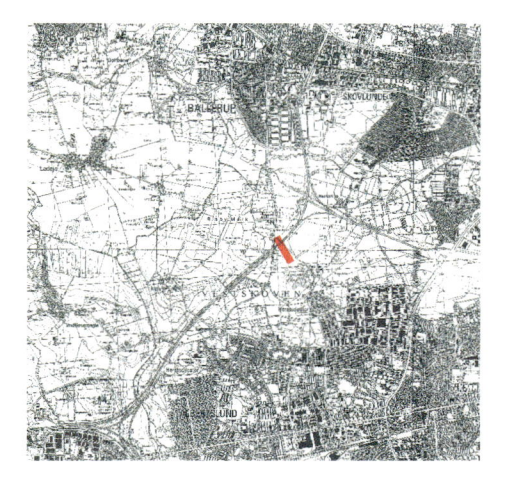

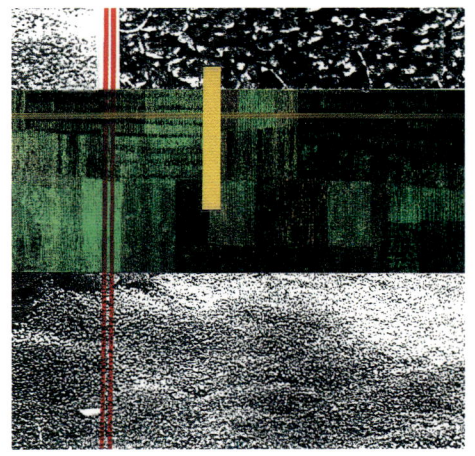

The Western Forest

can come into contact with the surroundings. A way of activating those parts of the forest that the local life does not exploit intensively. A way of supplementing the active edge with an active center. The rest stop is placed in the transition between the forest and the flatlands. It is spatially articulated as a stylized forest of systematic plantings of steel masts, Scotch pine and poplar. With its figures, the ground re-exposes the field structure that the forest has removed. The automobile culture's facilities re-evoke the image of the culture of cultivation.

Dybbølsbro/ The railway terrain

Dybbølsbro Bridge and the circumjacent vicinity lift you over a terrain with which you *may not* come into contact. You look down on to a different and – as far as the ordinary city life is concerned – forbidden world. The bridge puts you, at the same time, into a position where you can survey and perceive essential features in the city. You have now arrived outside the city and you can look in over the city and see it delineated and elucidated through its towers – as you are prone to explaining this to the city's guests. You can see the harbor, lengthwise. The directions become surprising when they are observed from this position. You can see, in glimpses, into the depth of Amager. Looking to the south, you can look right into Valby and Vigerslev, represented by their gas towers. And you can look back on the quarter of Vesterbro, from whence you came; you can see the borderline that you stepped over in order to make your way out to the bridge – no longer as an end, but now as a beginning. You have been set free from the conditions and rules that applied while you were standing in the city and now you can study them without being subjected to them. You have been lifted free from a specialized terrain. And you are hovering over that which previously had been water.

In its logic as a place, the Dybbølsbro bridge is the reciprocal of the Bispeengbue overpass: The local and regional traffic here is lifted free from the regional and the international. But in much the same way as the Bispeengbue overpass, it conducts the regional – and here, also the international – into the city without having it come into contact with the local. When you start out from Vesterbro and walk up Skelbækgade toward the Dybbølsbro bridge, the street's ascent continues right on to the bridge. It points up into the sky and articulates an emancipation from the city's rules and architectonic syntax. But it also conveys the openness and the surrounding world into the city, down to Søndre Boulevard. For some time, the prostitutes took up a position precisely on the spot, where the city's wholeness and control go into dissolution and begin to glide over into the uncontrolled and the non-controllable. There where you can enter in and do something else without being controlled by the city's normality. The railway terrain is otherness. This is a place for dreams and reminiscence and accordingly, for heightened awareness. A place where you can dream yourself away, because you are not confronted with the city's normality. Where just by being in a different kind of space, you can dream about other spaces. This is a different type of collective space alone by virtue of the fact that – up until now – it has avoided the economic homogenization and therewith represents an emancipation.

The railway terrain encloses just as many people into the city and sends just as many out as the largest of the approach roads. Nonetheless, the space is almost unaffected by these currents. Whereas the large approach roads are so hectic, and they crescendo to pure inferno and hysteria at rush hour, the space in which you find yourself when you stand on the Dybbølsbro bridge is virtually unmoved and unafflicted – as if some black hole had swallowed the movement whole and neutralized it. But the silence and the opening out toward a world outside the city, which you experience on the Dybbølsbro bridge today, will not be permanent. Dybbølsbro and the railway terrain will come to be influenced dramatically by the construction of the Fisketorv's complex and the building development running alongside the Kalvebod Quay. Previously, the Baneby project attempted to abolish the space completely and to draw the space into the city's normality. Where today, as you walk out on to the bridge, you wrest yourself free from Vesterbro and meet the openness, you can also see at the same time the huge silo facility and the Ørsted power plant's immense volume on the other side. Accordingly, you are situated in the midst of the most fundamental meaning of the concept of "transition" – namely in the middle of the transition between different structural types, between different spaces, between different worlds. And in an ambiguous or poly-coded transition. The industrial volumes insinuate themselves on you; they seem to be inside the space without being there at all. The openness in the railway terrain's space gathers them in, but it also permeates them and conveys the railway terrain's space forward toward the conjunction with the Commons. The industrial volumes alternately appear inside a space that encompasses the railway terrain, the harbor and the Commons, and these volumes establish transitions between the various spaces. The level of observation to which the Dybbølsbro bridge elevates you unifies these three vast spaces and sets them into reciprocal interplay. From having been an outer space in the middle of the city, which becomes part of this three-foldedness of meaningful space, the space of the railway, when the changes being made along the harbor are carried into realization, will become an inner space. The ambiguity will disappear, to whatever extent it revolves around the inner part of the railway terrain.

The fantasies about covering all of this will, rest assured, acquire

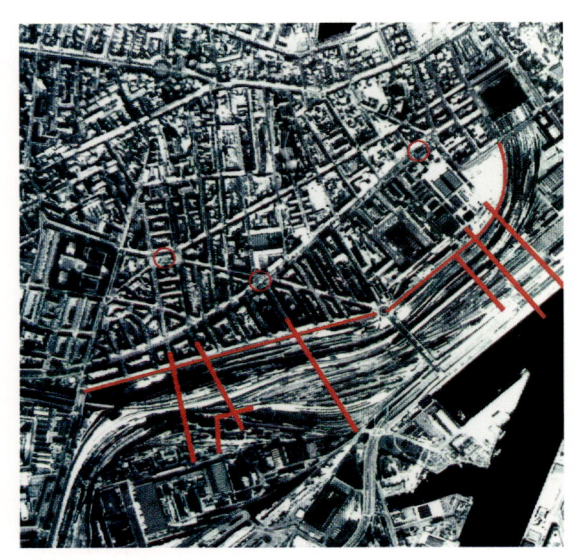

Dybbølsbro bridge / The railway terrain.

new sustenance. The railway is a luxury. It is a luxury to receive the city's guests right in the heart of the city – in broad daylight. In most other metropolises, incoming passengers are sent into a dark tunnel long before reaching the city's center. On your way into Copenhagen, you arrive in the daylight. Up until now.
It is a luxury, right in the middle of the city, to have a dream terrain which eludes the vested interests that measure value in constructional potentials.
If the railway terrain is not set into relief and rendered something extraordinary in the general perception, it will easily fall prey to being incorporated into the urban normality and to generalization. If the terrain is not rendered distinct by virtue of its role in the interplay with the harbor and the Commons – as boundary, as transition and as the initiator of new forms – then the remodeling of the Southern Harbor will gradually devour its way into the area and render it a fully uninteresting traffic cleft. The counter-strategy would be to articulate the railway terrain as the forbidden – in the sense of being inaccessible – garden of steel, stones, light plants, water, fire and movement.
At the same time, subject to and questioning the railway line's logic of linearity and repetition, curves and intersections and the spherically formed residual figures.
To build a bridge where today there is a separation, but without upheaving the separation. To stage and articulate the otherness and accordingly engender a consciousness about the space's qualities. Open to dreams about other kinds of spaces. To create a new type of public space, rendered public through experiences and impressions, which no other public spaces in the city contain and which concomitantly establish a resistance against the worn-down and the generalized. To articulate the emptiness.
A terrain and a world rendered accessible through five new bridges which take their mark in, or which are connected to, the most active points in the underlying urban structure and which accordingly open up for new connections, new coherences and new ways of understanding. As observed from these bridges, the long lines of connected railway cars will become elements in a veritable garden of movement.
Railway cars that move their way across a surface where the materials which already exist – gravel, steel, concrete, lumber, light sources of different kinds – are placed in new formations that interfere with the movement's logic, as manifest by the tracks – but without dissolving them. The residual figures that are established between the rail sequence's couplings are articulated as special surfaces or established as spherically formed spaces. The transverse movement is delineated in the surface by having the bridge's imaginary shadow on the surface constructed in light, in a transverse Corten surface, in a concrete or stone surface – in certain spots through a field of low protective planting demar-

cated precisely by steel or stone. All the new elements are subject to that geometric precision which characterizes the railway, through – respectively - the exploitation of the curvature and the confluence of long curves, and the contrasting of these with the transverse rectilinear right-angled forms and surfaces.

The lengthwise movement which is the area's constitutive logic is delineated once again by defining and appropriating a number of the figures that turn up in the interlacing between different groups of tracks. They become ribbons of water, fire and plants – or else they become closed spaces, which can be used for exhibitions, as experiential spaces and as connections between different bridges. The tracks' geometry is recapitulated and staged even further by arranging the freight cars as moveable gardens or exhibition podiums. The garden's materials are set into the surface with which you cannot come into contact. Presence and absence offer their commentary on one another. And the transition's dilemma and the ambiguity are rendered intelligible.

As you move around on the bridges, you can overlook the whole park and survey its relationship to the surroundings. But you cannot come into contact with its materials – they belong to the forbidden garden. A number of the new elements on the surface will only be capable of being perceived when you are positioned immediately above them. Many of the light sources will be shielded off in such a way that they can only be seen vertically, and many sur-

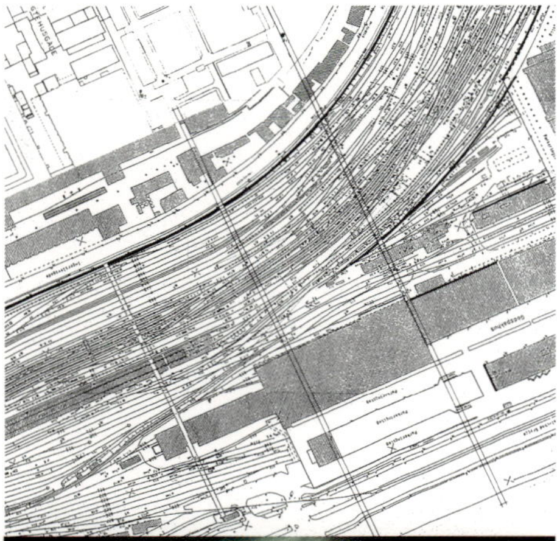
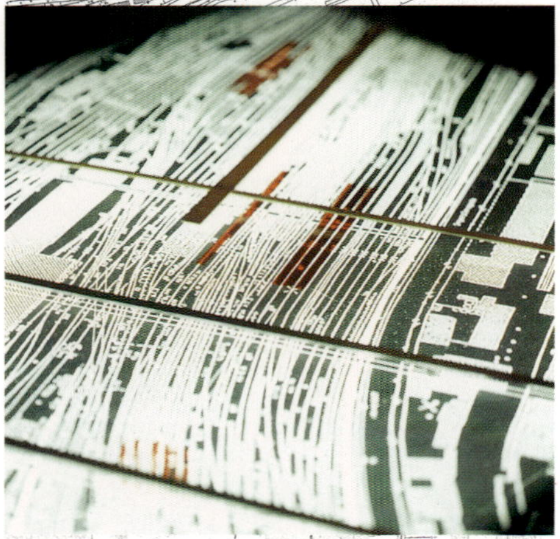
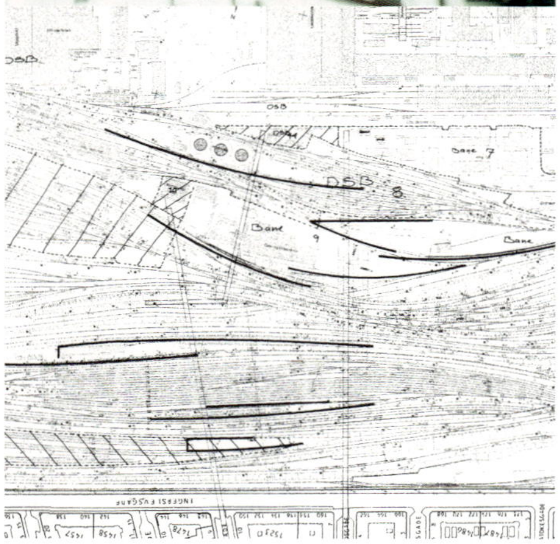
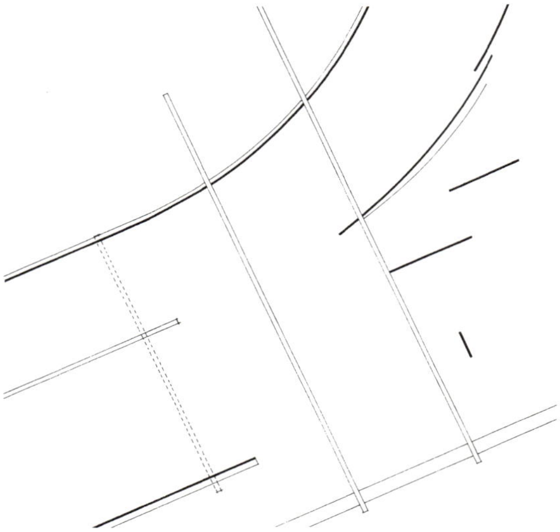
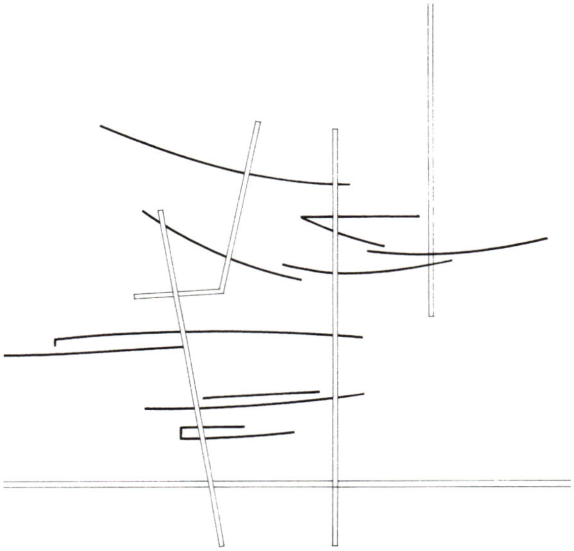

faces will be edged with the result that they can first be perceived when you are standing above them.

When you descend into the spaces that are established by the residual figures in between the tracks, you lose your sense of overview and you become enclosed inside a local world. The proximity revokes the overview. Silence and intimacy supervene.

The closed spaces fashion sensory spaces, light installations, paraphrases over the forest, the meadow, the formal gardens, sculpture exhibitions, discotheques – all of which will add an extra layer to the experiential spectrum of the park and facilitate its flexibility in being re-staged and re-coded.

The boundaries with Ingerslevsgade are specified explicitly and opened up. A lengthwise, elevated promenade is created, which simultaneously articulates the borderline. As it passes Kødbyen [the meat market] and the DGI-byen [sports center], this promenade is comprised exclusively of white concrete. As it passes Søndre Boulevard, it is paved with gravel and here it also contains trees on those stretches that are wide enough.

The new bridges are localized in such a way that they make contact with the most active points or pedestrian malls in the surrounding city. In the boundary between DGI-byen and Kødbyen, two steel-latticework bridges are placed, which lead past the freight yard to the promenade on Kalvebod Quay. There is also access to the bridge from the elevated promenade running alongside Ingerslevsgade and from a new promenade running below the Main Post Office. The new bridges are connected to the existing tubular bridge and further on from there, to a new pedestrian bridge situated on top of the long train's car wash. You can walk alongside, in the same direction that the trains are moving. In this section of the park, it is the movement, the light, the overview, the view out over the harbor, the activity on the ground plane - and the very capability of moving around over the railway– which together constitute the main attraction.

Where the through-going streets from Enghave Plads reach Ingerslevsgade – this means to say, in the prolongations of Haderslevgade and Flensborggade, and with the starting point in Arkonagade - three new lightweight steel bridges are to be built. With respect to their form and materials, they are akin to the frames that support the weight of the trains' overhead wires. They will conjoin the existing points of accumulation on Vesterbro with the coming railway museum situated inside the old workshop buildings. Around the workshop buildings, a form of industrial park is developed, which will establish an anacrusis to the Southern Harbor's new urban quarter.

The existing terrain is more heterogeneous in this part, and the combination of being able to move across and also being able to delve into the closed space or to cross between bridges via the closed space will fully unfold here and render the experience all the more composite – and make it possible for you, through your own choice of movement, to compile and compose your own experience.

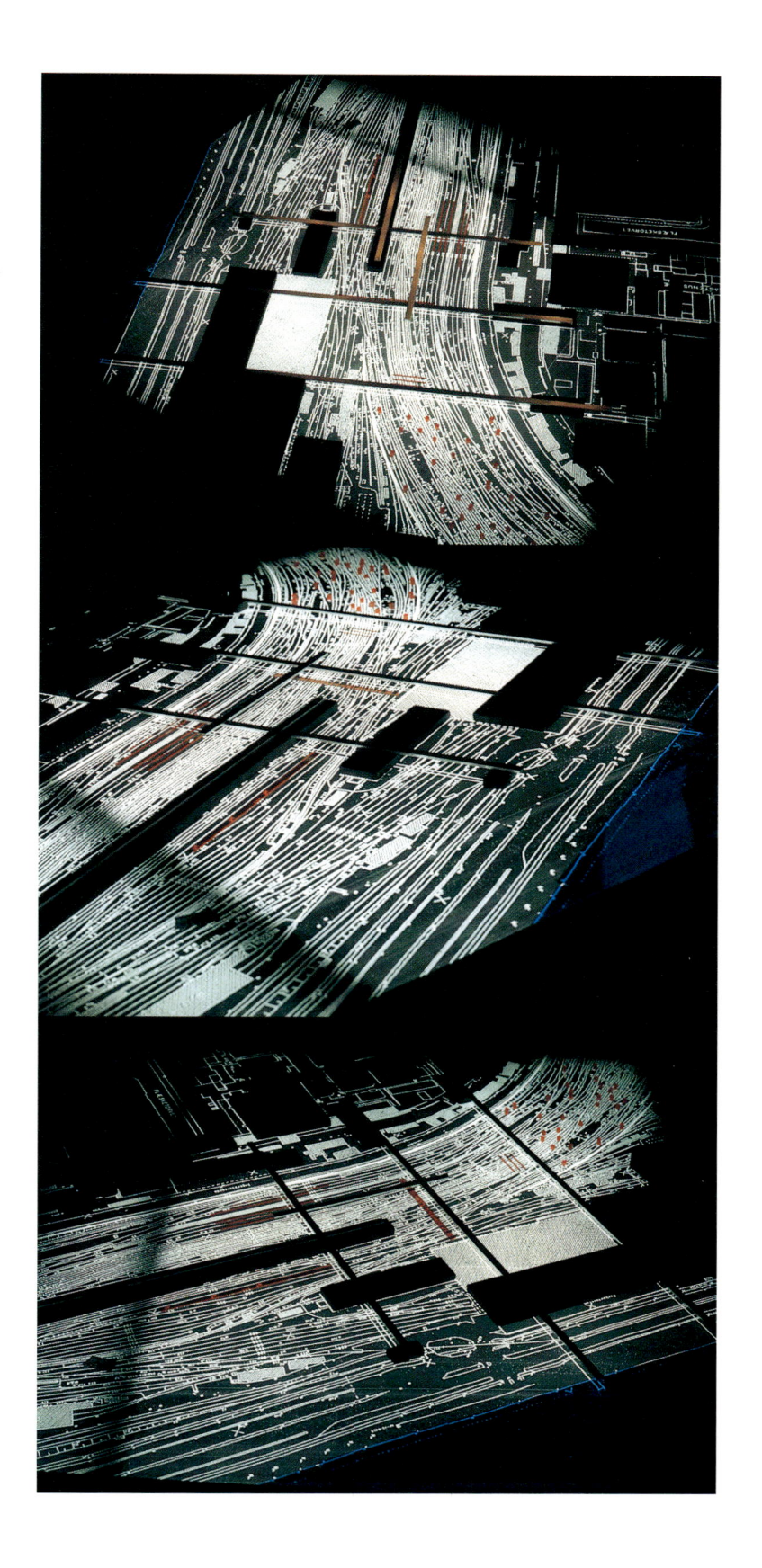

TAGE LYNEBORG

The Collective Space

The assignment can be enacted in the intellectual area. It can be characterized, on the one side, by finding the possibilities and seeing the poetry in the existing state of things, by turning our attention toward the immediate reality and by learning to see and describe qualities in this reality. On the other side, this area can be characterized in terms of the addition of governing, explanatory or concretely new and gathering facilities, which can bring about new understanding and quality.
This "contemporary space" can be said to be a pragmatic space, built up from differentiated and collocated constituent elements. Architecture is being challenged here to re-create the connection between the Body, the Place, the Community and its Horizon, in new coherences, with present-day needs, inside this present-day space.
One way of responding, then, might be to add elements and spaces to "the place" that can promote a new unifying perception and awareness, through the implementation of new functions that will alter the status of the place. In other words, instead of attempting to see "the beauty" in what is available, and instead of calling attention to the place's meaninglessness, the architecture could make an attempt to build further to a *meaningfulness*.

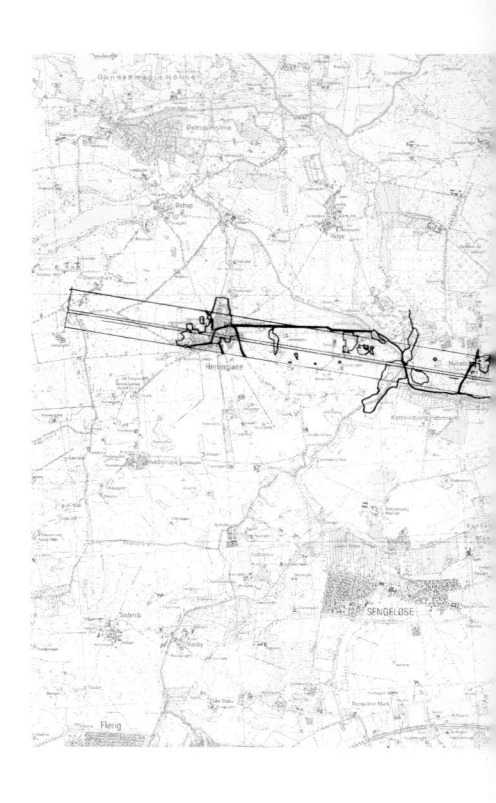

The examples
The places that have been worked with here originate from the introductory draft for the assignment: Amager Fælled, Vestskoven, Dybbølsbro and Bispeengen.
Amager Fælled [the Amager Commons] has widened and now deals with the water's surface south of Amager up to the Skudeløbet in Svanemølle Bay. Dybbølsbro has inspired us to call the Kalvebod Channel and Valby Sailing Club in the Southern Harbor into play. Vestskoven [the Western Forest] has now become sporadic incisions in the open landscape toward the west.
The city has many structures – the quarters' salient features, the road structures, the relation between the center and the periphery, the finger-plan and the harbor – which, layer upon layer, serve us in our apprehension of the city's space. The chosen examples touch upon some of these, and all of them are "places", all of them are peculiar and all of them occupy marginal positions! The character of a special emptiness or incompleteness imbues them with an affinity.

The Project
The project attempts to set the places into a new coherence and to make visible a new structure, which deals with the city's center and periphery, its construction and its landscape.
Two "imaginary" axes, perpendicular with respect to one another, with their point of origin in central Copenhagen, extend out into the open landscapes of Vestskoven [the Western Forest] and Vestamager [West Amager], as sequences running out from the city. They establish a new and supplementary possibility for understanding the city's immensely large scale.
The east-west axis, through Vestskoven, moves its way from the city out into the open landscape, and introduces a supplementary way of creating comprehensibility inside an already existing spatiality. The north-south axis, West Amager, moves its way through a landscape of landfill. It is, in one way, a vacant landscape created without any vision, but it also constitutes an axis of the possibilities.
The suggested proposals, in many ways, point out into a new space, an introduction of a new city's space in the water south of Amager and a fantasy about a new spatial and functional element – the energy landscape. This could provide harmony in the proportions between urban structure and landscape. As fragments, the structure crops up at two places along the axis.
As a parallel motive, the Harbor has come into being. The city's meeting with the harbor has now become a new opportunity for and new sensibility about a far greater articulation of the edge between urban space and landscape space, through the establishment of "terraces" facing the water's surface.
In the Southern Harbor, the Valby Sailing Club has inspired a sketch about a built-up area inside an extreme spatial density with the flowing water at the sluice.
The proposal for Bispeengen adds to a vacant spot in the city a new function within the collective space, and exemplifies the establishment of a new layer - an atrium inside the city's pulse, in a re-adaptation of the spatial notions of movement and stationary space.
Taken together, the project attempts to testify that ideas springing up in a free and independent manner *can* be pursued, and in a re-adaptation of the places, they *can* be developed and perhaps even stimulate inspiration for viewing some of the city's untested and untried possibilities in a new light.

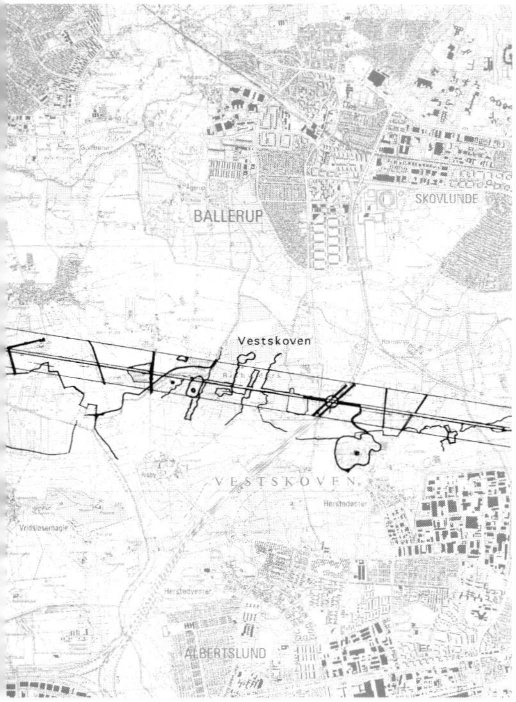
BALLERUP
SKOVLUNDE
Vestskoven
VESTSKOVEN
ALBERTSLUND

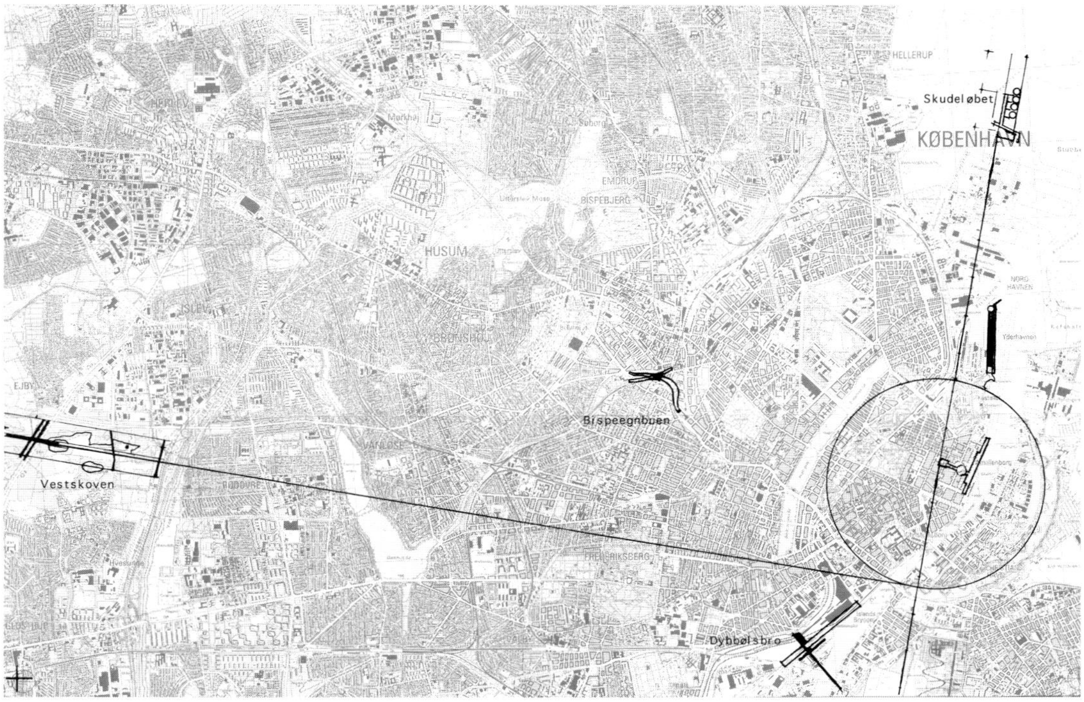
Skudeløbet
KØBENHAVN
HUSUM
BISPEBJERG
Bispeegnbuen
Vestskoven
FREDERIKSBERG
Dybbølsbro

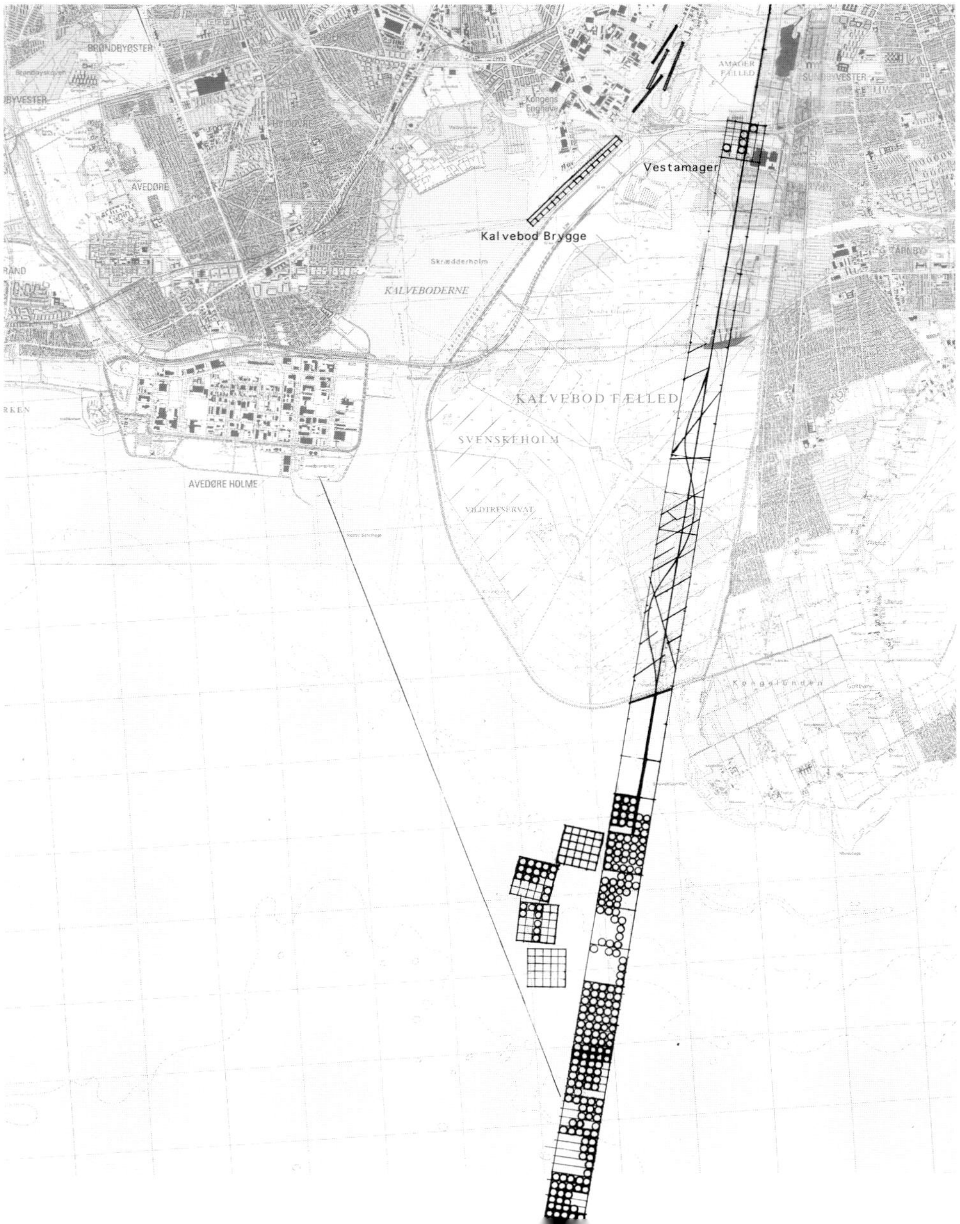
AVEDØRE
Vestamager
Kalvebod Brygge
KALVEBODERNE
KALVEBOD FÆLLED
SVENSKEHOLM
AVEDØRE HOLME

KØGE BAY

The landscape of Vestamager [West Amager] has in its background hundreds of years of landfills on the beach- and low tide-areas between Sjælland and Amager. This is an artificially created landscape, and in this respect, there is no clearly defined boundary between land and water. Moving out beyond the dike on the southern shoreline does not exactly constitute a giant step. Moving out into Køge Bay, however, is tantamount to discovering room for new possibilities.

The idea here is to establish a feature which, as an element in the great wide landscape scale, will establish a new place along a new axis that extends its way through the city's center and out into the open landscape, all the way to a point in the horizon.

An energy landscape which, as a new and societally created element, a technical facility, and with fragments of city, with the sun as a fundamental source of energy, will engender a new structure in upon the water's surface. What is envisioned is the establishment of a technical-physical structure, as a new urban formation, upon the water's surface. As floating coffers measuring 100x100 meters, they are linked together in formations. They take up no place on the land, but they fashion new ground over the surface of the sea.

Obliquely angled structures with solar energy elements establish space, and they revolve in the water, in time with the circadian rhythm's dance beneath the sun. The solar energy can be converted into hydrocarbon, which can then be transported to existing power plants.

Once and for all, they place their bets on filling the modern society's needs for energy. No sporadically-placed and noisy windmills in the landscapes here, but rather a response, based upon one certain technology, which could very well become the future's all-encompassing one.

As the settlement, through the march of time, has been articulating mankind's progress all along, a new settlement will crop up in the future's energy landscape.

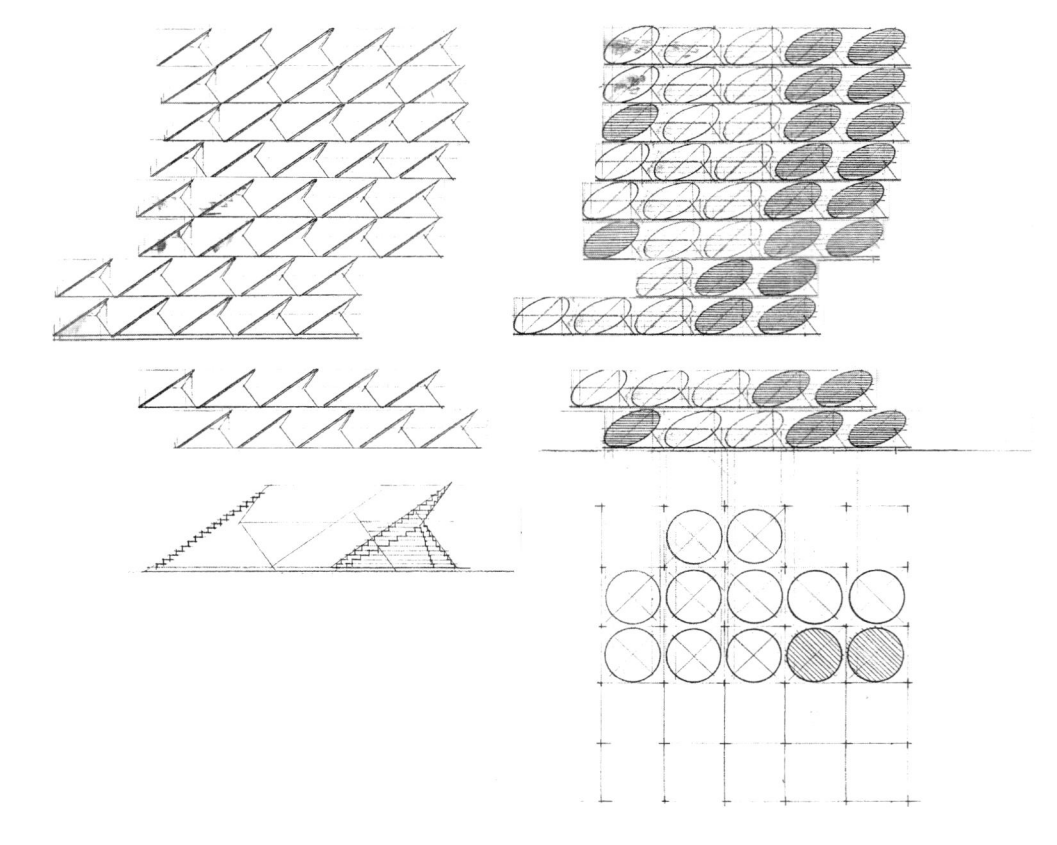

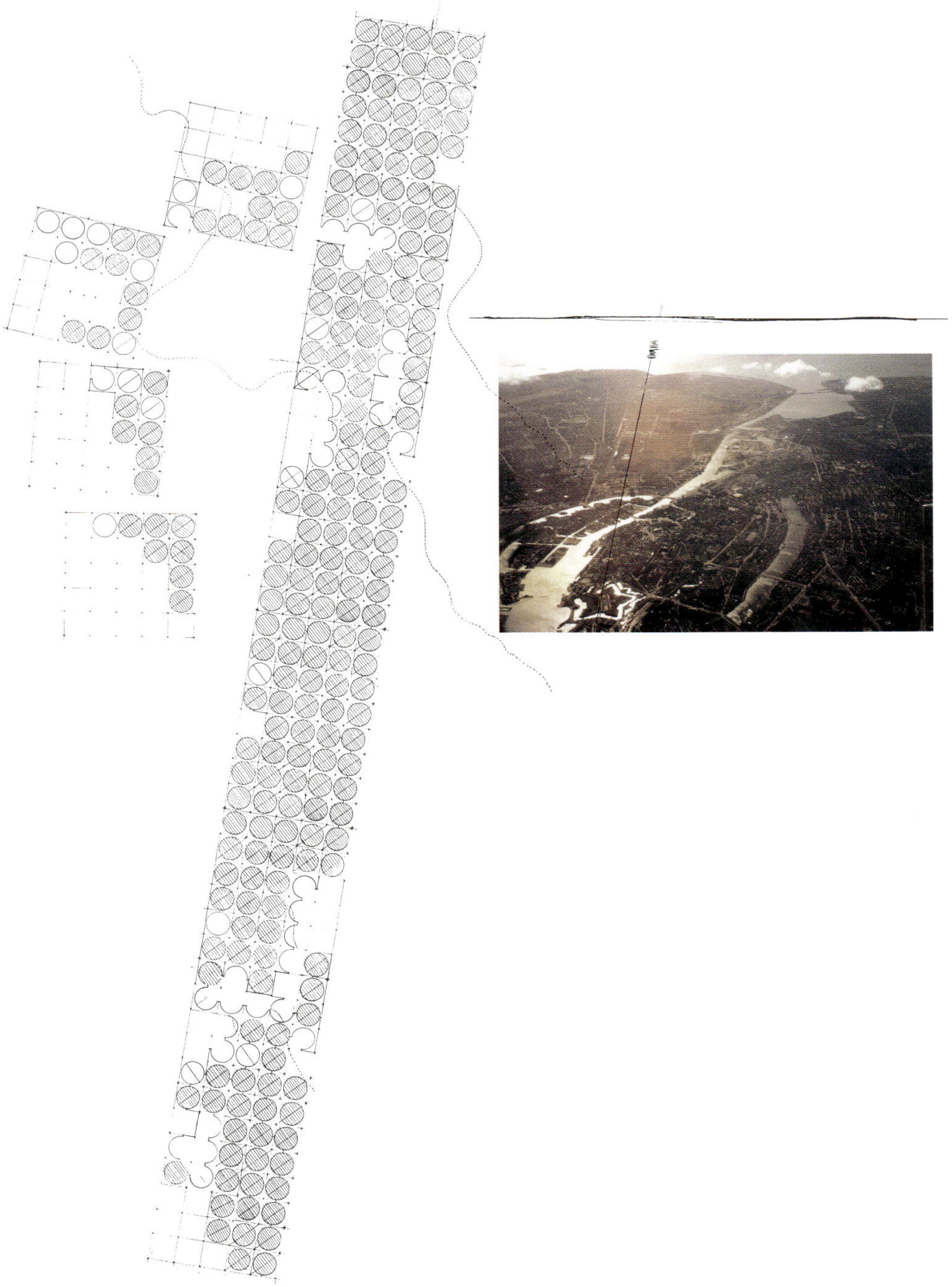

VESTAMAGER [WEST AMAGER]

In the transitional zone between water and land near Bella Center, we find the urban module with its settlement- and energy-structures springing up from the landscape's surface. This module tells something about what is being accomplished further to the south.

From here, and like a kind of gateway to the landscape, the spatial moves out from the proximate toward the remote horizon, in a line running through the landscape, over the dike, and out over the surface of the water in Køge Bay. The commons' landscape possesses its very own history. Landfills, drainage ditches, self-sown vegetation and valuable biotopes. The course of time changes all this, but what is unchanged is the eternal space, defined by the water – the surface of the sea.

The 500-meter wide zone is articulated in the graphic representation, but it actually does not stand in need of any physical addition. It can be perceived as images that move past: surfaces of grass, intersecting ditches, depots and thickets etc. - horizon and delimited space.

This provides an opportunity for envisioning this expiration of landscape as an intensely re-worked artistic project - an animal park for the renewal of Copenhagen's Zoo – an analogue – a biological contrast – to the energy landscape situated to the south.

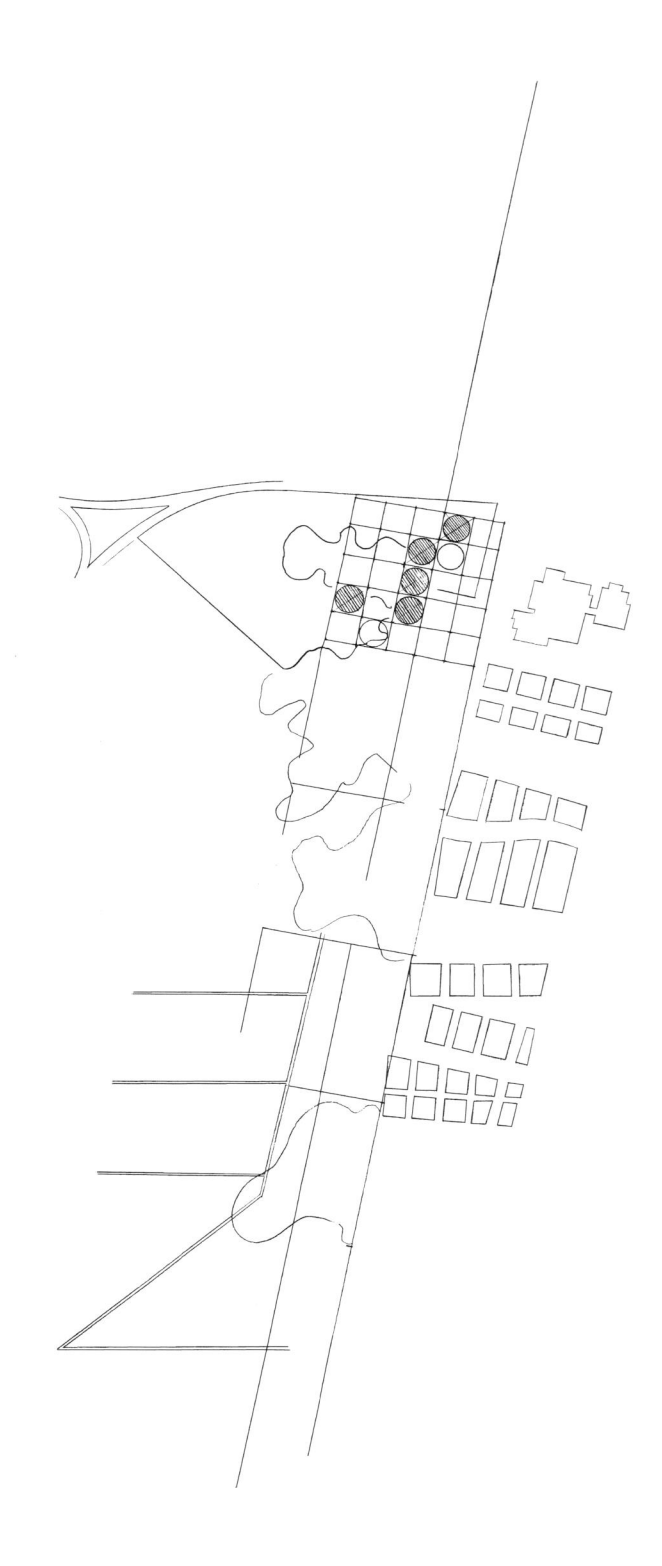

Skudeløbet

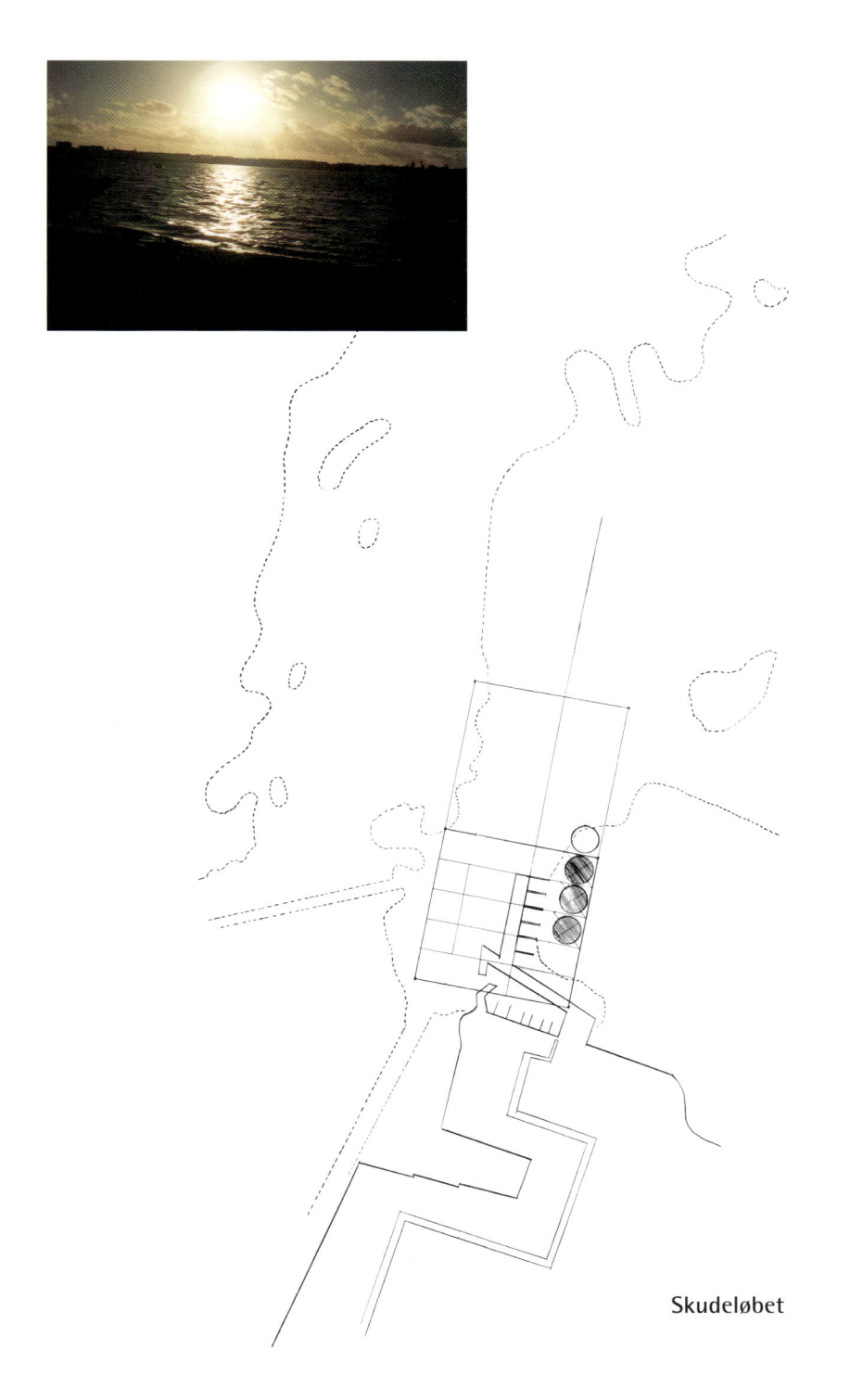

THE HARBOR

When one looks at a map of the present day, what is so striking is how the city is pressing its way forward toward the sea; it has been closed off as a possibility, for so long, for the city to expand all the way to the water. There is no place along the harbor front where any space has been created for the collective life, historically speaking. But now all this is changing. In recent years, the active harbor, as we know it, has diminished its demand for areas proximate to the city. This change has engendered new possibilities.

The harbor front can be seen as a series of plateaus or terraces in front of the city, most of which are just waiting to be endowed with a new function, in the open air, which could rightly be called the city's meeting with the prospective, grandiose, recreative blue wedge. Amaliehaven and Langelinie are examples of such urban terraces which have already attained such a distinction.

KALVEBOD CHANNEL

Sejlklubvej [Sailing Club Road], all the way out on Tippen [the Tip] situated to the south of the Musikbyen [Music Village], is an area which has cropped up on a no-man's land of land-fill. Here, a recreative milieu, which inflects the city toward the water, has been established. An informal terrace. The idea here is to add the already emerging milieu to a linear course of sailing club units, which will fashion a continuous sequence in a partial stretch of the harbor. A tilted beach plateau with club- and bathing-houses along the narrow Kalvebod Channel. Inasmuch as the new embankment facing the harbor is more than likely to be changed into a tunnel or retractable bridge, the navigation runs through the harbor will be taking place in a free and easy manner for the city's sailing aficionados.

West Amager

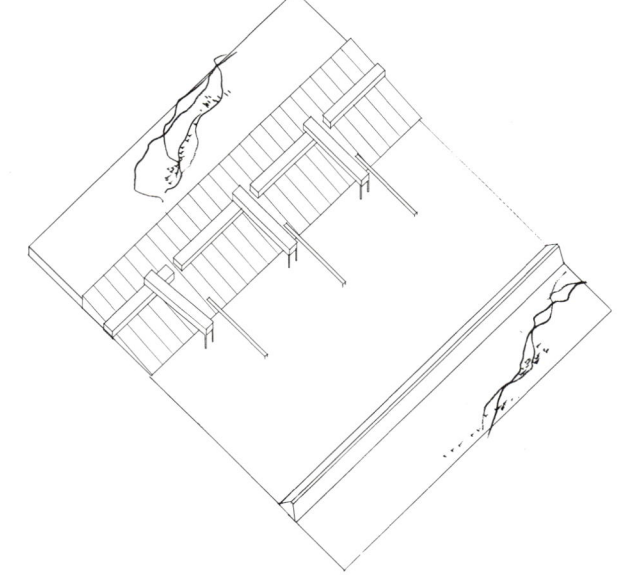

Kalvebod Channel

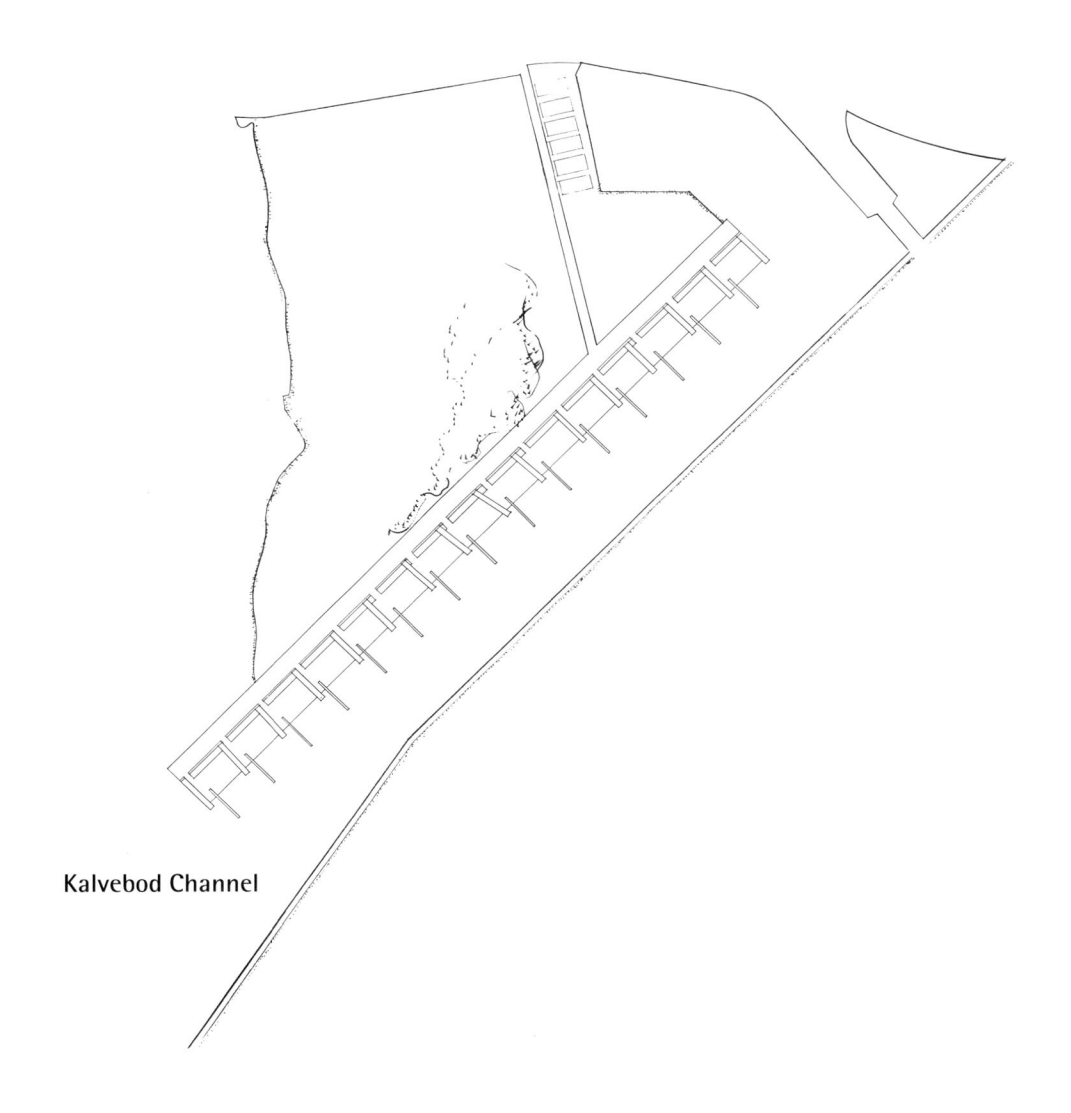

VALBY SAILING CLUB, SOUTHERN HARBOR
Immediately across from the sluice on the Sjaelland side, there is a considerable deal of activity going on in the Southern Harbor. The first business premises alongside the waterfront have already come into being. This is a business district in development. However, such functions have no monopoly on the course of events in the vicinity of the harbor.

On an edge alongside the fairway of the harbor, the Valby Sailing Club has established its domain. Right here, the harbor – on account of the system of sluices to the south – sometimes behaves like a torrential gush.

On poles set out in the water, and with its own urban formation and central open area, its row of houses corbeling over the water, and bridges out into the running stream – what we find here is an unassuming example of a "paradise established".

It's inspiring to stand on the bank of "the river" right here.

Were time to ever dictate that something new replace this unpretentious concentrate of "city by the water", or could it fashion a model somewhere else, I would choose to illustrate a more forcible rendition, which has carried along the proximity to the streaming current as its image.

Very tall and narrow housing slabs situated right on the edge and out in the stream, forming dramatic and intense spaces. Beneath the buildings, facilities for the residents' boats; above, the dwelling and other things. We know nothing of any such an urban concatenation!

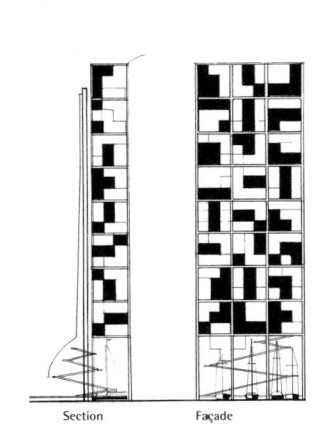

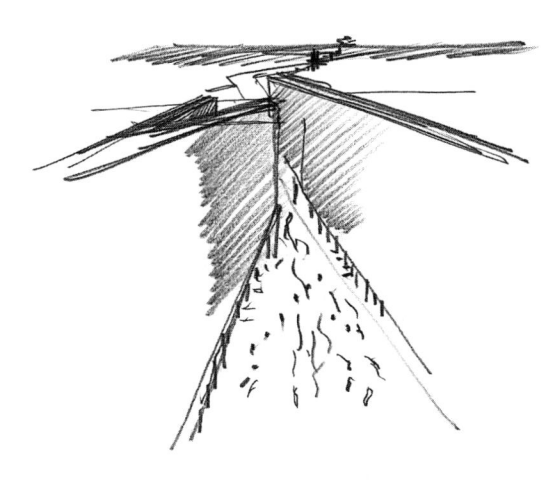

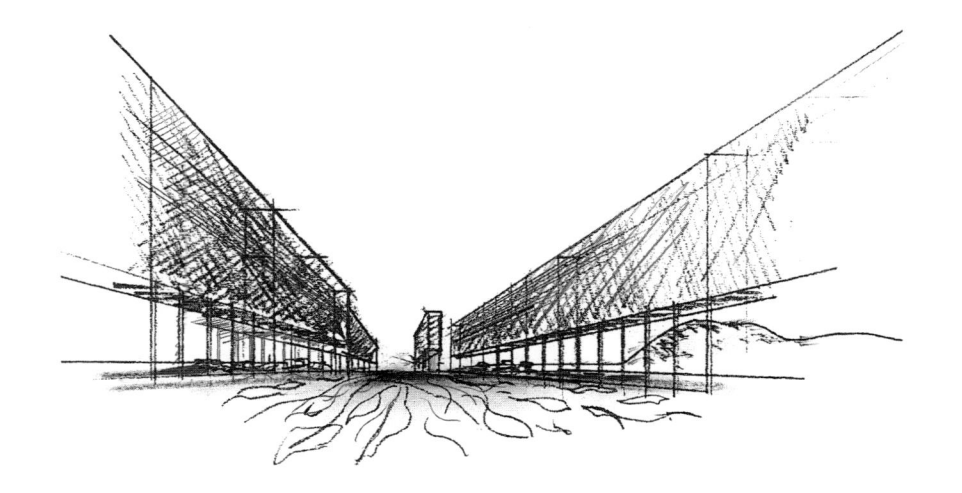

Section   Façade

Sydhavnen

Sluse
Sjællandsbroen

DYBBØL'S BRIDGE

The railway's terrain and the beltway running along the harbor separate the Vesterbro section of Copenhagen from the Harbor. Dybbøl's Bridge was set up in order to remedy this situation, which, as a matter of fact, was recently re-established. But it is not used all that much. The reason it is there is to bear witness to the fact that the urban quarter behind the railway tracks ought to have a connection to the harbor. Dybbøl's Bridge will form a bridge between a jammed urban quarter and the large re-creative element, the fairway of the harbor. With the establishment of a people's park, which would raise itself up above the 'infolded' problematic existence inside an urban quarter that is severed off from the horizon, a new urban element - a highly elevated park terrace - can impart to the urban quarter a view out over the fairway of the harbor, and nudge the quarter forward into a front-row seat.

On the 1300 meter-long plateau, what could be established are sports facilities, halls, gardens and promenades. There is also sufficient room for building underneath the plateau.

The freight terminal is situated beneath the new park plateau, and in the future, it could be set free for purposes connected with the urban quarter's park; a vast interior urban plaza inside the ground plane's immense hall.

A delicate and slender bridge connection can conjoin the urban sections on either side of the harbor.

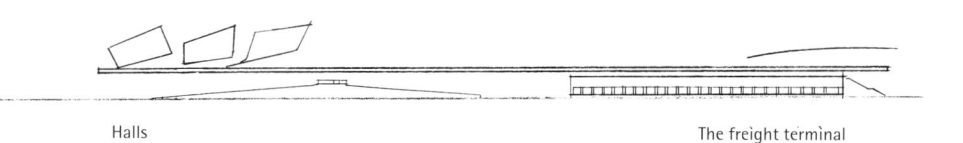

Halls   The freight terminal

The Harbour   Vesterbro

The freight terminal

Dybbøls Bridge

The Harbour

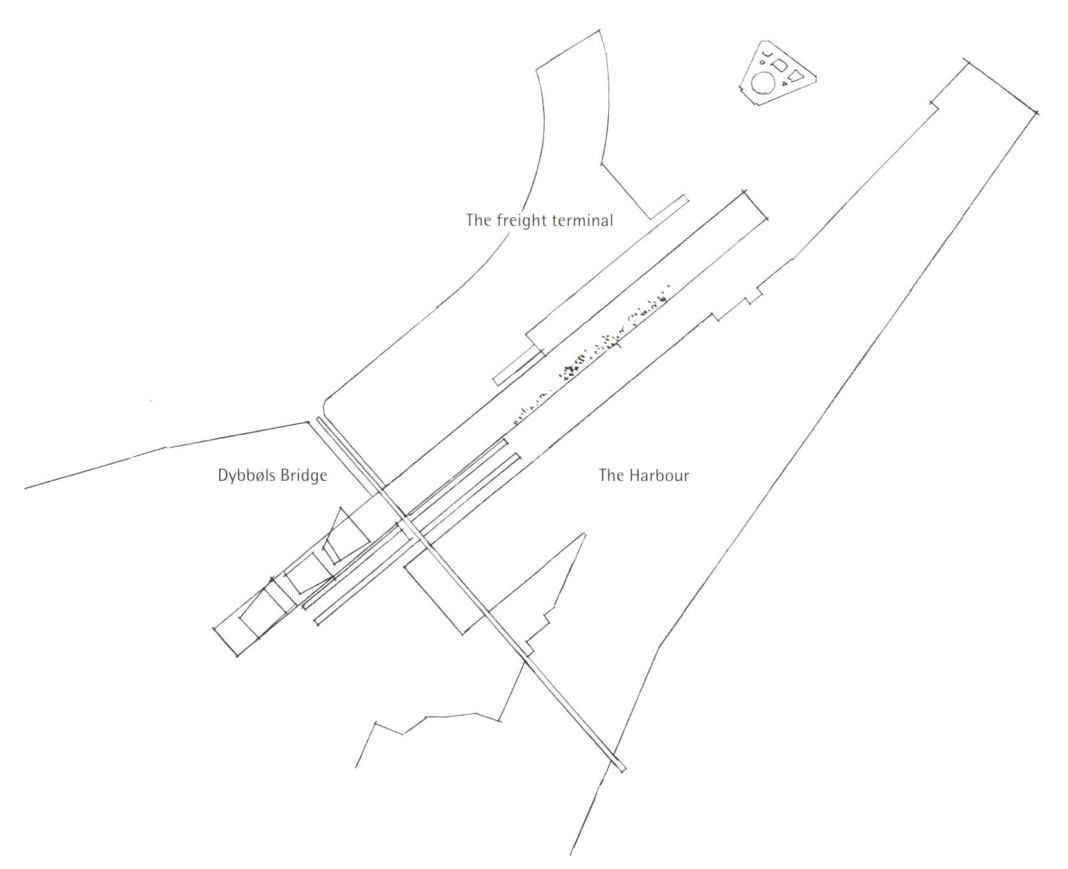

BISPEENGBUEN [THE BISPEENG OVERPASS]

It was as if Bispeengbuen was originally supposed to have levitated itself in order to make room for a street life on the city's floor while preventing any interruption of the city's pulse.
But the area beneath the overpass-arch remains a desolate place. Up above, trains and cars speed on by. But the urban life has never flowered here.
However, the place is actually grandiose, inasmuch as two infrastructural facilities meet in their dynamic layout-lines up above the stagnating urban plane, and elevate themselves in order to make room for a commonly shared space for the two urban quarters!
This space can be exploited by a re-working of the ground plan in a new plastically super-ordinate form that follows the inflection of the overpass's arch and the elevated railway line and amplifies their movement's forms and layout-lines into urban elements, and allows these to take on urban functions. Along the elevated railway line, right over its course, a linear building is formed.
A tower establishes the connection from the ground plan.
Beneath the overpass, a vast collective space is created. When this space is covered with glass around the periphery of the overpass, it can establish a space that could become a gathering place for the circumjacent neighborhoods.
A new spatial element that can put this no-man's land back into play and get some life moving between the neighborhoods, and consequently replace an empty space with a cultural and commercial junction.
The new figure is established by four layers: the street level, the urban expressway's overpass, the elevated railway line and the linear building spanning the railway line.

The collective space under the overpass

Section

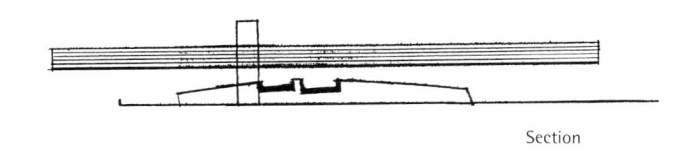

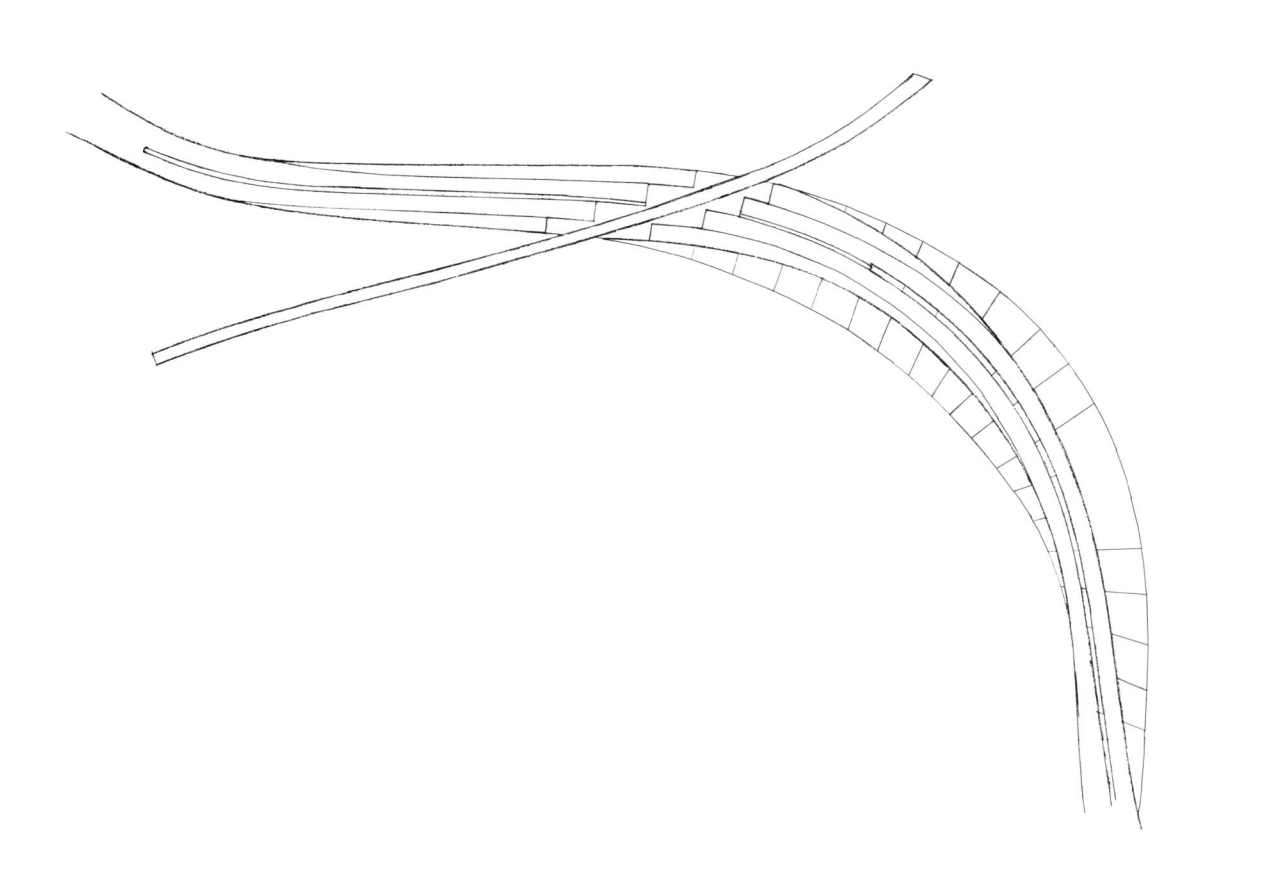

VESTSKOVEN

Vestskoven [the Western Forest] constitutes a forward-looking provision and an element in the city's overall plan.

As of yet, it is strangely lacking in character – well, you might say at least that it is a work in progress.

It consists of many different kinds of landscape terrain, in a haphazard sequence. The transition to the open landscape is imperceptible.

In order to elucidate the elements and the landscape types that exist here, what must be established is a line of sight from east and out toward the west, running right through the landscape. This new element can, in a physical sense, be imaginary. Or it can constitute a perspective. Or it can even be a path in the landscape. In any case, it constitutes a visual space.

This line of sight running through the landscape will offer to the visitor a certain route and a certain way of contemplating and of being inside the landscape space.

In the movement from the city out through the landscape, certain particularly characteristic prospects will be thrown into relief, as sporadic sectional incisions, or as set pieces of the landscape's diverse types.

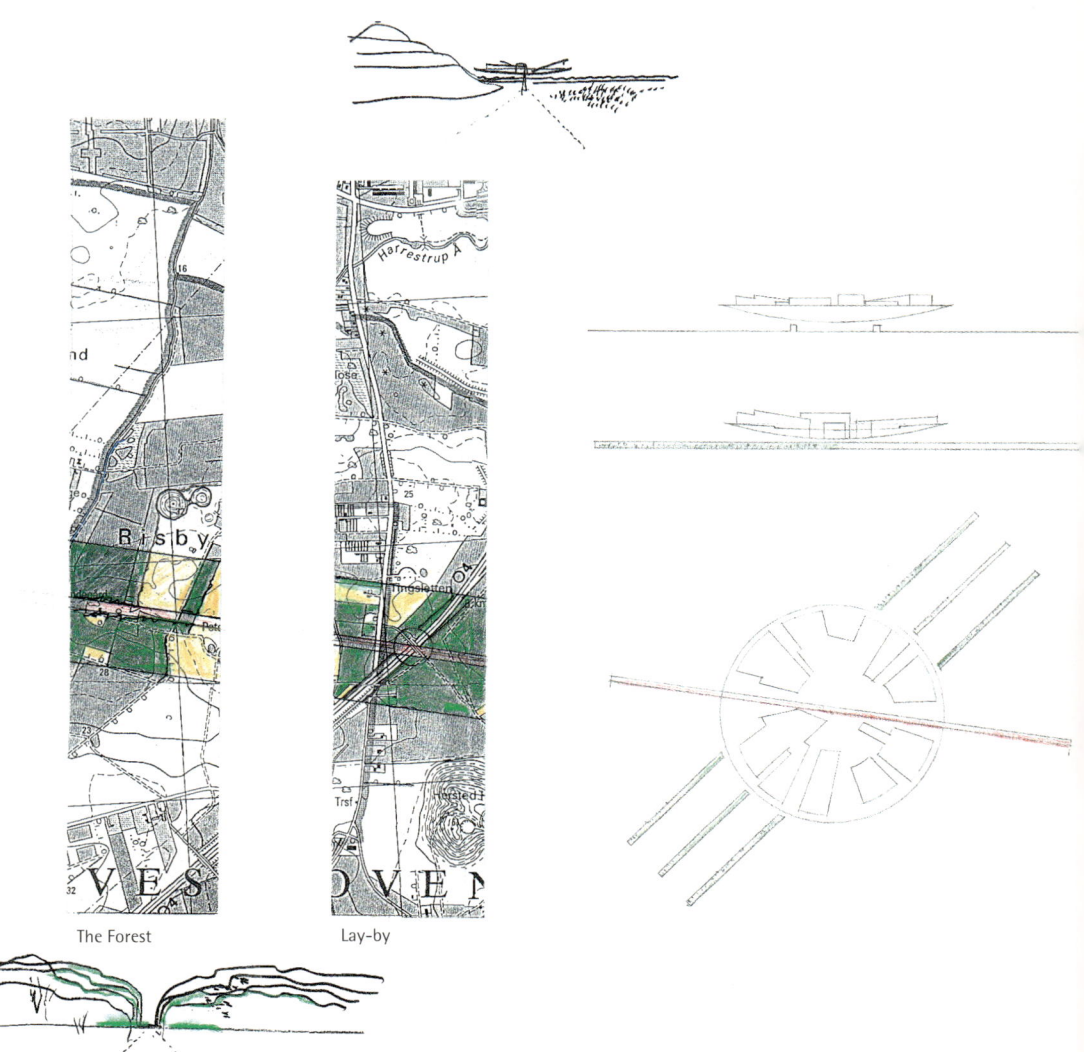

The Forest   Lay-by

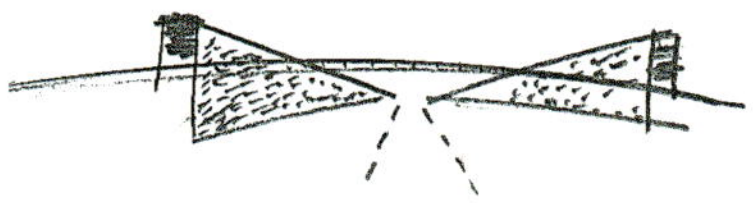

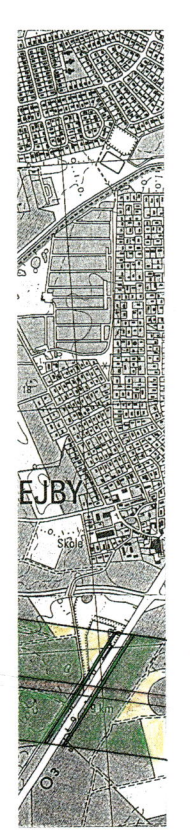

Noise protection 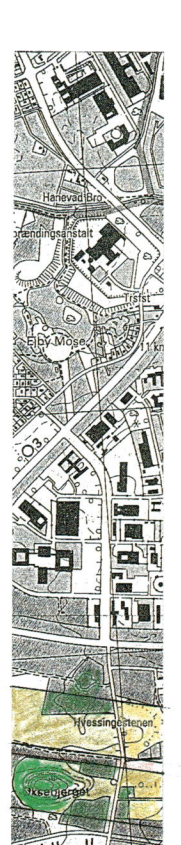   The Hillock 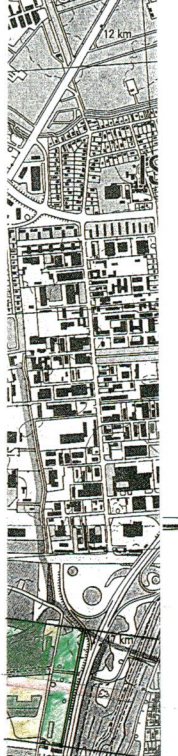   Highway

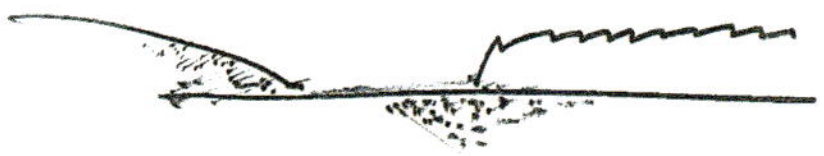

VESTSKOVEN

Vestskoven [the Western Forest] is pierced by the immense highway layout, and split up into disconnected segments.

This visual and spatial interruption and the terrible noise from the roads serves to belittle the experience of the Western Forest as nature.

In response, we can screen off the forest from noise with high stone fences running along the highways, and establish passage over the road via bridges.

However, there is the special situation that the largest group of people who are passing through the forest, via the highway, have no access at all. You cannot stop your car and walk into the forest. What is proposed here, then, is the establishment of a place to pull over, - at a particular point where the line of the road intersects the line of the landscape, and accordingly a spot where a presentation of the landscape can transpire. The rest-stop area is to be formed as a plaza-like, circular and bowl-shaped plane hovering over the road's profile. Consequently, the wayfarer looking out from the plaza will obtain a bird's-eye view of the landscape. The plaza's buildings can even accommodate urban functions that are specific to the needs of traveler and he/ she who is visiting the landscape. From the plaza, the pathway will lead out into the open landscape.

Vestskoven

The Village

Small river

The River valley   Marshland   Forest road

KRISTINE JENSEN

Transitions – architectonic form and coherence in the contemporary urban landscape
– a few remarks about the space's mid-ground

Reading the city as a landscape is, in principle, a method of apprehending the city which has found favor among architects over the course of the last few years. In this is seated not merely a change in connection with the firm differentiation between city and countryside that previously characterized architects' perceptions. What is primarily going on here is an acknowledgement that both issues have to do with matters of extended process, whose components are also subject to the influences of time. When focus is being increasingly directed toward the process – it makes sense to talk about transitions. In the city's spatial coherence, where we play witness to change and where we take part ourselves in the alterations, central points of anchoring are displaced, and our common fixed points seem to be fluid. But in my opinion, the fact that the force of attraction is no longer situated in the center of the constricted space need not entail a waiving of the three-dimensional perceptual structure. In such a way that has been more or less maintained, and which has consequently provided the occasion for long passages about the city's lost structure in triviality's set of accidents. For it is only in time's monument, the Moment, that gravity as a matter of your own sense, misfires. When the space falls once again, this transpires in the depth as well as in all other nuances and definitions of length, width and height. And this entails, if anything, that we can obtain elements of attraction without necessarily having to prostrate ourselves before the dogmatics, seeing that nobody believes anymore that the formal construction of the central perspective establishes absolute value as the mediator between the city and the landscape. Inasmuch as the identification points of spatial- and pictorial-composition as foreground, mid-ground and background are no longer relegated to merely serving a priori assigned functions within a code of practice, they can now form new and essential entities in the city's spatial composition.

Within the domain of landscape gardening, which landscape architecture has shared its history with, the mid-ground has always played an essential role. It is tempting to say that this way of tri-partition into background, mid-ground and foreground constitutes a fundamental artistic definition, which originates in formal gardening – stemming from when Francis Bacon, as far back as 1597, already divided this branch of art's tasks into a triadic program described by these points: Terrace, Main Garden and Wilderness. And almost 200 years later, Humphrey Repton, albeit under the influence of a whole other style, transposed the program into the pleasure ground, the park and the landscape. In this (garden-)architectonic purpose, these considerations apply to probings concerning scale, atmosphere and especially the various conspicuous transitions, which are inscribed in between intimate/ private space, common/ public space and all the way out to the completely remote, the outer or the undefined landscape space. Landscape gardening defines its special effort around the main garden and also the park, (which, incidentally, constituted one of the most important elements in twentieth century urban planning) and accordingly, in the anchoring of the mid-ground, and has presumably always, both as craft and as artistic discipline, formulated its implements and its effects within that set of cultural transitions situated in between the near and the far. Between the proximate placement of the foot and the eye-point's remote invitation, as a genuine disclosure of scale, involving the whole body, in the full ingestion of the surrounding space's extent.

In the landscape picture, the mid-ground is formulated in the picture's construction and composition. The English landscape painter A. Cozens offers an account that is almost identical with respect to the aforementioned tripartition in his Compositions of Landscape, – a new method, dating from 1785. According to Cozens' method, it is possible to divide any given landscape horizontally in relation to the different distances that they emanate, moving out from the eye. These horizontal partitions can be referred to as grounds: that which is closest to the eye constitutes the picture's foreground – and so on and so forth with the mid-ground and finally, the background. For each one of these "grounds" there are certain appurtenant objects which organize a certain order and establish the desired atmosphere. In a more general sense, the method can be employed for deciphering certain codes that appear in the landscape pictures of different epochs. The mid-ground tends more or less to define the locality, whether this be a scene depicting the hereafter, an exotic image or a past scene (via paradise symbols, Chinese or Greek temples; later on, with the advent of national-romanticism, Norwegian huts or Danish beechwood trees were also employed for this purpose). In between the foreground and the background, the space's very atmosphere is distended, that is to say, both the external and the internal atmosphere, the latter being what is today called the psychological. And if you hereby conjure up here in your recollection Caspar David Friedrich's painting of the wanderer at the peak's abyss, you will certainly understand something about the astonishing play of confusion that is continuously being carried out between psychology and beauty.

In the 1950s, the American painter Mark Rothko, moreover, dissolves the whole issue of the mid-ground as being a field for objects – through the means of a distension between foreground and background of delicate, livid vanishing lines, which make their appearance as transition-less gradations between the pictorial plane's top and bottom. This kind of fundamental weightlessness places the entire orientation of time, space and place on the shoulders of the psychology of sensation. One could say that psychology's internal space supersedes, as it were, the body's external locality. And in keeping with the abstractionists' figureless renderings, the mid-ground folds up, collapses and disappears as an objective field – with the result that all becomes foreground and/ or background.

Modernism's architecture complements the picture, insofar as the building assimilates landscape gardening's elements and space. The once so graceful paths and the disintegrated terraces are executed instead as the building's in-folded space of open-air balconies and airy roof-terraces. The interior's living rooms are fitted with windows as large as the exterior's panorama – without any disturbing mid-grounds or softening transitions. The architecture of the buildings makes its insistence on the difference and takes a radical stand as relation to surroundings – and this changes not only the image on the landscape but also architecture's way of understanding landscape gardening, insofar as both its territory – the mid-ground – and its object – the garden – have to be reformulated and articulated differently, in the light of the modern architecture.

Even though this scenario more or less plays itself out within the construction of the central perspective and even though this relation, obviously, cannot be correlated with a new awakening today, what we have here is really a matter of viewpoints which continue to be relevant to the establishment of orientations. In Helsinki's new museum for contemporary art, Kiasma, architect Steven Holl has been working in a completely consistent manner with eliminating the mid-ground's position inside the building.

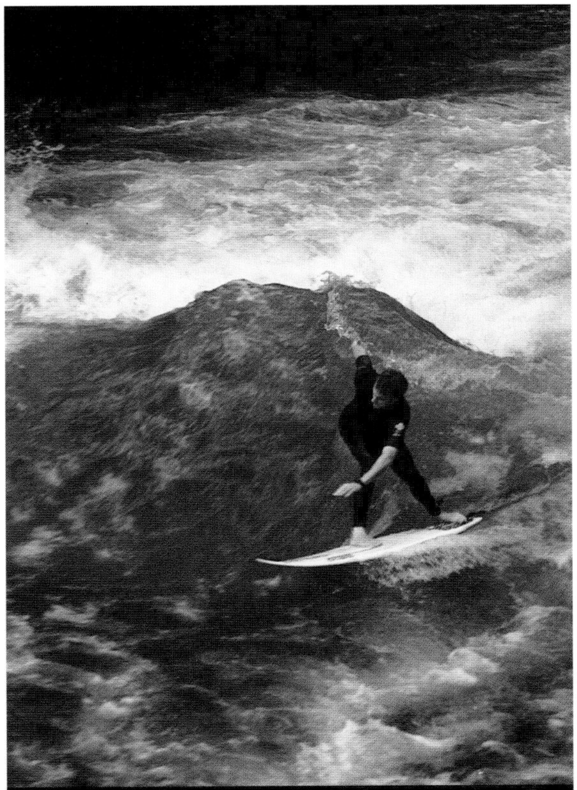

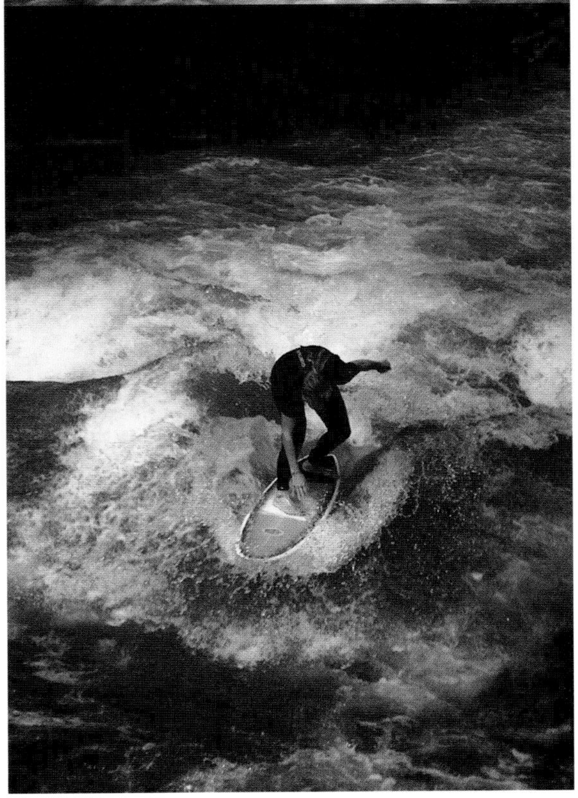

The Kiasma building thus makes it appearance, in the classical architectonic respect, as background. As a frame where the foreground is earmarked exclusively for the meeting, such as the body's contact with the detail, for example, the door handle, or the window opening that leads the eye or the ramp's upward incline that can be sensed by the foot, etc. According to the architect, the mid-ground is reserved exclusively for the art itself.
The Mid-ground – as place and space is thus, in both a figurative and practical sense, a marginal place, or free space, understood as that place and that space which eludes functional- and specification-demands' expectations with regard to any specific conduct. Last summer, in Munich, I experienced that the situation can transform fixed perceptions of the city's space and place. In itself, Munich is an endearing and somewhat somnambulistic place, which simmers with that extraordinary and secure metropolitan life style which in Europe is fastened to the background-heavy urban space. Space and place accompany one another in the historic style formations, while the standardization of life styles operates athwart the locality's urban emblems. Chanel's and McDonalds' global clothing and fast-food chains are indeed situated side by side, along with other chains of local events from past and present, utterly separated and yet entirely juxtaposed. And yet, again these brands and labels of the fast food and clothing-fashions' temporal updating hardly provides any complete picture of the changes that are happening in our cities. The changes that, of course, rock our very perceptions about space and place while simultaneously opening up for an urban existence that does not permit of being organized along the lines of the aforementioned outline - the slippery friction between the past's and the present's social-economic boastfulness. At the entrance to Munich's famous expanse of park– the Englisher Garten - down below one of the city's most trafficked sections, I saw some five or six people standing on surfboards positioned up against volumes of water from a very small dam. Through their way of ingesting it, I perceived that these surfers were reorganizing the space, and the place, as a genuinely worldwide frame for physical action and experience. Seen in this light, it is never the world that we are tired of. What we do tire of is the wearisome experiential descriptions about the whole plethora of things that cannot be done in this world. The surfers refurnished the conceptions of both the city and the landscape, and the actual action in its relation to space and place can be expressed with Carsten Juel-Christiansen's words: "The articulation of the space's middle ground is an organization of the locality's place as a bodily space which renders the individual world a part of the others' world."
The mid-ground, - a dynamic dimension. In Århus, the area between Klostertorv and Frue Kirkeplads is characterized by the medieval convent-buildings conjunction with Vor Frue Kirke (the Church of Our Lady). The buildings constitute the area's identification, - its distinctive mark, but the area is also a socially strained place, whose urban surroundings bear the mark of many years of routine treatment, - here it is neither really ugly nor really beautiful. Small garden rudiments alternate between painted parking bays and heavily anchored bus stops. Huge quantities of urban inventory, like road signs and dog toilets, old-fashioned light poles and new-struck planting hardware, are supposed to secure the functional surfaces, to frustrate social 'elements' and to improve the locality's somewhat diffuse orientation. The area's appearance is a textbook case of a prevalent urban planning aesthetics that continues to build upon a functionalist approach. The areas around the convent buildings and the church have by now become zoned and sub-divided into ever smaller fields which simultaneously, albeit sub rosa, have the purpose of making the areas controllable inasmuch as, in this way, the non-controllable elements – the so-called socially-strained clientele - are 'stressed' and marginalized.

But it is the method that is unsound; it implies that the plaza is both fragmented and filled out, all at once. With a simple deduction, the space can be defined instead in its primary elements: the surrounding chains of houses, typified by a more or less anonymous red-brick architecture, fashion a 4-6 story edge which in the best Aldo Rossian sense can be identified as sterling background architecture. A kind of architecture which allows the convent building with the church's light green spire to come forward, as the singularity, and to play the role as foreground. In this spatial set, one large refreshing surface of grass could spaciously establish the mid-ground of this space. A surface of grass of this caliber would regenerate the area's spatial constitution, - and precisely on account of its form – and with respect to functionality, just by taking it easy and letting the mid-ground fall back, the possibility would be fostered of letting something else come forward and of making room. For everybody and everything, in fact – admittedly, with a little help from modern gardening-technology. Well-known dissimilarities, such as artificial surfaces up against natural surfaces or altmodisch up against hyper-modernity; the city's edge up against landscape surface could test out a kind of de-parallelism which would overhaul the customary procedures by establishing transitions between various epochs. The surface of grass would, in such a way, draw the past (the convent building) into the present – without the occurrence of the converse tendency, that the present would be pulverized back into the past (as any adapted style-formation will always wind up in). The mid-ground can, then, also be seen as a rather dynamic dimension, a variable in more than one respect.
The Mid-ground, as architectonic articulation. In Sten Eiler Rasmussen's book, On Experiencing Architecture, there is the famous story about the boys who are kicking the ball up and down the stairway of the Santa Maria Maggiore church. Although the author does not provide any exhaustive description of the stairway, we understand that it constitutes the transition between one particular ridge and one particular church, and this is an architectonically masterly articulation of a mid-ground. What is so

fantastic here is that the articulation takes hold from within, from the very heart of the landscape's morphology – and continues all the way to the local space, as the stairway continues the church's concave and convex forms, ever so consummately, down the ridge of Esquilin. One of Rome's seven mythological hills. And this truly constitutes an articulation of transitional forms, in all gradations of scale, from the body's space with the foot in the perfect step to the culmination at the eye's point, where the stairway in the unit's compressed form fashions the foot and the base for the church's corpus.

Moreover, landscape has been penetrating the city's space ever since eleven huge aqueducts, from a distance of almost a hundred kilometers, carried the waters of the surrounding territory into the thousands of fountains and bath facilities in ancient Rome. As Ivan Illich recounts in his book, H_2O and the Waters of Nepenthe – if we could, in this way, stop our tinkering the world, we might just find that it is a far better place to be than we could sense at first.

I imagine that transitions can be defined, somehow, just as broadly as one can envision the distance between two opposites: the way we leave this world, respectively, one abrupt and one slow. This notion serves as the foundation for the working concept behind the following parallel study of the two transitions – both defined by the mid-ground.

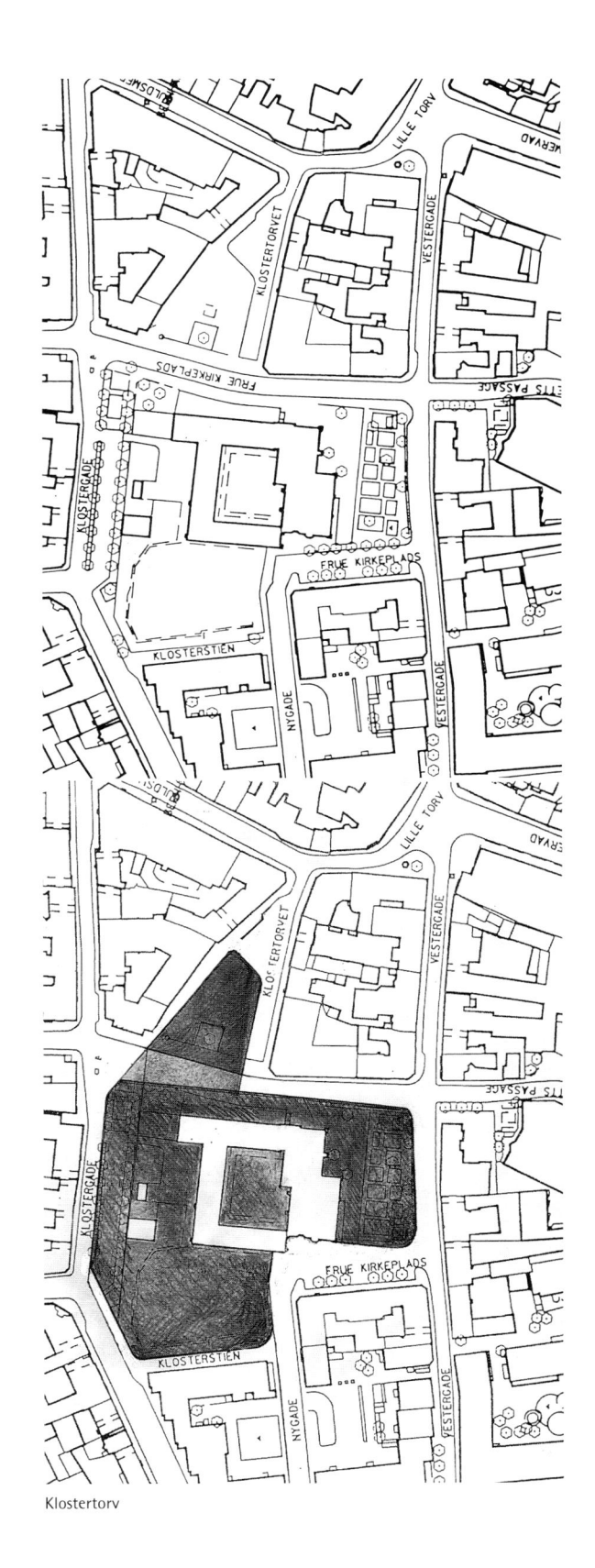

Klostertorv

Aerial photograph of, respectively, Sydhavnen (Southern Harbor) and Nordhavnen (Northern Harbor): The mid-ground's potential fields are disposed as left-over ground areas. Boundaries between the city's edge and the vast landscape features, which are constituted by the Southern Harbor's wharf edges and the Northern Harbor's basin edges, are marginalized here. Areas that can be re-experienced inside the transition's form.
Parallel to the Southern Harbor, running transverse with Dybbølsbro, a water element is positioned. This element is distended as a horizontal middle-region on the marginal territory running along the railway cutting and the roadways behind Kalvebod quay. A mid-ground which defines the water's place between the city's solid anterior edge at Ingerslevsgade and the southern harbor's overall features. One could venture to describe this as a variegated field: a slow transition that assumes the form and the color of its surroundings' stream of roadways, waterways and permanent ways.

At the Northern Harbor, parallel to the permanent way and alongside the Kalkbrænderihavnsvejen (Lime Kiln Harbor Road), a long and slender stretch of park area is defined. It makes its appearance as a vertical stretch of park up on the marginal territory's terrain gradients. A mid-ground characterized by the vertical columnar growth of the trees, just before the foot of the streets situated at the edge of the city, like a park wall that rises up right there on the other side of the northern harbor's surfaces.
What we are dealing with here is the essential difference between the Northern Harbor's airy surfaces and the city edge's dense firmness, – an abrupt transition, articulated as a gateway between two distinctly different parts.

Perspective Southern Harbor

Perspective Northern Harbor

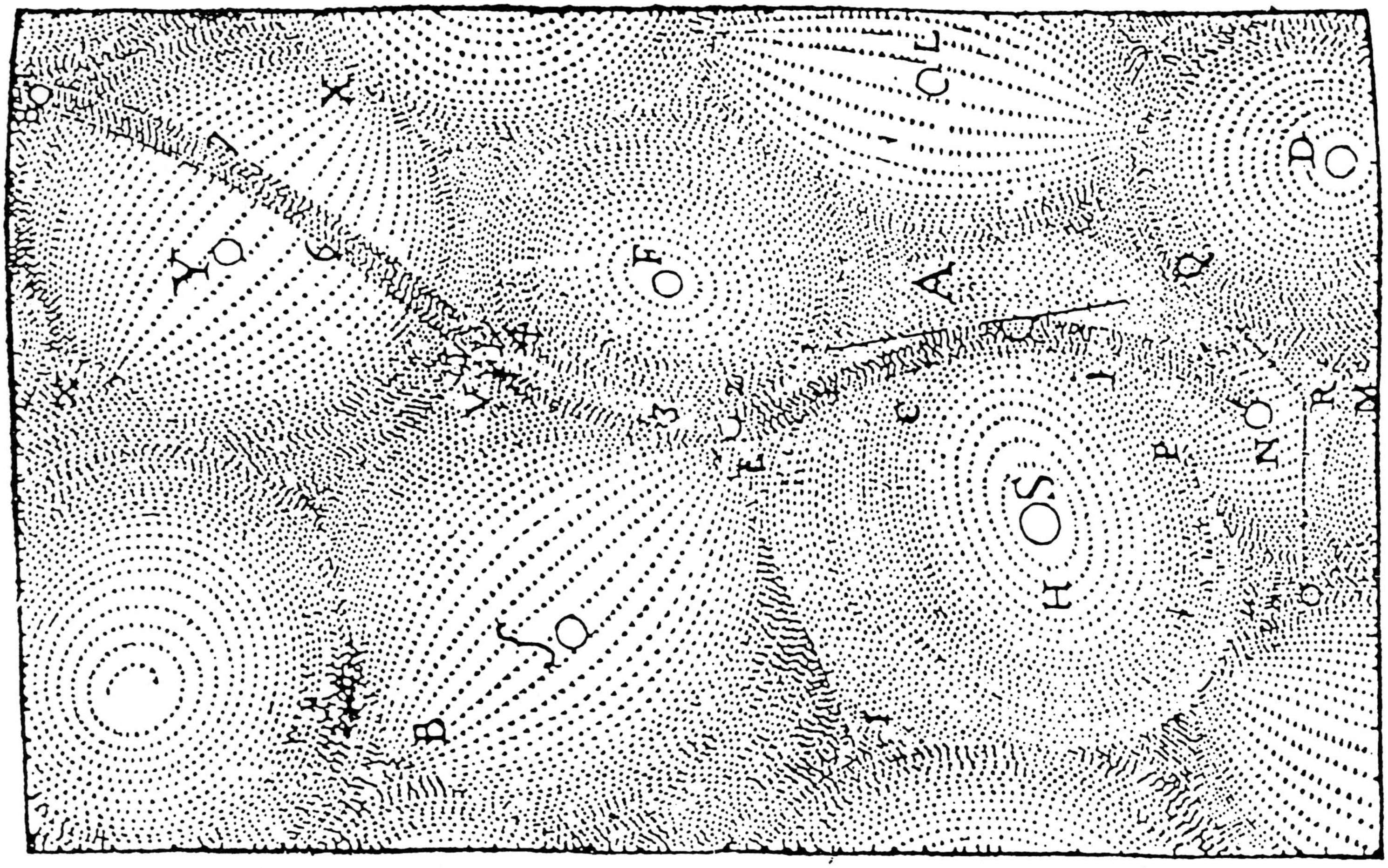

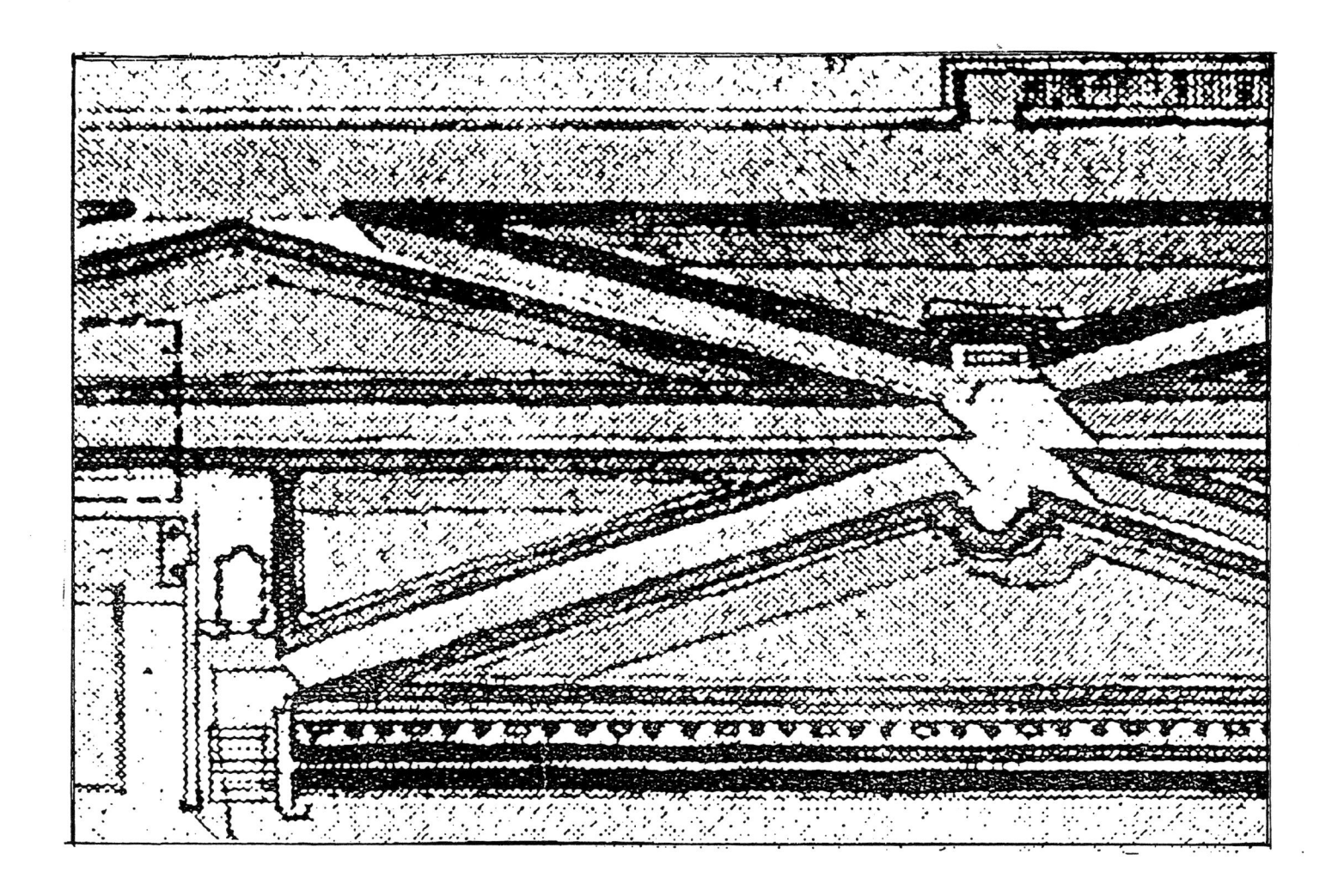

Both the park- and the plaza-elements are characterized, above and beyond the reference to water and trees, by an autonomous modeling of the terrain level. For this internal modeling, which in this particular instance can rightly be called 'the content's form', what is employed is an already existing form which is fastened to the conception of the fantastic form. The existing forms are gathered from the past – from the middle and the later parts of the sixteenth century. At that time, Descartes made a drawing wherein he visualized a segment of the universe's energies, moving in eddy currents. During the same period of time, Ligorio created a garden that has become better known by the name Villa d'Este. The garden is disposed in levels out upon an edge, as a chiseled contour, which in a manner almost contrary to nature zigzags its way down over a slope's precipitous decline.

The garden, in this way, constitutes a transitional form that plays on the change from one plane to another, consequently between the vertical and the horizontal planes, in between the wall and the garden paths. The plate reproduced here illustrates a section of the garden's upper levels.

The Southern Harbor

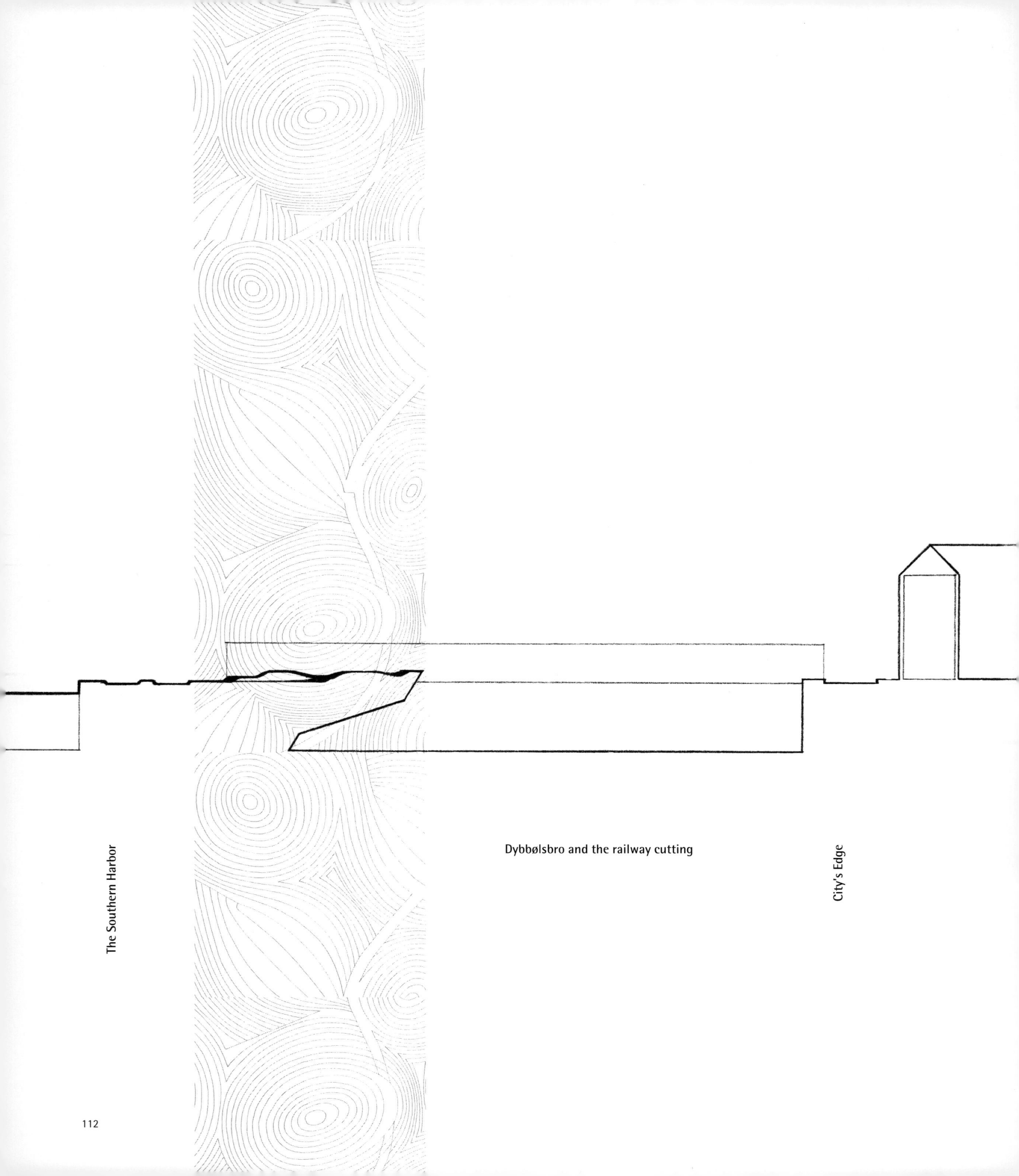

Dybbølsbro and the railway cutting

City's Edge

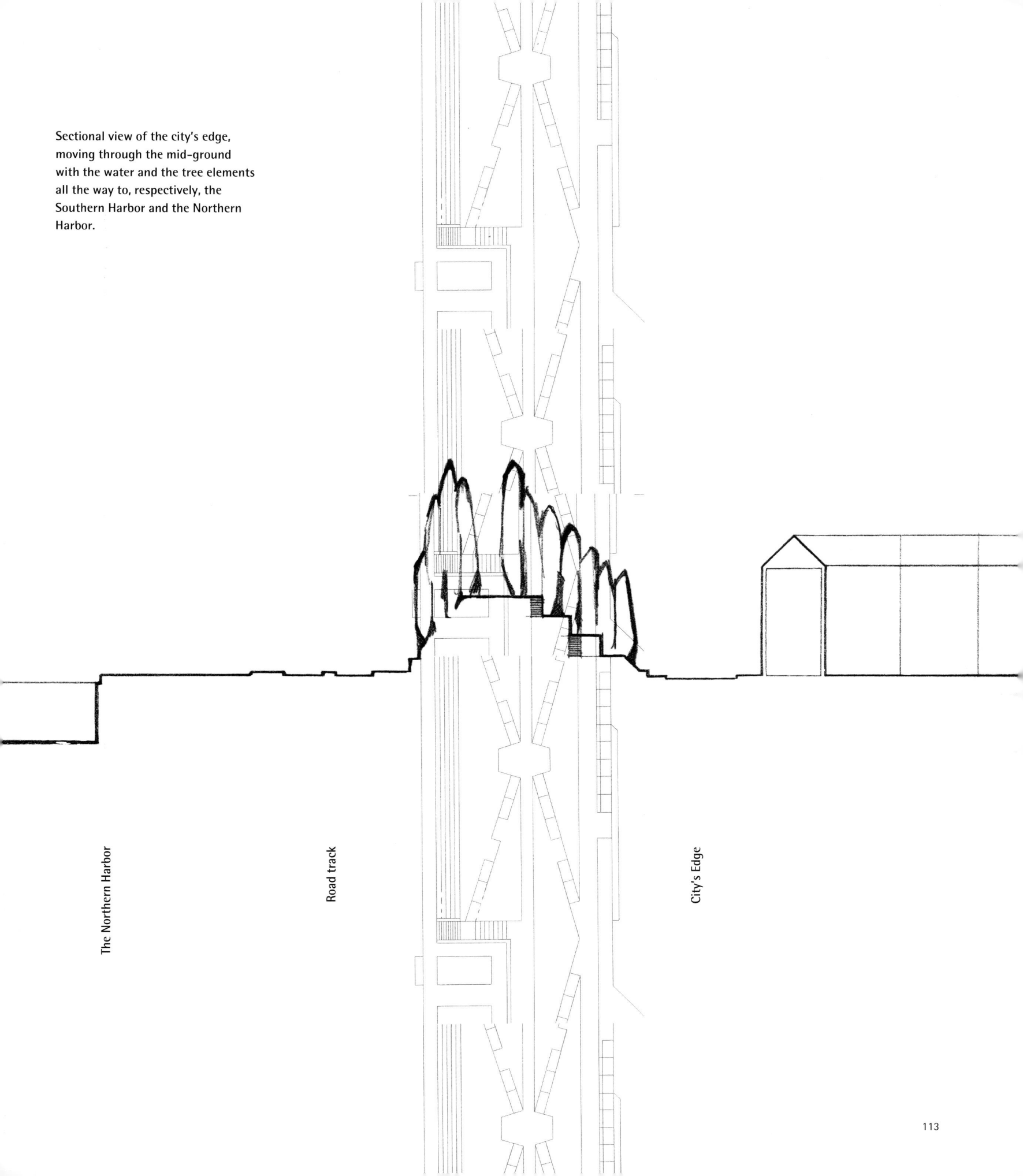

Sectional view of the city's edge, moving through the mid-ground with the water and the tree elements all the way to, respectively, the Southern Harbor and the Northern Harbor.

The Northern Harbor

Road track

City's Edge

114

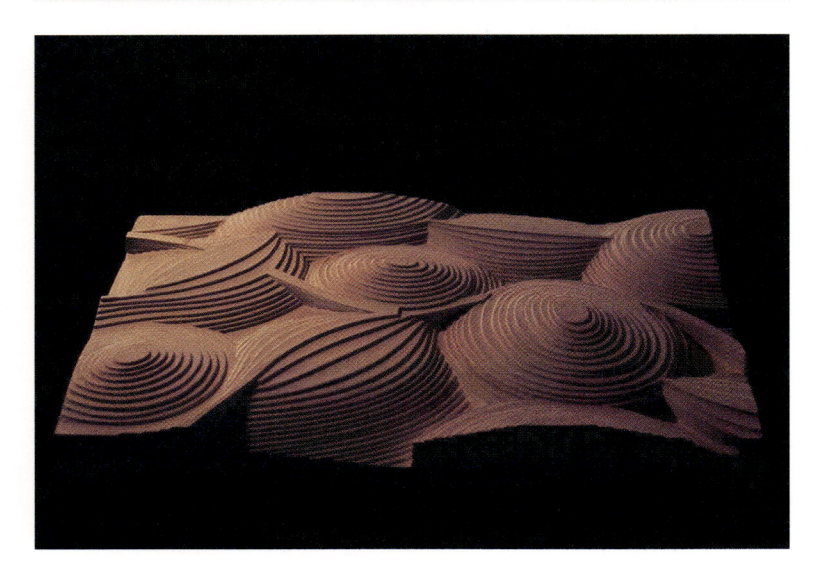

The execution of the park-/ plaza-elements'
internal form is envisioned in modules, and
thus the modeling of the terrain is executed
as a fundamental ground element which
can then be assembled in the length.
The park/ plazas consequently become contractors' parks of a kind, which can be constructed in stages. In principle, the module
can be superadded indefinitely – but in this
case, within the limitation of the demarcation of the left-over ground areas.
The model photos illustrate the two fundamental ground elements, with each of the
modules' terrain forms.

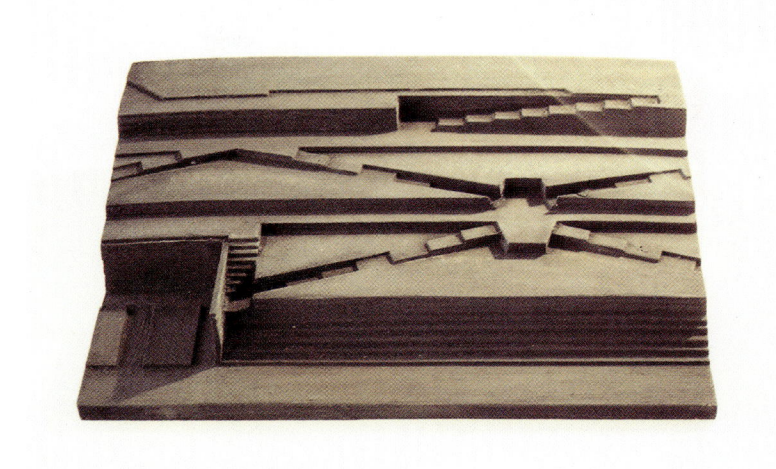

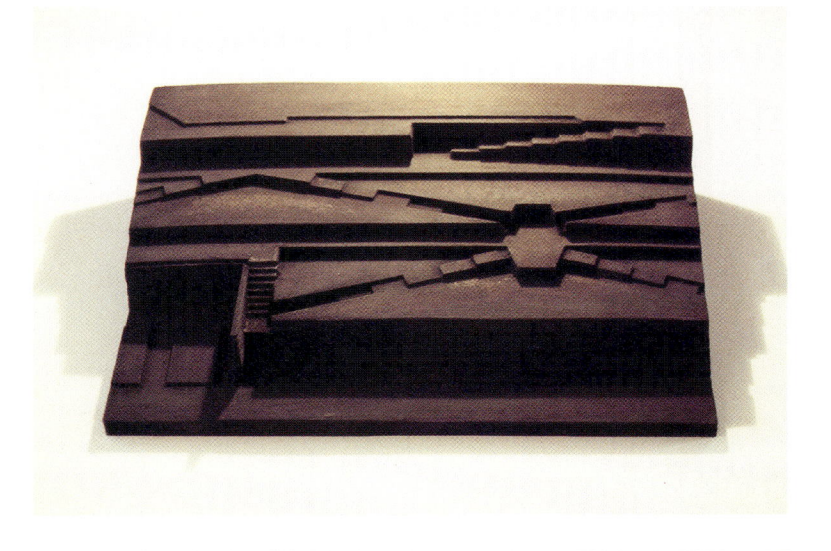

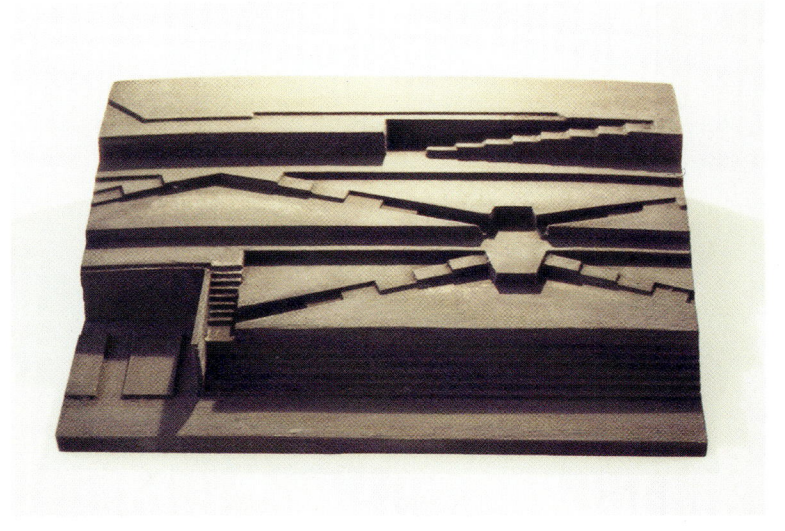

The Water

The Tree

SVEIN TØNSAGER

The Space's Middle Ground

1.
I can remember visiting my paternal grandfather once in the beginning of the fifties. In a section of Oslo, where there is today virtually not so much as a "trace" left over from that time. In a working-class housing area, there was a redbrick building that had actually won a gold medal at the world exposition in Paris on account of its cast-iron stairway and an 'advanced toilet-system'. Across the street, there were the bazaars, on two levels, also in red brick, and with immense, round arch-formed apertures. My grandfather was blind, and his craft was making wicker furniture. Without being able to see what he was doing, he sat and "looked right out", as his hands kept busy all the while. I still remember the articles of furniture – they were very beautiful. When he was finished with a certain number of pieces, a truck from "The Blind People's Store" came and picked them up. They were sold at the store's facility in Oslo.
In this account of childhood/ past, there was a coherence. The residence, the workshop, the harbor in Oslo, the Town Hall, the distance to Karl Johansgade (Parisian Boulevard), to the Castle and to the Movie House. I can still very easily draw a significance-map pertinent to this coherence.

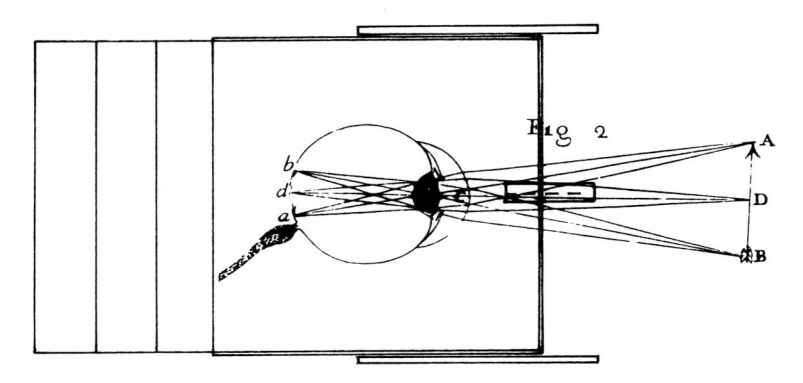

"The field of vision has always seemed to me comparable to the ground of an archæological excavation." *Paul Virilio.*

2.
About fifteen years ago, I sat on a train moving through Holland. Sat, as one does when travelling by train, looking out the window at the surroundings passing by. In the flat, cultivated landscape, there was a row of trees. Far away, but by virtue of the fact that they seemed to be situated in a 90-degree angle with respect to my motion, it suddenly dawned on me that in just a few minutes, I would be seeing the row of trees from perspective to elevation. I availed myself of the time that I still had before this would transpire to envision what kind of arrangement there might be here. Was there an avenue? Maybe even a canal in between the trees? Or would there be a yard at the end (in the perspective)? I was thinking about my own direction of movement, about the avenue and about the potential canal.
In the fraction of a second that it took me to see 'the picture', I observed the avenue, the canal and the house. Afterward, I looked back with "longing" – from the other side. Knowing full well that if I wanted to contemplate this entirety I would have to get off the train at the next station, take a bus or rent a car and find the avenue, the canal and the house. In doing so, I would be delaying my trip home for at least one whole day, having to wait for the next train. So I just kept on riding, and I have always preserved this partially incomplete picture in my memory about something that I assumed was a complete arrangement.

3.
These two stories both have to do with the part and the entirety. They both deal with a form of coherence. This "project" deals with what is removed, disturbed in the physical, cultural and social coherence – where a "project", a strategy, can attempt to establish "a new coherence". In its physical form, the city's parts, its buildings, streets and plazas - the city's topographical relationships – have articulated the relationship between the private and the public, in

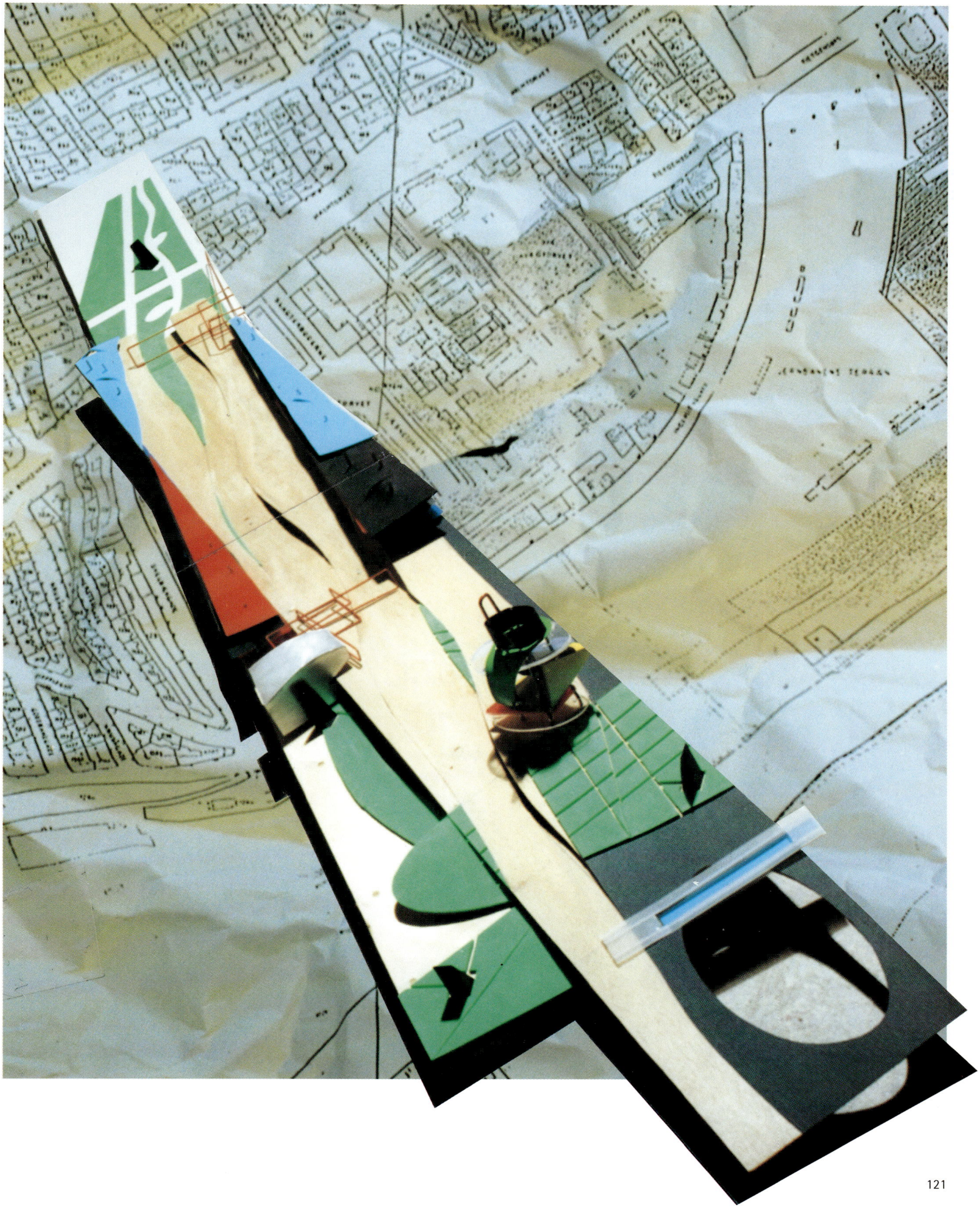

The Penguin Pool, London Zoo.

functional, social, cultural and political respects. The living rooms were oriented toward the street and the bedroom looked out into the backyard. And the window-mirror and the view over the yard apportioned voyeurism's and the window-mirror's functions.
But there are 'crevices' that have been struck into this tale. The radio-scanner that taps the neighbor's cell phone and the video camera that can be linked up to the Internet, with the result that private interiors are becoming globally accessible, constitute but a few examples of how both privacy and public-ness in the traditional sense are being eradicated. To be private is no longer fully possible, and what is meant by "the public" is in the course of losing its original significance.
In order to establish a new coherence, a field is being spread out. The field is the experimental site for testing out the new coherence. The field is a ribbon, where the landscape, in a cultivated sense, "stands across from" the city's buildings. Inside this system, place is made for the areas, the marginalizing functions that the presently existing city has suppressed. The new "neighborhood" possesses surfaces and vertical connections rather than "streets and plazas". It embodies complex coherences rather than distinct functionality, unlimited rather than limited possibilities. The surface's arrangement suggests a possible disposition rather than a finished programming.
"As architecture is a social art the value of a building must lie chiefly in its ability to create environment out of human situations." Peter Cook, *Architecture: action and plan.* Studio Vista/ Reinhold Art Paperback, 1967.

(Thanks to Morten Stubgaard, Dept. V, AAA, for conversations about the project and for his model-experiment.)

Drawing: Svein Tønsager

'Rupture in Space',
pencil drawing,
Svein Tønsager.

123

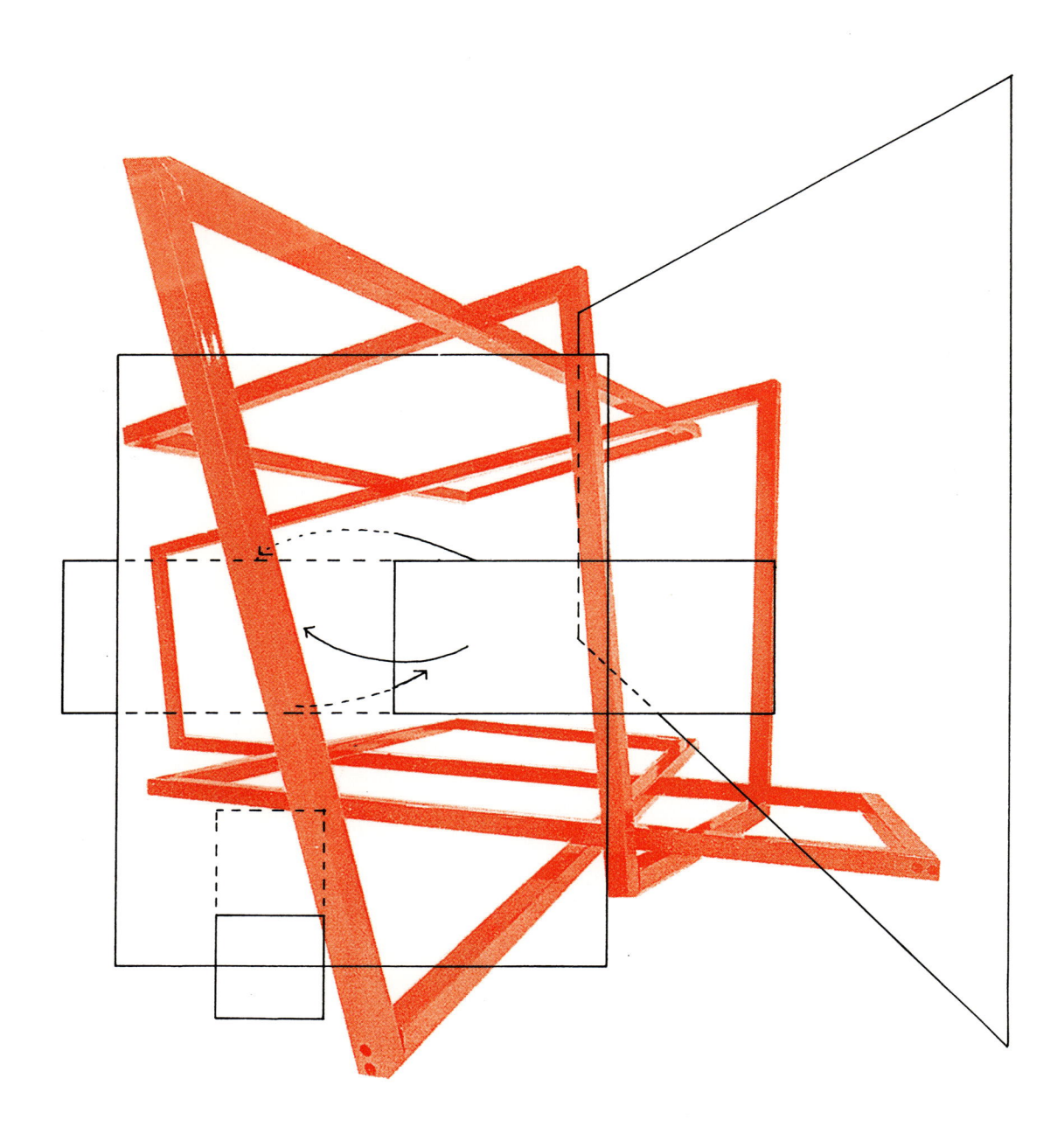

Continuous lines in space. The place's reference to the ribbon.

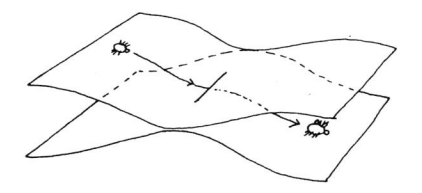

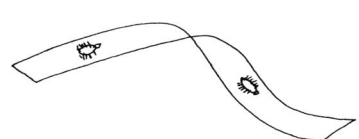

Riemann's 'cut', multi-folded connected surface.　　Elastic-ribbon.

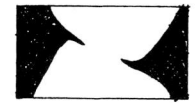

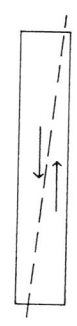

Above: Vesterbro. Interweaving of city and nature.

To the left: Incision though two three-dimensional forms, which contact each other and intertwine into one another (Raoul Bunschoten, Oslo Workshop).

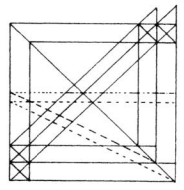

Jonathan Marvel: Fractal model (after Mandelbrot). "Investigations in Architecture", Eisenman Studios at the GSD, 1983-85.

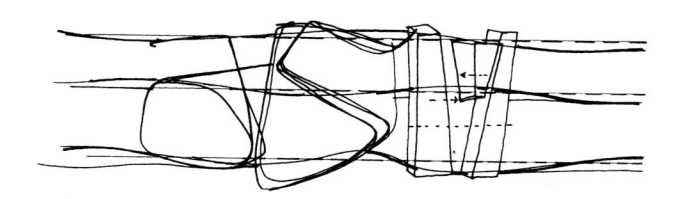

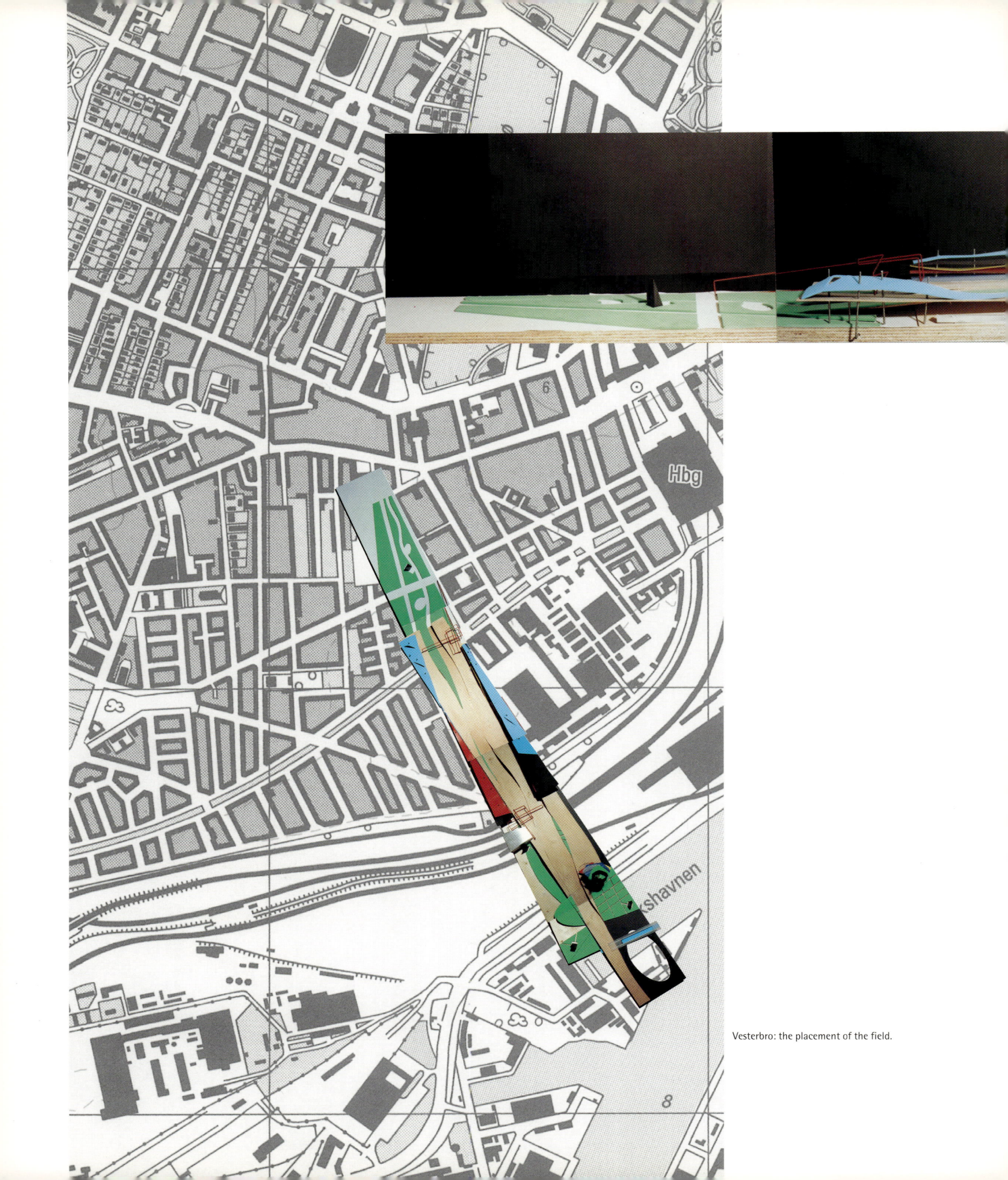

Vesterbro: the placement of the field.

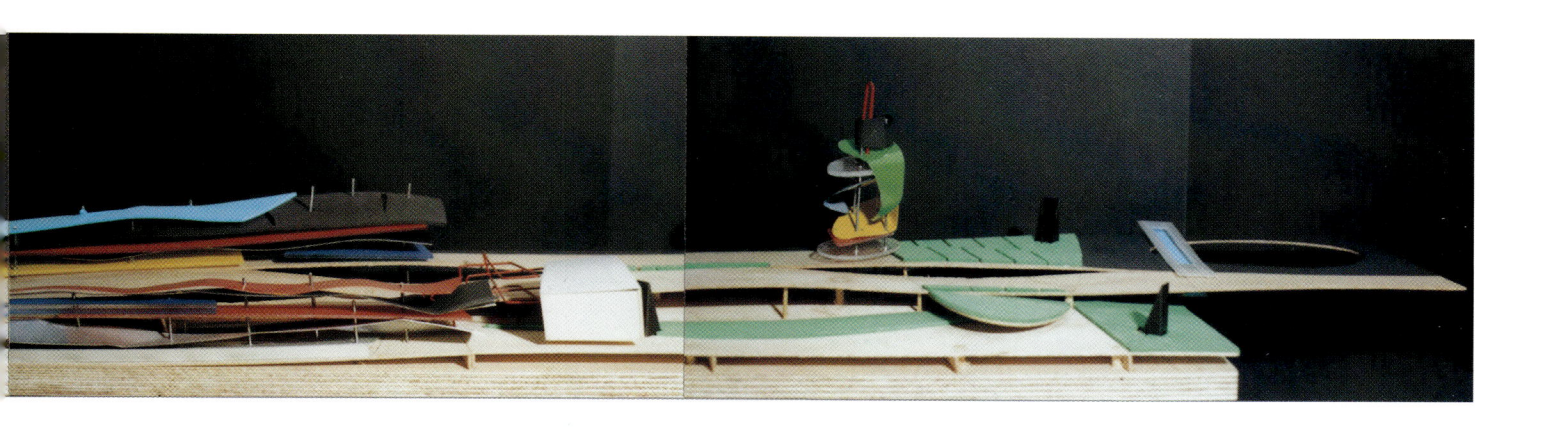

Media House.

127

The swimming hall

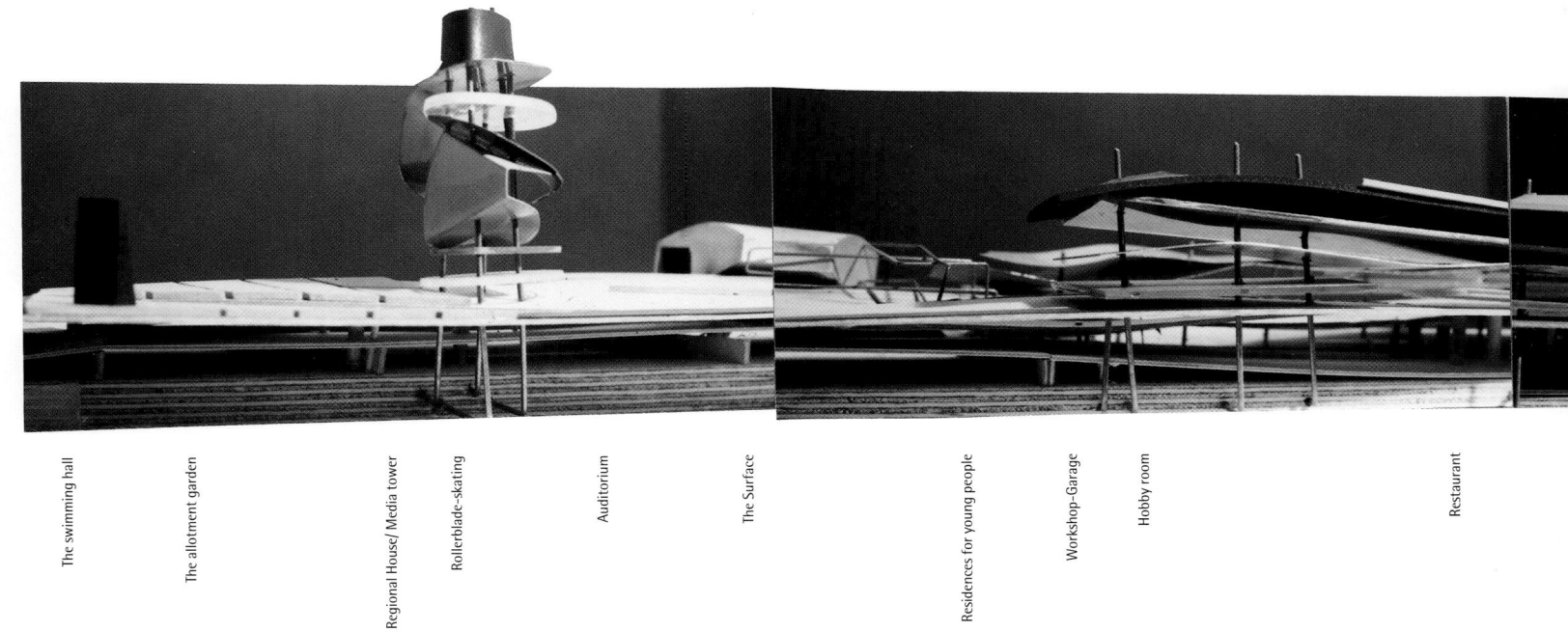

The allotment garden

Regional House/Media tower

Rollerblade-skating

Auditorium

The Surface

Residences for young people

Workshop-Garage

Hobby room

Restaurant

sløjfen

haven

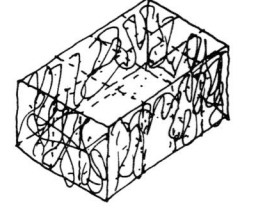

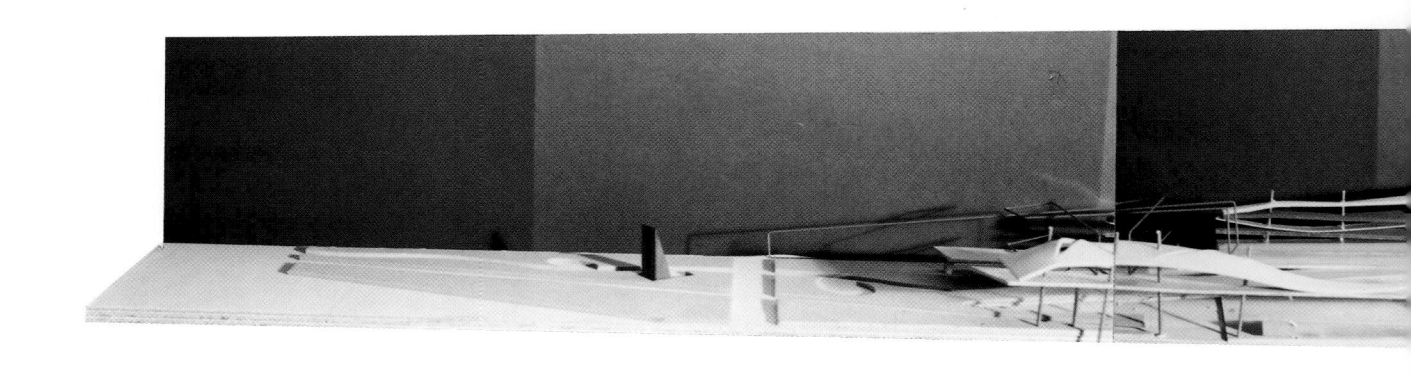

Café Laundry Aerobics Shops

Model Vesterbro "girder".

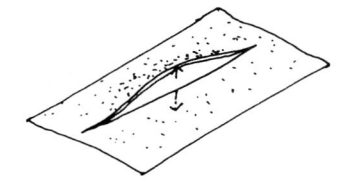

Snittet

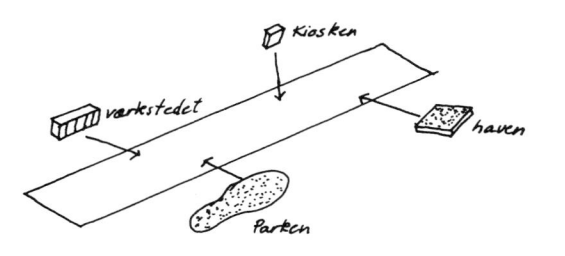

130

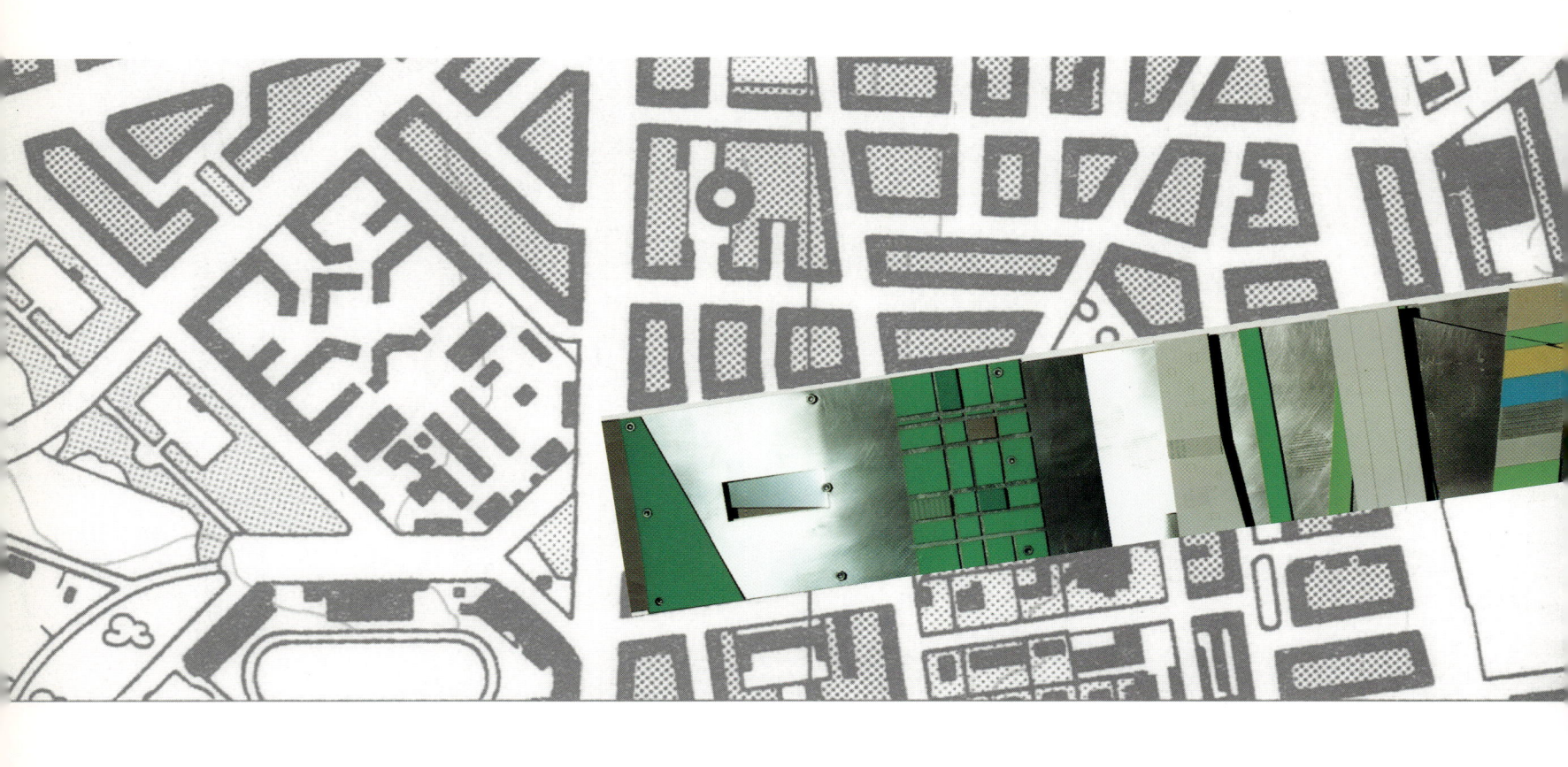

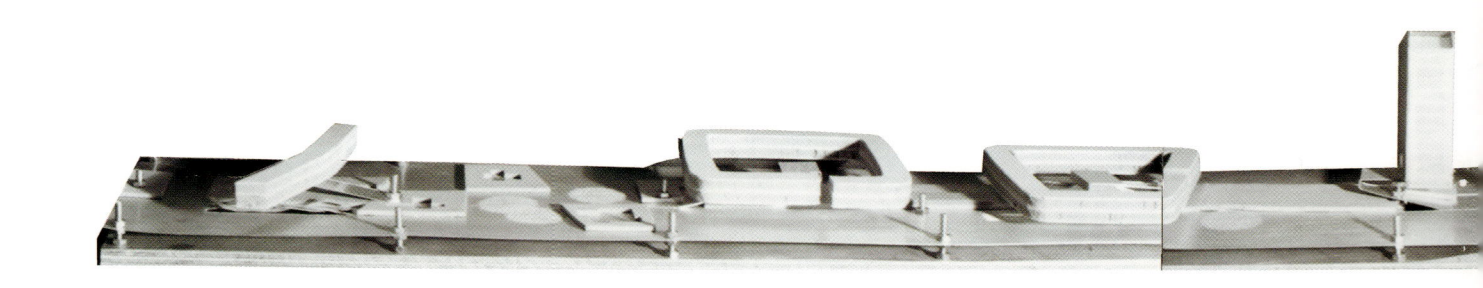

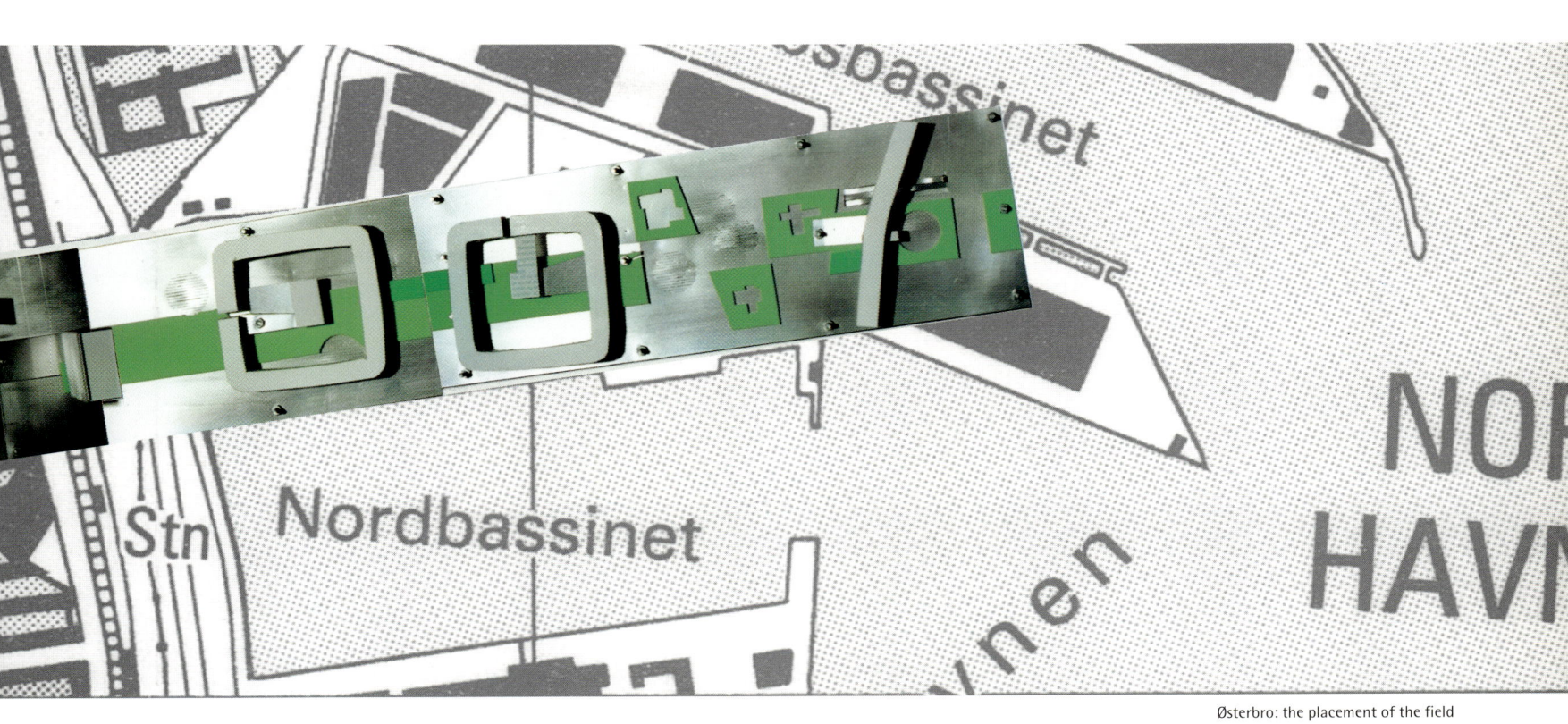

Østerbro: the placement of the field

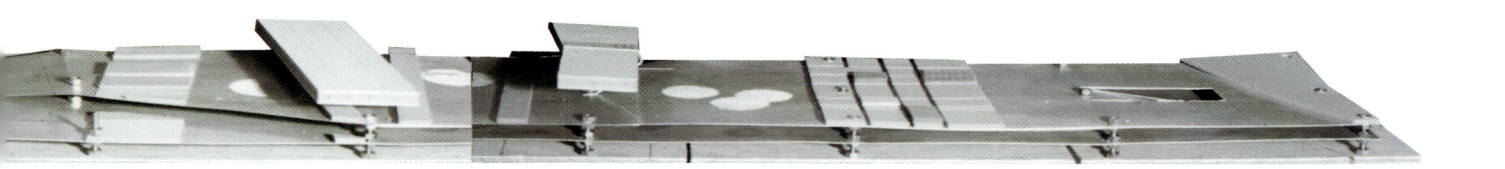

131

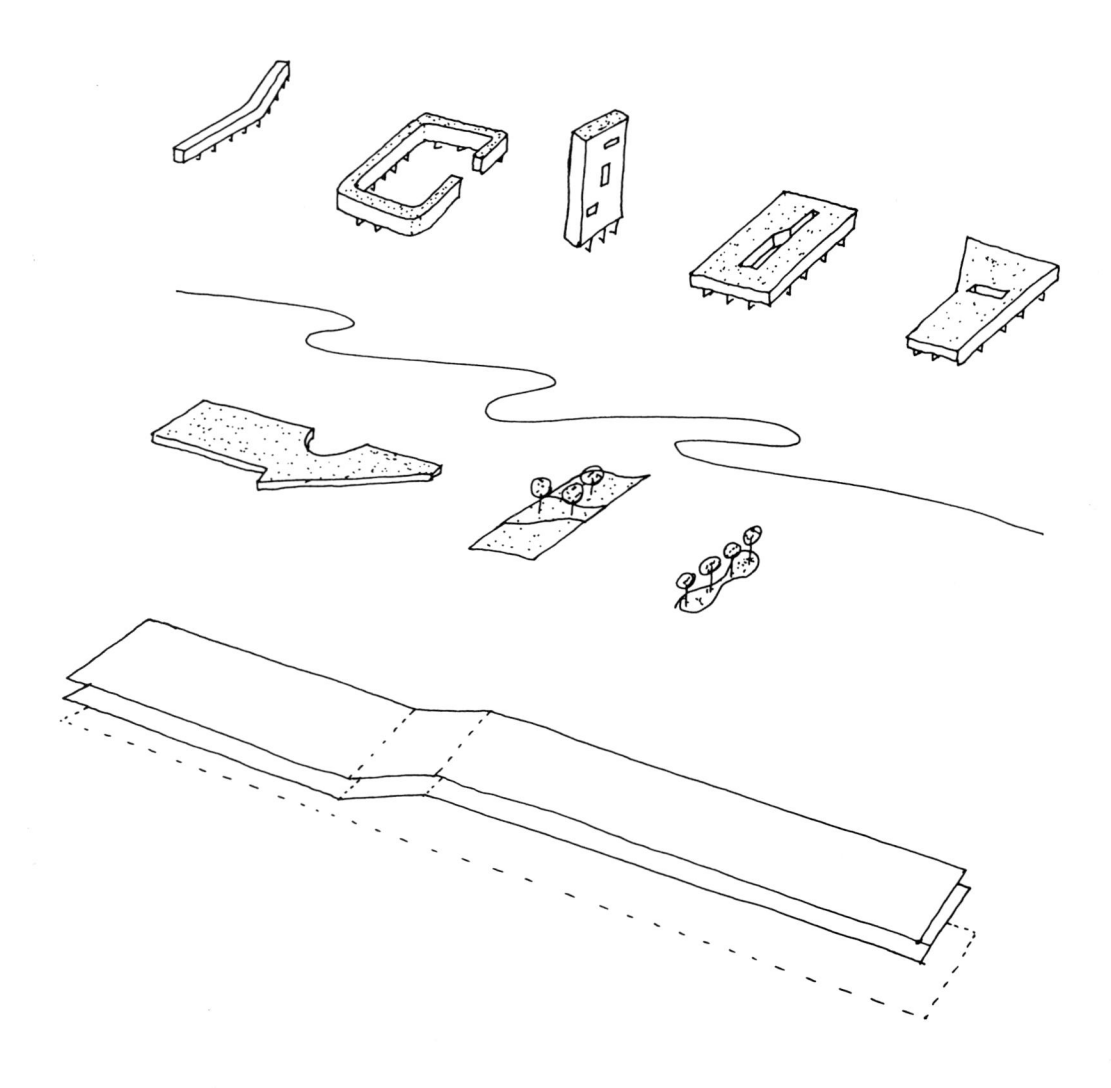

Typical elements for the "girder" on Østerbro.

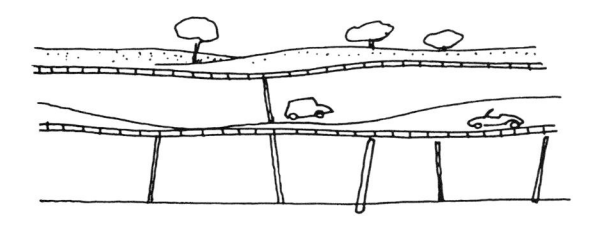

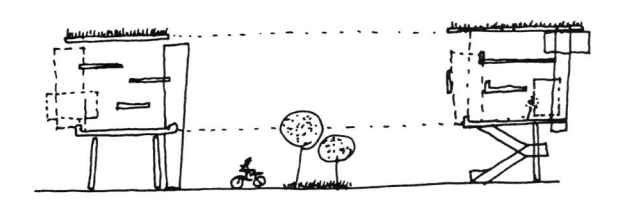

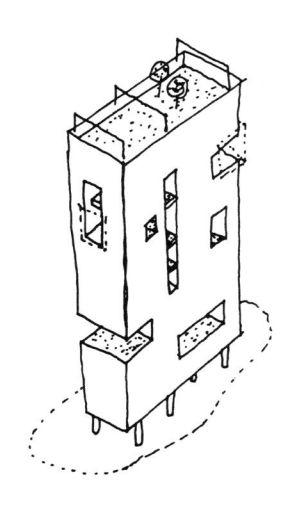

Vesterbro

Østerbro

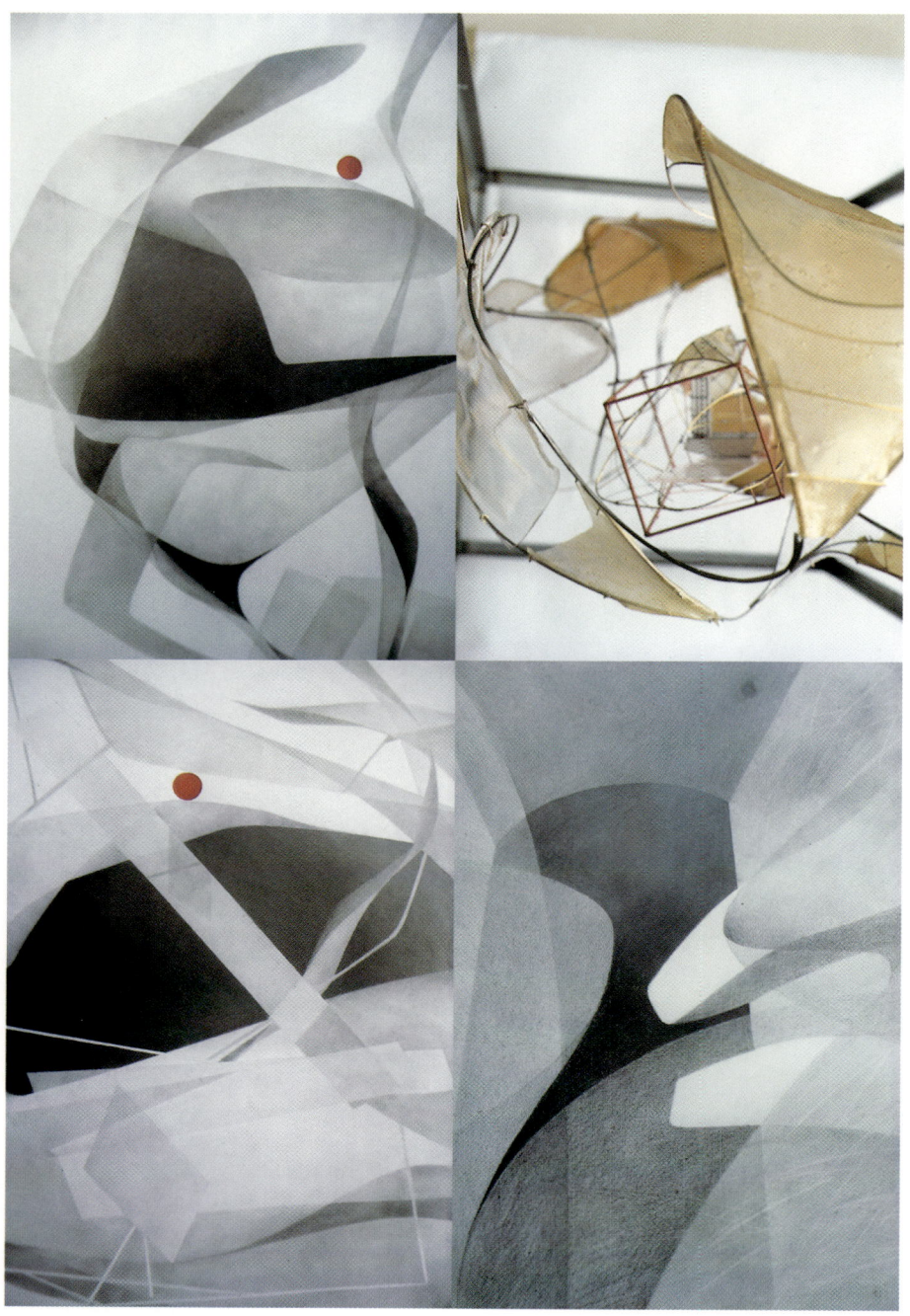

Drawings and model: Dynamic movements in space.

137

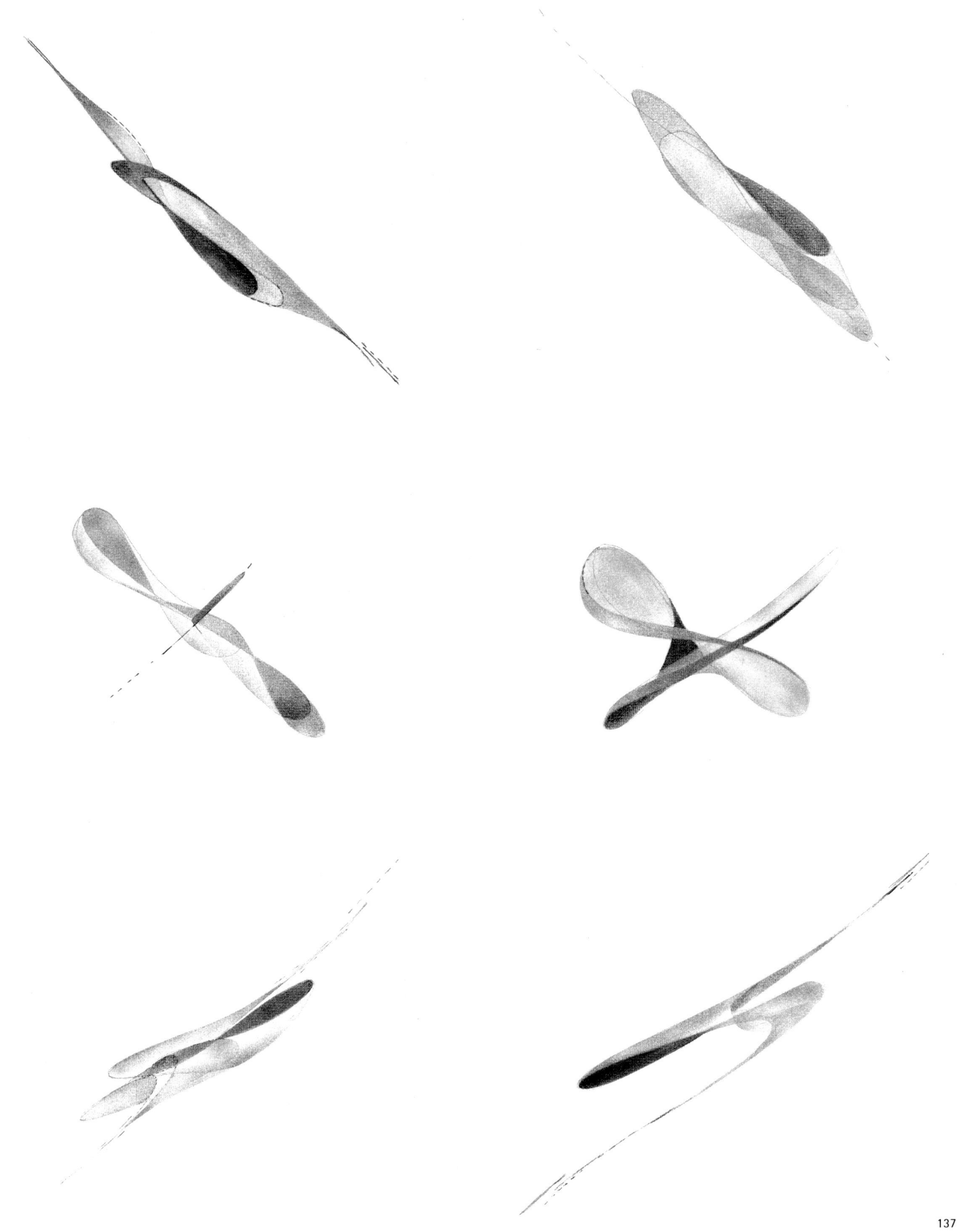

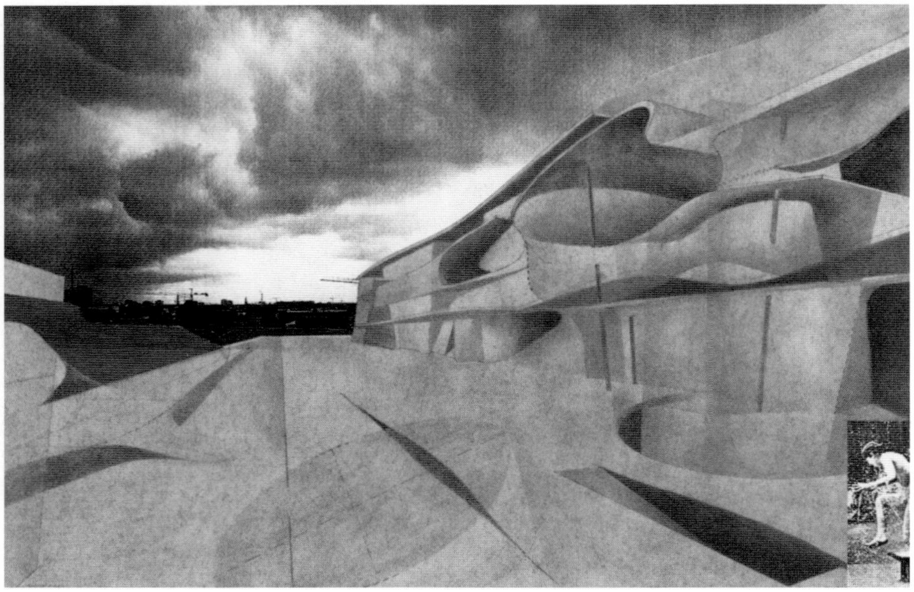

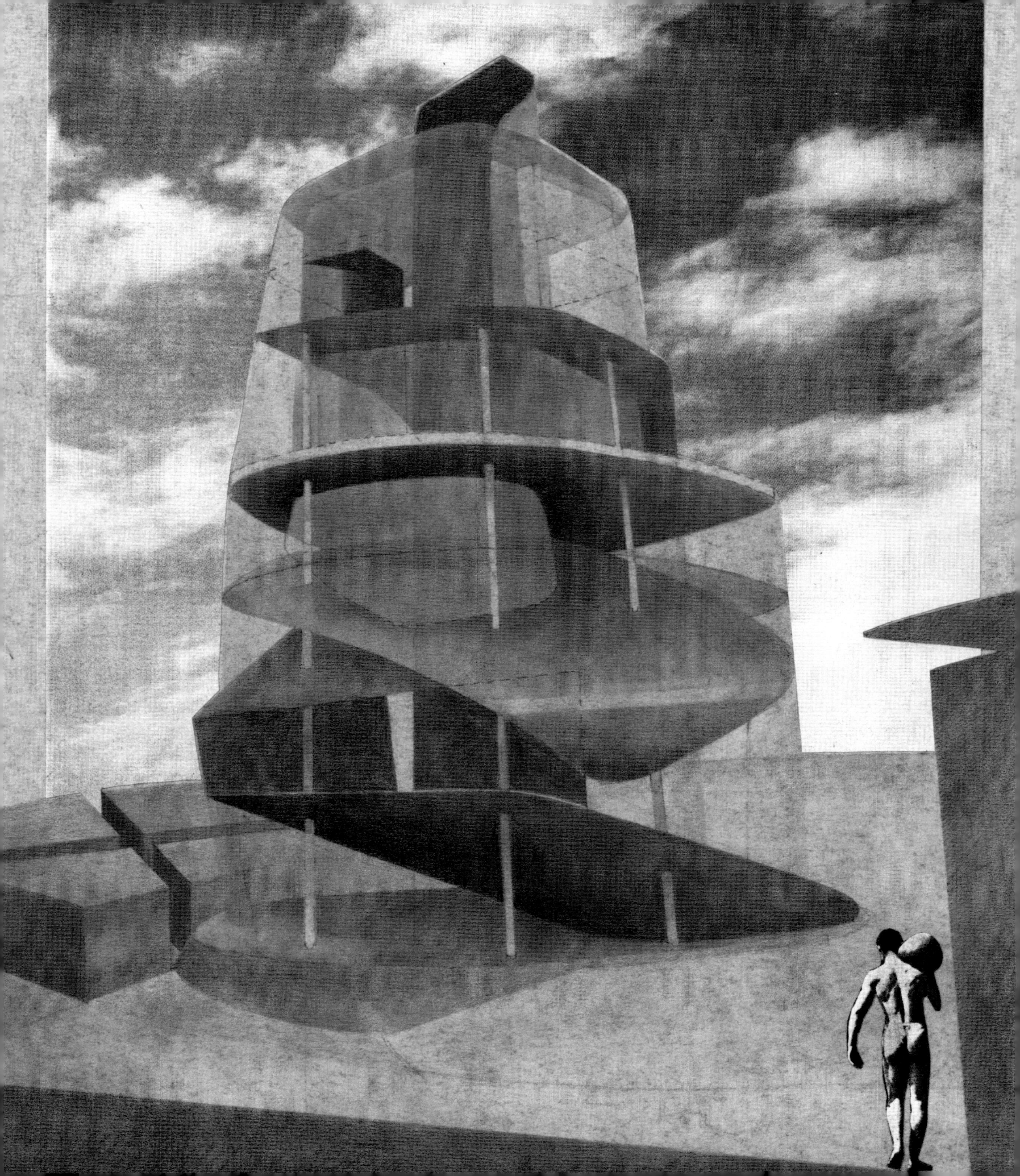

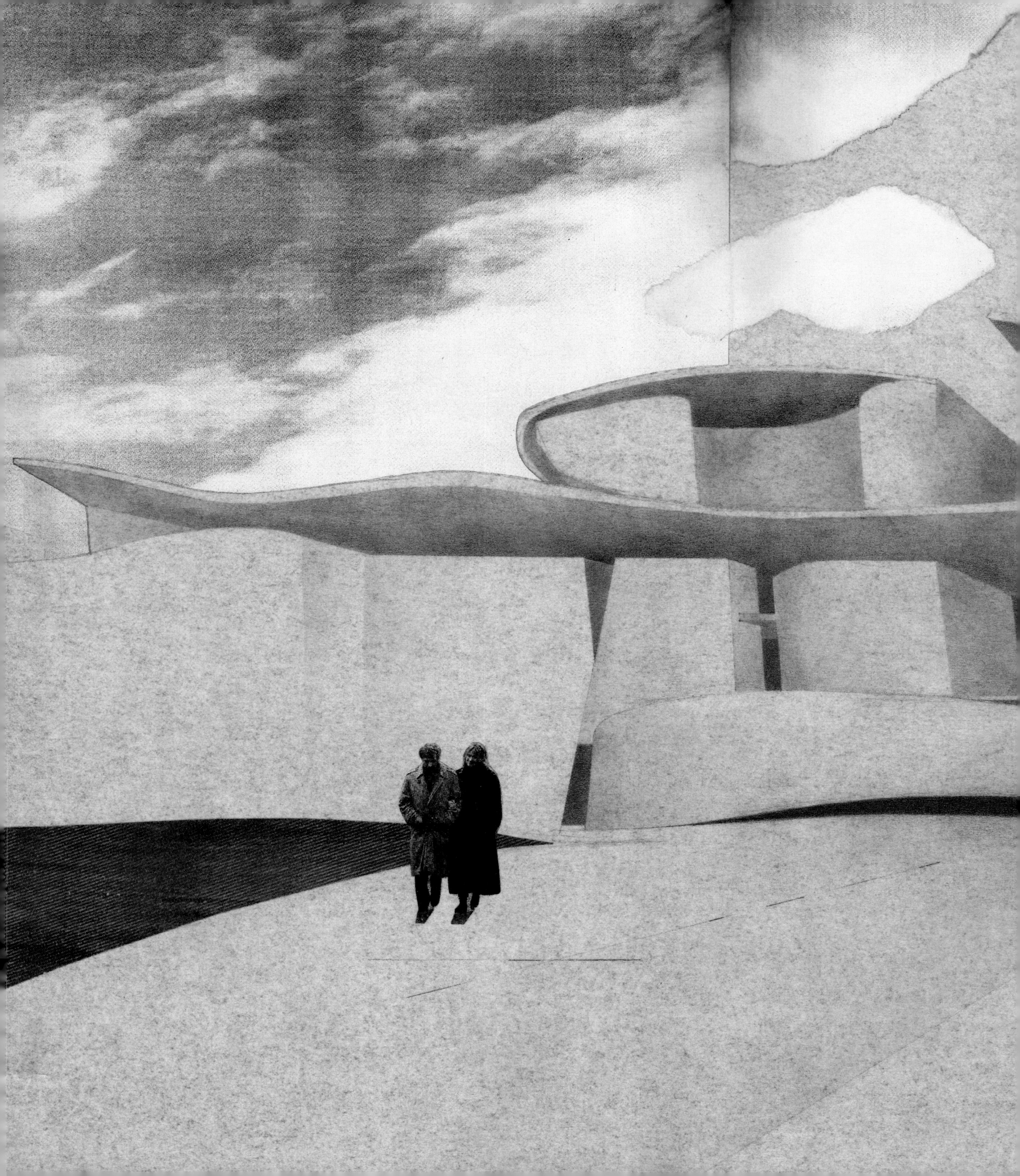

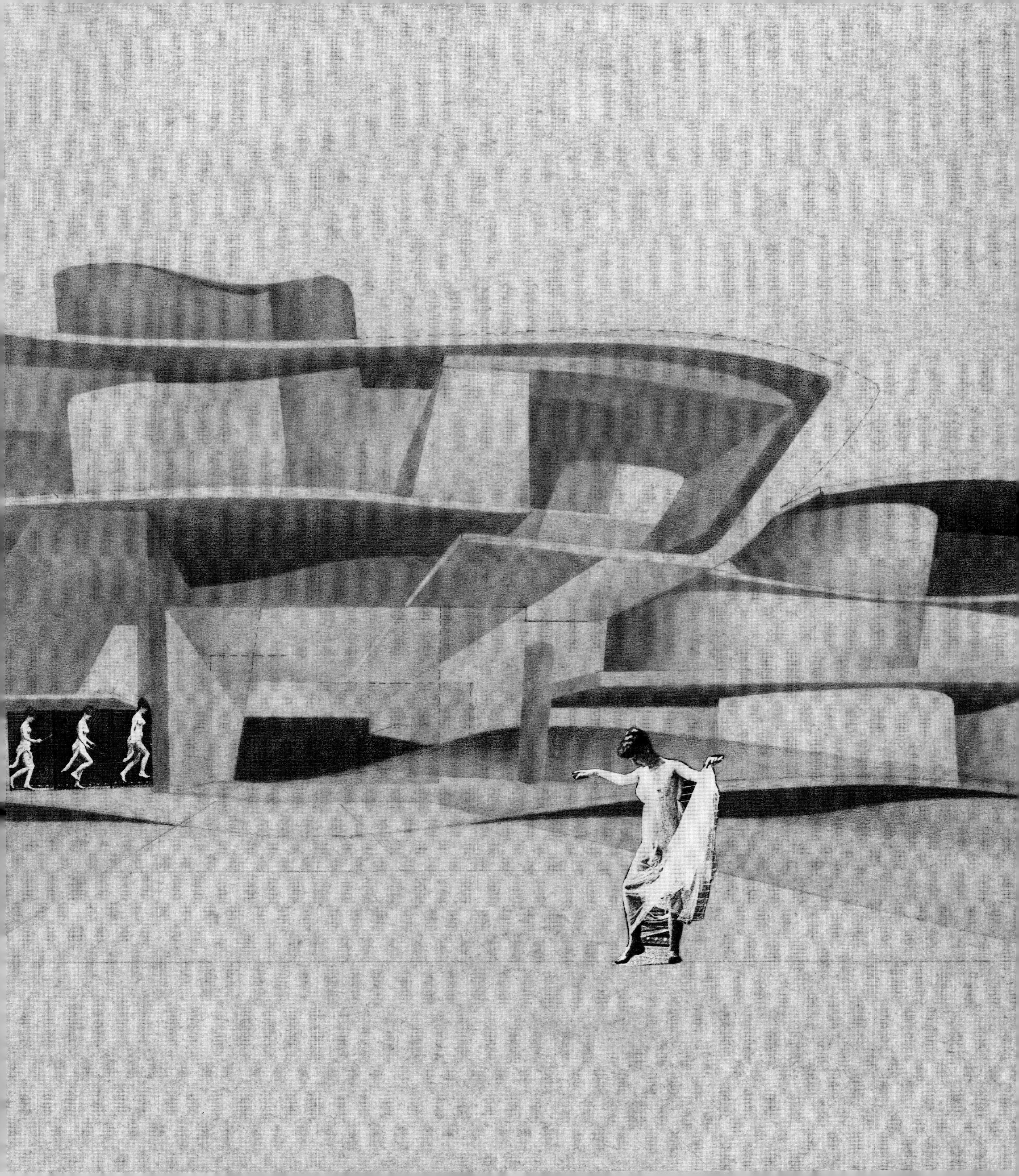

NIELS GRØNBÆK

THE MIDDLE GROUND
On the Metaphysics of the Delay.
A draft. Short-circuits in the Relationship of Uncertainty.

> *born in brackets*
> *the falcon to the air*
> *the shark to the sea*
>
> *the human being*
> *not conclusively*
> *for this*
>
> Ivan Malinovski
> - from *Poetomatic*, 1965

"... By and large, it is typical of the economic, technological, social and sign-related development that the middle ground is being forfeited as a mediating transition and symbol for the connection between near and far, or between 'the innermost and the outermost'.
"... The articulation of the space's middle ground is an organization of the locality's place as a bodily space which renders the individual world a part of the others' world. ..."[1]

SVANEMØLLEHAVNEN
SKUDEHAVNEN
CONTAINERVEJ
SKIBSFARTVEJ
ORIENTBASSINET
KALKBRÆNDERIHAVNEN
ØSTRE GASVÆRK (NEDLAGT)
ØRESUNDSHOSPITALET
ORIENT
PLADS
ORIENTKAJ
SUNDMOLEN
SUNDKAJ
KRONLØBSBASSINET
FORTKAJ
LÜDERSVEJ
SUNDKROGSGADE
NYBORGGADE
STRAND BOULEVARDEN
VORDINGBORGGADE
KORSØRGADE
KOLDINGGADE
ÅRHUS PLADS
ÅRHUSGADE
HJØRRINGGADE
VIBORGGADE
VEJLEGADE
KRAUSESVEJ
NORDENSGADE
GAMMEL KALKBRÆNDERI VEJ
NORDBASSINET
TØMMERKAJ
MARMORKAJ
UNICEF PLADS

LEVANTKAJ

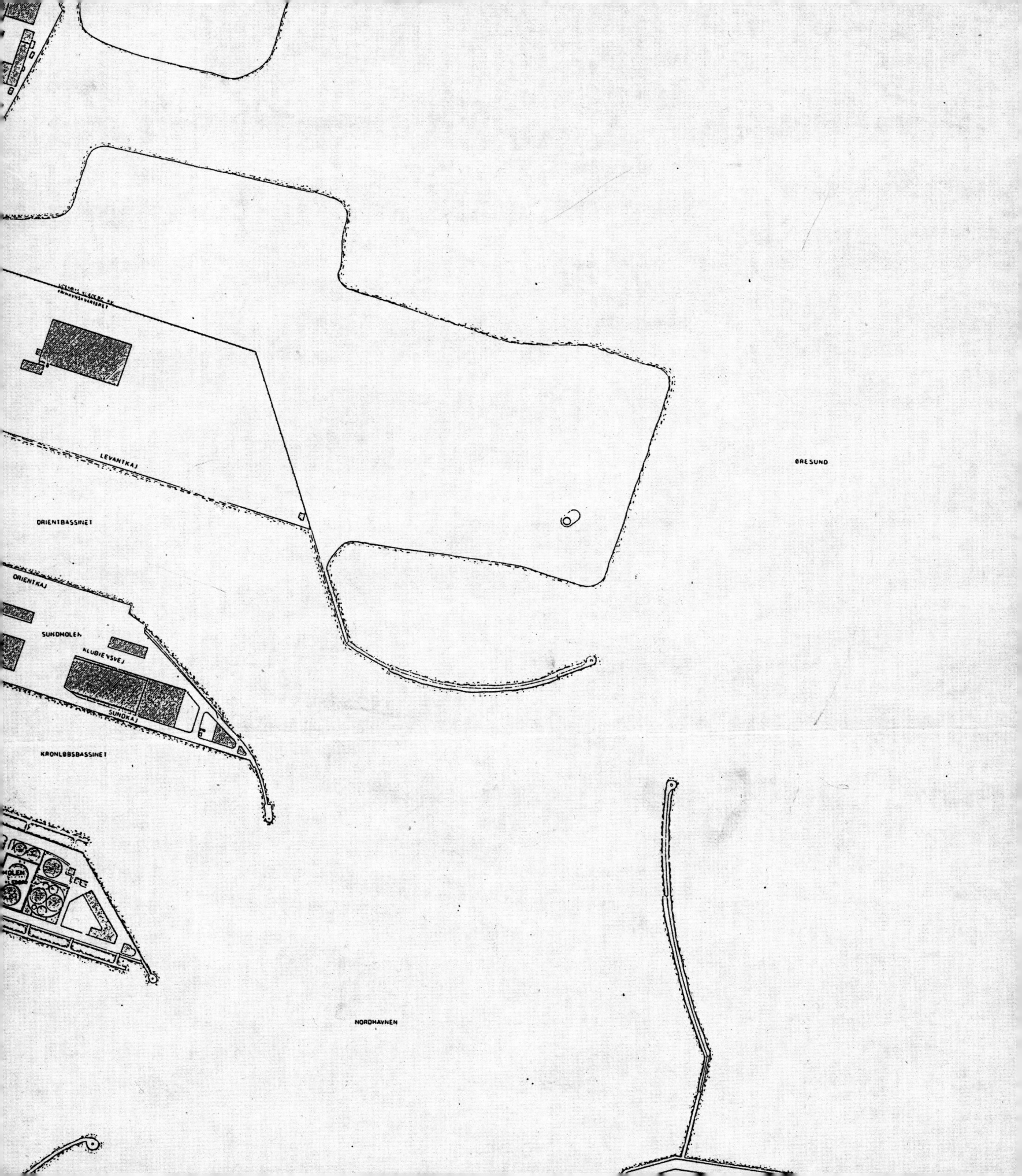

ORIENTBASSINET

ORIENTKAJ

SUNDMOLEN

KLUBIEVSVEJ

SUNDKAJ

KRONLØBSBASSINET

ØRESUND

NORDHAVNEN

I define the space's middle ground as that space I step into when I leave my dwelling's lockable private sphere. The dimensions of this middle ground are bounded by my senses' horizons, in diagram form, as concentric circles, when I turn my head. The horizon in the middle coincides with the body's form and the skin's purified membrane, from where the rings spread outward and inward. With the intervention of the skin, an internal space connected to the external, through the funnel of the senses, is ligated. What supervene in the bottlenecks are *delays,* which occasion the account between the brain and its horizon. The delay vanishes in infinite perspicacity, or as the bottlenecks disappear. *In the universe's heat death, all delays are annulled.*

Outside and inside the skin, the variety of species and the quantity of independent living individuals are enormous. The ground water and lymph are conveyed in vessels that divide themselves into capillary swamp and capillary flesh. Everywhere where there is fluid matter, bodies are formed like "the falcon to the air / the shark to the sea", brain and liver. The senses' horizons do not coincide, but rather create discontinuities of something that I hear but don't see and of something that I see but don't hear. The horizon is my sensory area's boundary. A bit like the light, which becomes visible when it strikes something. The visual field is irregular when it becomes delineated by something that is near – most dramatically when something gets in my eye and simplest toward the dip of the horizon on the open sea. The horizon dissolves in a fluffy blue in the cloud-free vault of the sky, in which the flight of the eye loses itself; it is more infinite toward the remote stars of nighttime.

"... Traditionally, we call body that part of substance that is caught in the sack of our skin. Certain things such as mirrors or language have us believing that it is indeed a coherent whole, ... As it is, what we take to be our body is in the first place a toric envelope. ... But we are all already caught in substance, that complex fact of concavities and convexities. The torus goes back to the torus; forever. ..."

"... Along with Bergson, we will call 'body' any zone that introduces an opacity in the transmission of interactions. ... There is thus body in nature wherever there is an indetermination with respect to a milieu ... Thus there are bodies in rivers where unpredictable whirlpools form ..."[2]

The city's space partitions itself on the borderline between the private and the traffical collectivity. The borderline is softened in the butcher's shop and at the café (the taxi in "Taxi Driver") and less so on the train platform. Canetti sits himself down inside a café and contemplates the throng, which - as an aggregate body - he was inside of, just before he came in. This throng continues to move on by, outside.

Inside the sports arena, the spectators are amassed - when a goal is made - into two organisms, which split themselves up once again into individuals whenever an injured player is carried off the field.

The middle ground overlooked. "...the middle ground is being forfeited as a mediating transition ... between near and far ..."[3]

Formalization can raise the level of complexity when it captures and fixes an invention, when it forms a body in the perishable indeterminacy that surrounds it. The local capturings can be taken out of circulation to constitute a larger body through a process of organizing the potentials inside the smaller formalizations. **They will accordingly for a while be tamed** in a critical balance between the larger constituted body of formalization and – through temporary drainage – the simultaneously constituted *outside* of an increasingly forceful vacuum of *otherness* proportional to the size of the body. This *Aufhebung* of smaller bodies into larger will lower the complexity on the original level and make way for a higher, until the bodies have attained a certain size. Complexity is furthered by the increasing frequency of bodies between different levels of potentiality. The duration of the ongoing presence or the maintenance of a body increases along an interval whose outer limits are constituted by the abolishment of delay, in the one end, and absolute difference, in the other. Towards the limits, the body's ability to form complex relations decreases. Towards the middle, there is an increase of contagion, invention, mutation and fertility. A zone of increasing complexity. A zone of transition and short-circuits – thunder and lightning.

"... The taking of the Bastille is symbolic of this state of things: it is hard to explain this crowd movement other than by the animosity of the people against the monuments that are their real masters. ..."[4]

The monuments have become homeless signifiers, follies. Without turmoil, they have opened themselves up to new codes. They leave behind a void, which is filled out with an atmosphere of crisis, devoid of theme. As material, the city outlives its progenitors and is entrusted to others for whom it was already there, as a landscape, which with a dual effect of languidness and variability encourages new ways of living.

The city upholds symbolic orders with its material's constancy. Politigården (Copenhagen's central police station) and Domhuset (the Courthouse) are still active in the mïse en scène of the practicing and judging power.

"...Whereas chaos stands as the contrary of linear order, where one system's development can be predicted, in principle, infinitely far in advance, complexity constitutes something that is rather an intermediate form between order and chaos. ...

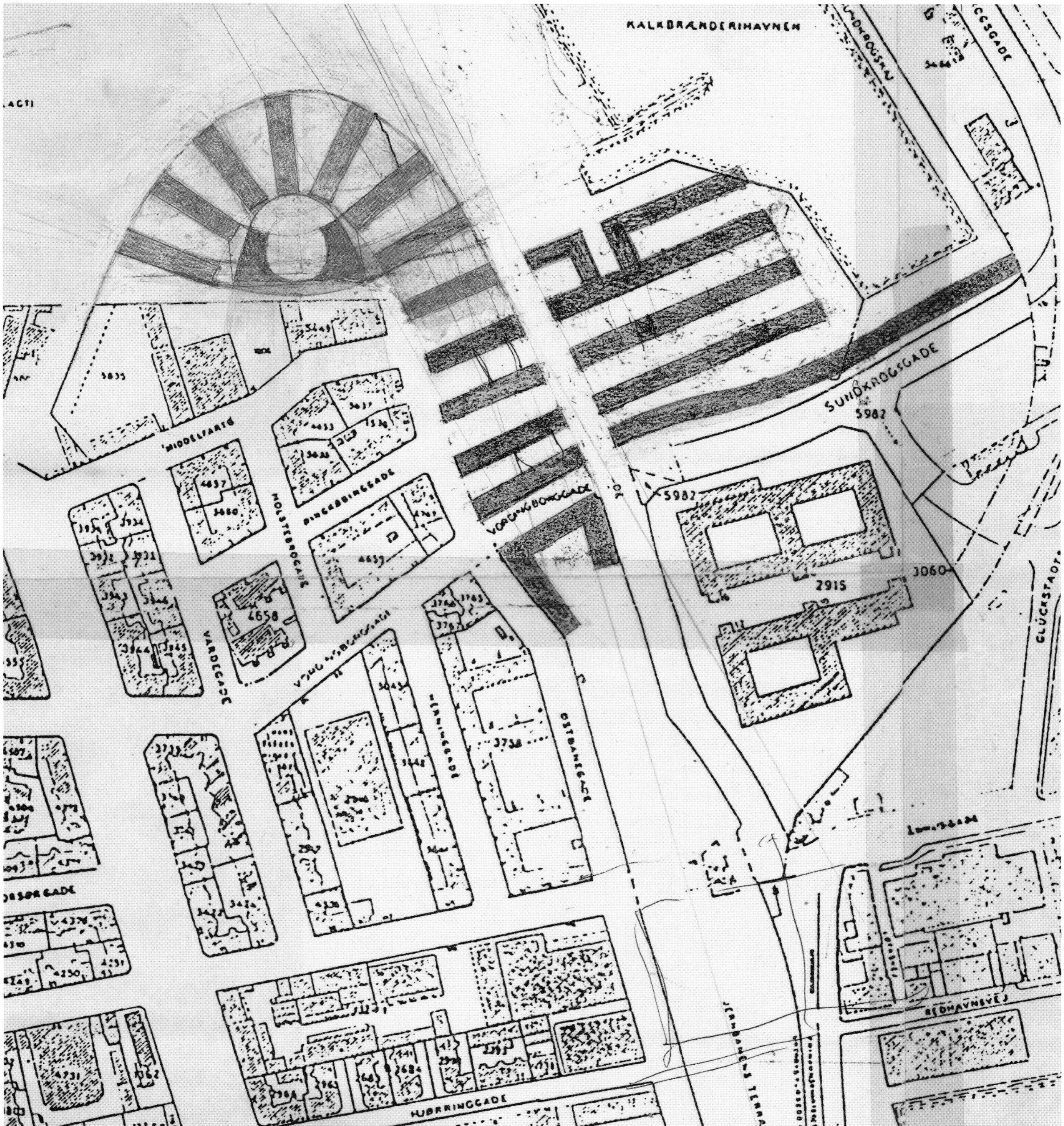

KALKBRÆNDERIHAVNEN
SUNDKROGSGADE
5982
3060
2915
HOLSTEBROGADE
VORDINGBORGGADE
VARDEGADE
ØSTBANEGADE
HJØRRINGGADE
4658

although the development inside a complex system - in the long run – is unpredictable, as in the chaotic system. But in contradistinction to chaos, complexity displays developmental features where nothing happens and only every now and then is this substituted by abrupt, discontinuous events. ... As opposed to chaos, complexity nurtures systems that are far from equilibrium, i.e. systems that are constantly pervaded by energy, that can code and re-code the individual elements' mutual relationship. Complexity further entails, again in contrast to chaos, the possibility of a certain memory in the system in question: it has the capacity to adapt itself to certain conditions in the surroundings, and therefore renders evolution possible – thus the Santa Fe school's notion of the "CAS" - Complex Adaptive Systems. ..."[5]

Projection

In a sense, the project is political. It is political and, as far as that goes, unnecessary. Under the heading of the necessary, we categorize all the efforts to uphold the society and its economic foundation. *Our time's politicians are more economists (matrons, housekeepers) than they are politicians.* The political work couples an ambition with a volition. Politics points out across the necessary and is conditioned by the desire to make that which is into something else, not in a general sense, but into something specifically different that can already be glimpsed. The political volition reads that which exists, with an underlying thought that is not blind to what lies immediately before us. Therefore, it does not think in utopias. In this respect, this project is political. It is unnecessary and borders on the unrealistic. But it is *not* unrealizable. It proposes a vast infrastructural encroachment that will involve an expenditure of perhaps 200 million DKK. The encroachment will have to be regarded as a gift, something that will alter Copenhagen, with a generous gesture. The idea is so obvious that somebody must have stumbled upon it before.

Unfurling its way across this area, where Øster Gasværk (the Eastern Gasworks, now shut down) once lay, a narrow patch of railway ground runs as an embankment. Outside of this, facing the Kalkbrænderihavnen (Lime Kiln Harbor) (the harbor area close to Østerbro - a large residential area dating from 1900), there is a 4-lane road. What is proposed here is that the railway and the road be sunk down, so that the cleared ground area of the former gas works and the cleared area facing the harbor can be linked up with a large open *field*.
Østerbro will be conjoined, in this way, with the harbor. And by establishing connections with Fælledparken (the large expanse commons situated in the center of Østerbro) and further in toward the lakes, a large urban area can carry the offshoots to the water. An immense urban area is potentiated and opened up for the roaming of unpredictable and unconcluded con-sequences.

Toward Østerbro, the city is built up of courtyard blocks, like a mass or a cake pierced through by streets. The houses do not delineate themselves as objects. The distribution is even between intruding and protruding corners. The figure/ ground relation alters itself as we approach the cleared ground area of the former gasworks. This allows the buildings to become more object-like: The National Council for the Unmarried Mother and Her Child, the lighting company's very special wooden building and the gas container, which sucks the entire Gasværk's ground area to itself. The new building alongside of this ground area veils the contrast between surface and container. The Svanemølleværk (electric power plant) is situated facing the harbor like a sphinx, which fetches an entirely different scale from somewhere downtown. Demonstratively, it turns its back and steers it way around all the axes and patterns. The power plant lays out a game concerning eccentricities, whose middle it does not itself occupy, positioned as it is - on the edge of the Sound.

Field and building volumes, placed across from the city of courtyard blocks, articulate a certain opposition. The work here transpires in between a flat field and a dense building volume, with the specific intention of engendering new forms that constitute an admixture of these two, situated in between. Transitions are examined as *double localities,* borne by scalar relationships, local dissolutions or incorporated ambiguous spatial orientations between field and courtyard block, and between courtyard block and solitary building. The construction of courtyard blocks expands further out on the Gasværk's ground area. The mass of the blocks flows forth out on the field. But this transpires in such a way that the blocks delineate themselves faintly from a distance, as one single object, among others. From a distance, object. Closer up, as a gathering of blocks. Close to or on your way in between the blocks, all of this changes. Constructed connections are intertwined with gardens and scrub between the wings. Facing Kalkbrænderihavnen (Lime Kiln Harbor), what is further conceived is a development that accordingly latches on to the blocks, as a detached mass of building on its way from one condition to another, through an indeterminate process of condensation or dissolution in a transition from the city of blocks to one single house volume even larger than the Svanemølleværk. The building mass is divided by traces of streets, which appear to be too small and unarticulated in their line and their profile. Here and there, these traces are fully dissolved, or else they are filled up with competing orders. Cars have access, where the streets are supplied with ramps running down to a semi-submerged parking level.
The drawings hint at a coherent layout. In themselves, they are continuous constructions, which are not in search of a conclusion. This establishes a strategy for the building's erection. Between the phases of drawing and building, what we envision is a gradual transition and later on, a continuous, reciprocal influ-

ence, with the result that drawing and building constitute one simultaneous and ongoing work. In this respect, the construction has already started to be, to exist, with the advent of the very first drawing. Offices, housing and workshops must, in every instance, be commissioned, financed, drafted, and built with a close cooperation between architect and client, regardless of the job's magnitude. What is built is gradually taken into use, when it is finished and ready. The architect's most important contribution, then, is his/ her work with an edge zone between the less complex external urban space and the internal density. On the inside, the uninterrupted extension can move toward extreme densities and, here and there, toward inner eyes. The architect is linked up with the development as the in-house architect, for perhaps twenty years.
Is the form of the constructed buildings' clarified exterior – of their bodies – becoming thinner, harder and more extrovert, in keeping with the holes in the middle ground? Almost like holes in an ozone layer.

Language determines reality, inasmuch as it reduces the special *otherness* and fortifies the general in a standard distribution's apex. The general and the special approach ligation on either side of a body – "an opacity" – which is the body of meaning, in the narrow sense of current usage. Dictionaries and grammars harden this body from two sides, gradually vulcanizing the zone of transition and delay. Language splices itself to what it refers to, if its meaning is entirely fixed, since the current *meaning* constitutes a third level between the special and the general. This meaning is always so close that it is beyond one's scope. Therefore, meaning is the medium for surprising splicings between the always special otherness, the general and itself. The splicings open up a complex field for the displacement of meaning, which attains its greatest diversity around the apex in a standard distribution. The extreme dearth of language and the extreme surfeit of language constitute the outer limits of this distribution within which the referral's otherness is, respectively, completely predominating or completely vanishing. And the probability or complexity of new splicings suddenly arising is thus nil.
The double bearing is like an ongoing reconstruction of a meaning-producing trajectory, in the moment of the spoken and written word, which possesses no doubling in the territories of either language or otherness, but is its own. The advancing line's sharpness, in the now of actual writing and speaking, reveals itself in the construction of the borderline between the converging territories, and looking back, as a comet's tail, which in its gradual thinning out is less and less a boundary and more and more a whirl of line and territories into a coherent and meaning-filled cultural landscape.
Nature and culture are conceptions that refer to entities which are not clearly delimited but which do make sense. A closer inspection of what they each refer to would allow the adjacent indeterminacies to merge. The indistinct body of meaning keeps the signifiers open.

The concept of alienation ensnares and marks a sensation whose nuances, attuned toward a potent restlessness, are erased in the signifier's shadow.

With words like quarter, street, plaza, market place, sidewalk and district, particular notions about dimension, density and situations are associated.

The language recognizes an infinitude of things and situations, but the individual word, seen in isolation, is normally at a want for associations.

Words like street, market place and quarter designate sections of cities that have attained a certain size. They are spillovers that have arisen in the course of the city's gradual growth, and they link themselves up with actual (and not relative) dimensions.

No longer is the city held together as it was before – the space has become more loose-knit, and the system's self-organization will not, in the near future, approach a critical state. And the spillovers that this will occasion cannot be predicted, or else they will crop up and disappear again before even being noticed.

The self-organized shows itself very clearly in the outskirts, from the satellites' and the planes' observations of a – like some mycetoid structure - coherent city. This coherence is experienced down in the suburbs as a sensation that supervenes in the place of overview.

"Bak accordingly took a pile of sand and supplied this with a continuous flow of sand from above, and then observed the development. At the beginning, the pile grows evenly, but by and by, as it becomes steeper, avalanches or landslides start to occur, which in the beginning only involve a few grains of sand. But eventually, as the pile becomes higher, this can involve more grains, until the pile reaches a maximum when, on account of the landslides, it cannot get any higher. Now what reveals itself is really interesting. In this condition, there are landslides occurring on every scale, all the way from the very small, with only a few grains of sand, up to enormous avalanches, which affect the whole pile. The smaller landslides are the most frequent, while the larger avalanches occur less frequently, the larger they are."[6]
The heap of sand has entered into a condition of self-organized criticality.

In an extension of Louis Kahn's speech concerning the city's own will and Per Bak's concept of self-organized criticality, it seems as though the city for the time being, does not have the will and the complexity it once had. The tendencies are weak and diverse, and the city is not pointing toward any unequivocal directions with respect to its ongoing construction. The architect is reinforcing the city's weak will by amplifying what he observes with a linguistic doubling. The articulation of the space obtains the language as its first level. The signification functions, in the first instance, as a metaphoric intensifier of tendencies in the locality: the five-finger master plan of Copenhagen, *the theater,* and *the bastion.*

The city occupies new domains, which will in turn give rise to completely new patterns and spillovers. Quarter, market-place < *double locality*[7].

Seen from *here,* the otherness is losing terrain, inasmuch as our codings establish with them an ever-increasing intersection of sets ... a shared-amount ... whose delimitation has extended further out than the individual horizons. Out there on the side that is always turned away from our initiative, it supervenes in dealings that are unaffected, and as of yet beyond our reach.

The city is on its way into a state of complex indeterminacy and the graphs for the weaker tendencies interweave themselves, loosely, for as long as the city seeks outwards in its ongoing building. As has always been the case, the powers that be are afraid of uncontrollable densities.

"... Blanquis wanted to make a survey over how many he had with him. But since the conspiracy was, in fact, a secret, the inspection of the troops could not transpire in the ordinary fashion. He knew from their appearance only the leaders of the individual units. The parade came to occur in this way: Blanquis stood by a tree on the Champs-Elysées. At the appointed moment in time, his unit leaders came past, in the crowd, each of them with their unit following behind. In this way, Blanquis could see his 'army' in the middle of the crowd, without this being visible to anyone else."[8]

The passing from the outskirts into the heart of the city is less presence and journey and more relative delay of the arrival.

In the metropolis, it is the endless collocation of residential units that is the cause of the commuting time and the extent of the commute. The light, the weather and the delay are the surveilled oppositions of otherness, abstracted into daylight savings time, the weather report and the radio's traffic reports.

The meaning-exhausted situated across from the comfortable.

The place becomes point, in hermetic microcosms. The point approaches absolute stagnation in the picturesque, isolated from surrounding terrains and regions.

The speed increases in vehicles whose degree of closedness is directly proportional to their increase in velocity.

If there is one fundamental problem, and this is only the case when the city is observed as being stopped in time, in a glimpse, then it is that the car has appropriated that same territory that it has opened the system up toward. *Problems are projections borne by revolutionary, nostalgic or other motivations.* The proximity to the others and an especially strategic spot are the city's origins. The urban formation which, where it struck, teleologically pointed toward the metropolis, is now in the midst of a transformation of its telos. The vectors are the computer and a little bit of friction between the cars and the roads. The roads don't provide much resistance; there are few bottlenecks. The transportation times are short.

Speed and delay are relative dimensions, inasmuch as they are always on the way toward becoming, respectively, faster and shorter. But they set down concrete trails in the city. The density of meaning diminishes logarithmically with the territory's size.

The recognizability of the home is made more profound behind hedges and outer walls which, as osmotic double membranes, divide the space up into an excessively well-recognized interior and a meaning-light exterior.

(caricature) A system is bound up with human long-windedness as the factor that threatens - while holding tightly to the one end of the vectors - to let them drag themselves across. This rupture will entail a complete compartmentalization of human life into a pseudo-authentic self-narrative and a hyper-specialized work, without any other wishes regarding coherence than a one-way economic relationship. Such a rupture will entail a de-formatting of the cultural criterion as correlated with the mythical-historical abysmal upcoming of the Germano-European peoples, which accordingly will bring its cultural sphere to a conclusion right before our eyes, without our even noticing it. The less we notice, the more it closes up.
In the course of society's organization, personal history has been superseded by national history and the administrators of this nation and this history are the politicians, who now have to see that the super-society (the Industrial-nations, the G7, ASEAN, the West and NATO) has taken the floor in the narrative of this history. The nations enter into alliances, according to a principle of proximity, and the organizational vector points toward the European Union, a super-protagonist among its peers, a co-author in the history of the huge conglomerates. Within this global narrative, there is but one dominant affective agent, but one gather-

ing abstractum, the whole dynamics in the continuation of history – economy. There is nonetheless one history that can become just as comprehensive: the expansion's counter-history – ecology, which moreover could become the largest, insofar as this history could subsume everything. All affective conquests would be undermined for a reality internalized as the *constituted Eco-system*. The ring of civilization – this closing of history, as seen from above, would be closed right where it began: as a spiral staircase, which has wound its way back to its stepping-off point, but now one level up. A deep, closed outer string would have internalized the global culture's steps of development, and would have laid them open to the scientists' consummate *durchsicht* (a stairwell, through-sight).

The relationship between the apparatuses' relatively simple functions introduced into the system and the ensuing unpredictable change in the system. The city at time t=0 becomes, with its material's imperishableness, a resistance and an independent vector in the system's self-organization on the next level.

The city will not manage to organize itself for critical states before the self-organizing conditions are altered and before the provisional formation is trampled.

The grains of sand cannot organize themselves into the heap's conical form in mighty side winds. But after some time, and under special conditions, they will call the wind into the self-organization, and form dunes of desert sands.

Substance that has received mankind's minting, even the printed letter or the spoken word, embodies an outside that has moved its way back across a border zone. From the other side, rats get into the sewers and foxes enter the backyards.

That which is not grasped by the brain and is not the object of its good graces will obscurely form part of the self-organizing. To carry this further: The self-organizing subsumes everything. But it does so in an intermediate zone between the all-organizing outside and the some-organizing brain, where their organizations are blended in a complete entanglement of vectors, in all sizes, following the pattern of 1/f-noise. There, the trace of organization often would not be larger than instantaneous deflections. In a split second, there's a deflection, which constitutes the only trace of organization. *1/f-noise or fractals over time are complex noises, situated between white chaotic noise and monotonous or single-toned noise.*

The human being lives in an ever-increasingly hermetic space. The multiplication of way and time has still not achieved its optimal articulation outside of the experimental set-up.

The free individual vectors are ensnared and detached over and over again. The largest corpuses like planets, seldom or never fuse with others of a similar size, only because they are so rare. *Does interplanetary and interstellar dust constitute a quantity of matter that corresponds to the substance in planets and stars?*
The distribution according to the bodies' size follows the pattern for 1/f-noise.

The sea is being monitored, like a patient under observation.

The city is not chaotic. It is a mass, relatively complicated, but as a place in the meeting with the inhabitant, it exchanges its own degree of complexity between the indistinct in the outskirts and the alternating in the densities.

The TV news's inverted picture storm reduces the space because presence, as a third dimension, is subtracted: I am excluded from the studios and the battlefields; they are not spaces within which I reside. The camera's inverted picture cannon sucks the angles in on to the digital retina, which is imperceptibly transformed into my own, and then disappears. The apparent complexity is illusionary, and my arousal over the events, as they stream through the eye of the needle, approaches interactive zero. A flicker is sucked right through a naught, in a multiplication that counts out what is complex in the relation.

The space and the material do not run up against one another on a borderline, but are rather tangled up and correlated. *"How long is the British coastline?"*

"Nonetheless, |Chuck| Yeager routinely took his students up beyond the first atmospheric boundary (70,000 feet) where the sky goes black and silent but the air's molecular structure sustains aerodynamic buoyancy - to give them a taste of the 'outside'- that is, of space. ...
"Aerial dogfighting, more than anything else, is like space time arbitrage: one must exploit discrepancies that appear between parallel flows (the twisting vectors of adversarial aircraft). But these flows are so far from equilibrium - so stretched - that the critical discrepancies must be snatched from any dimension that is not already strained to the max. ..."[9]

The extreme positions in a particular standard distribution constitute the extreme thinning out of the substance of the universe's horizon of expansion and the black hole. In the first position, the mutual distances in between the dust particles have become so great that they can no longer attract one another. In the second position, the mass-attraction is so powerful that even light cannot escape. Between these extremes of substance's dispersion, there is a swampy middle, where the most complex accu-

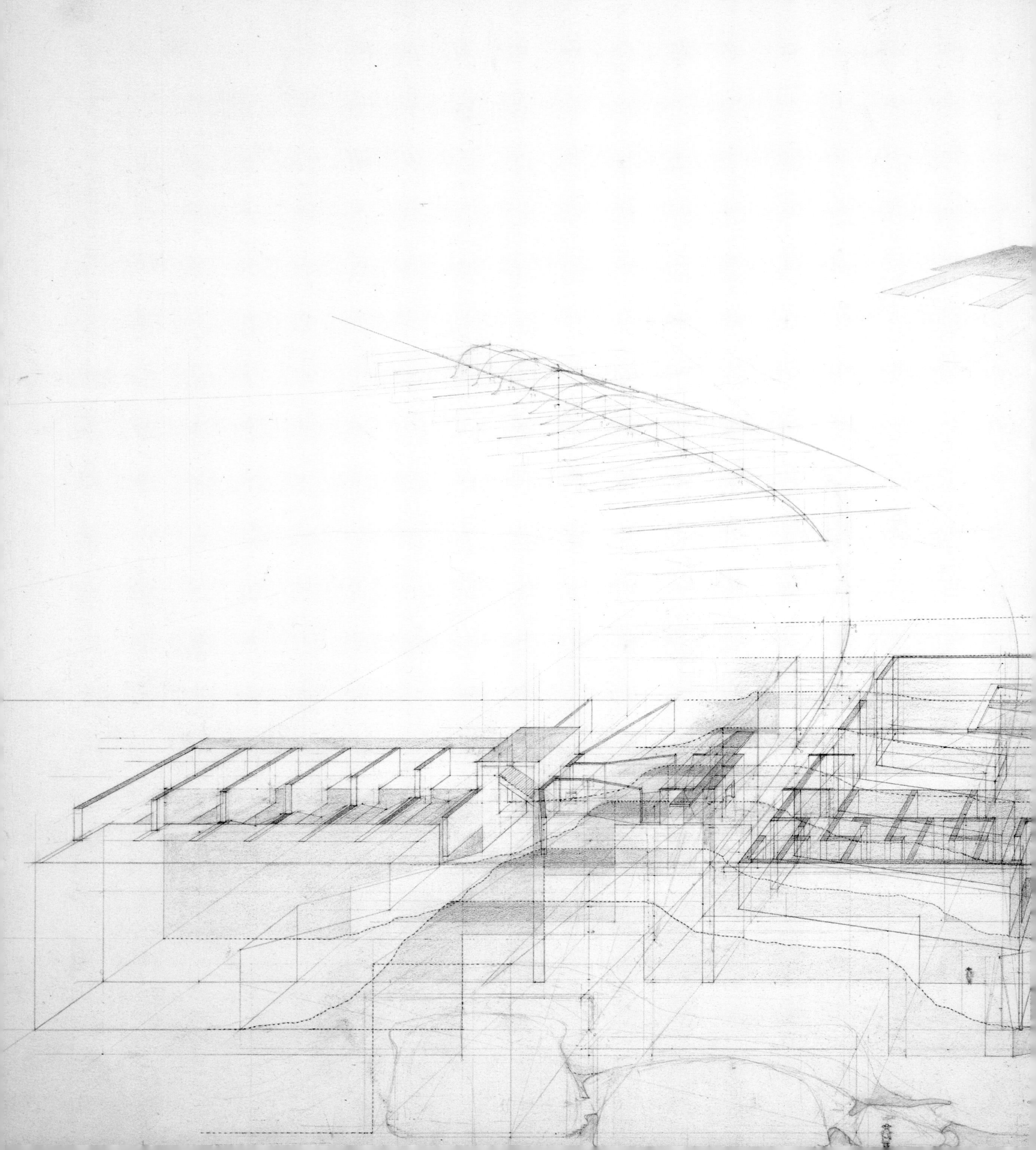

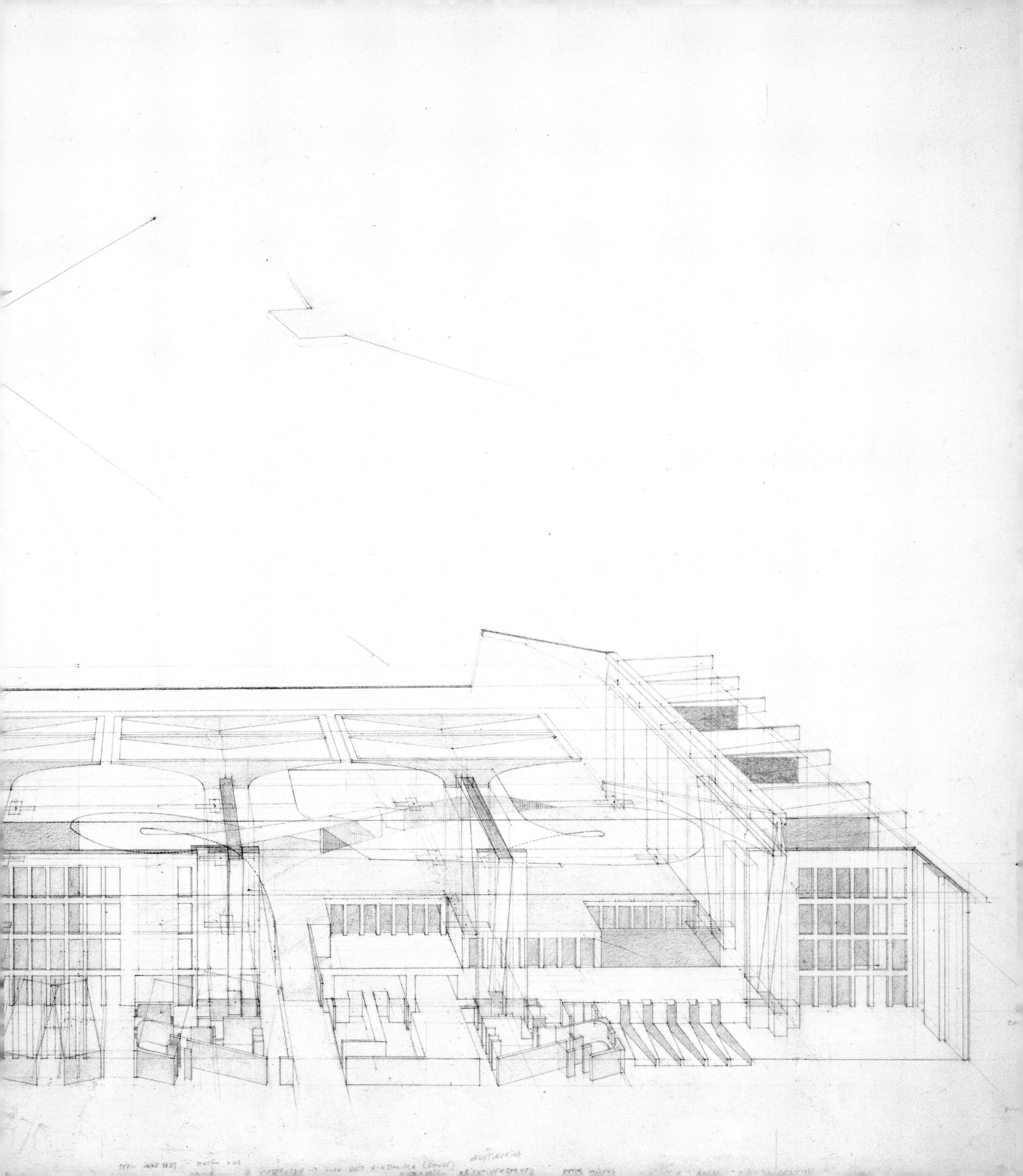

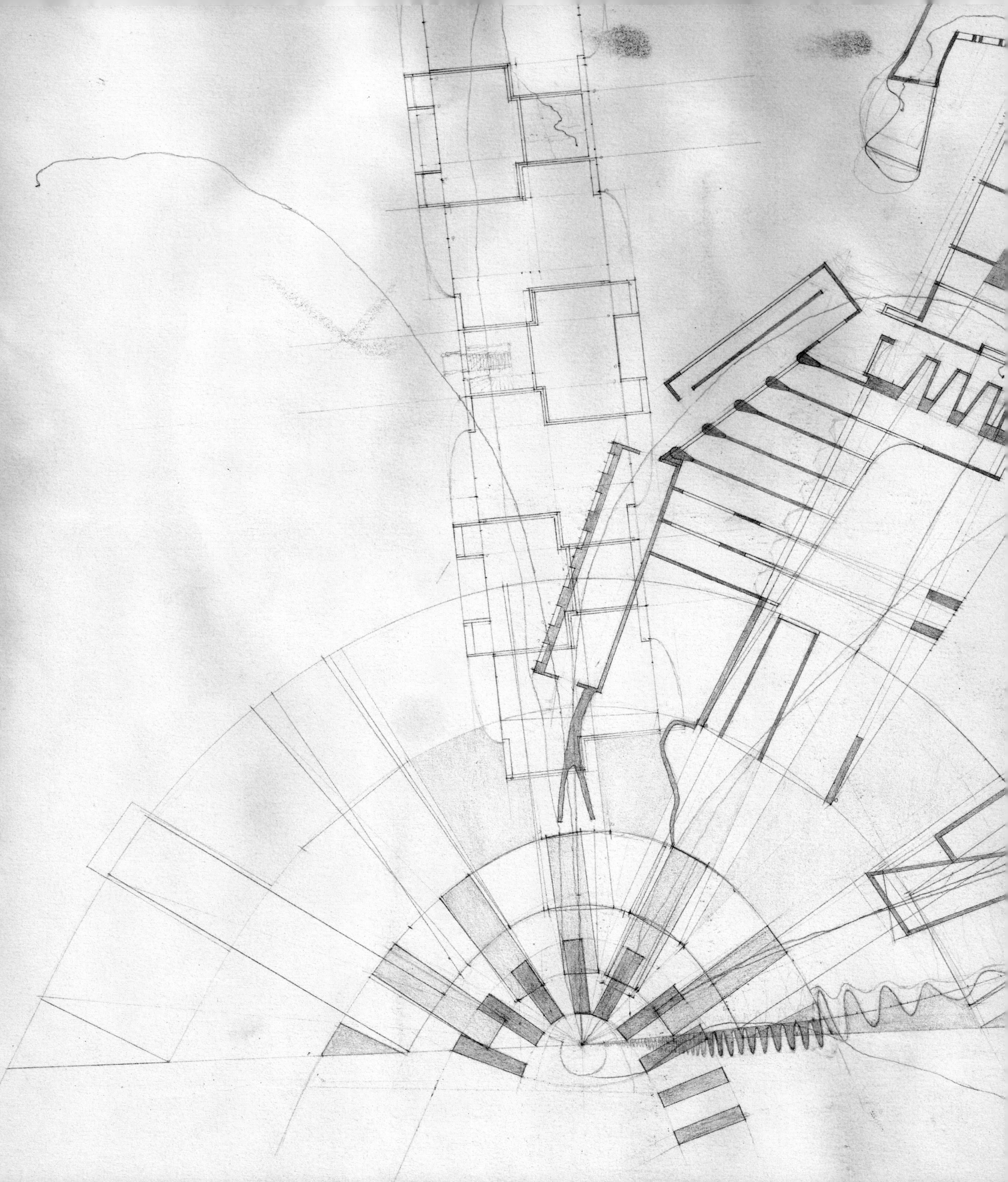

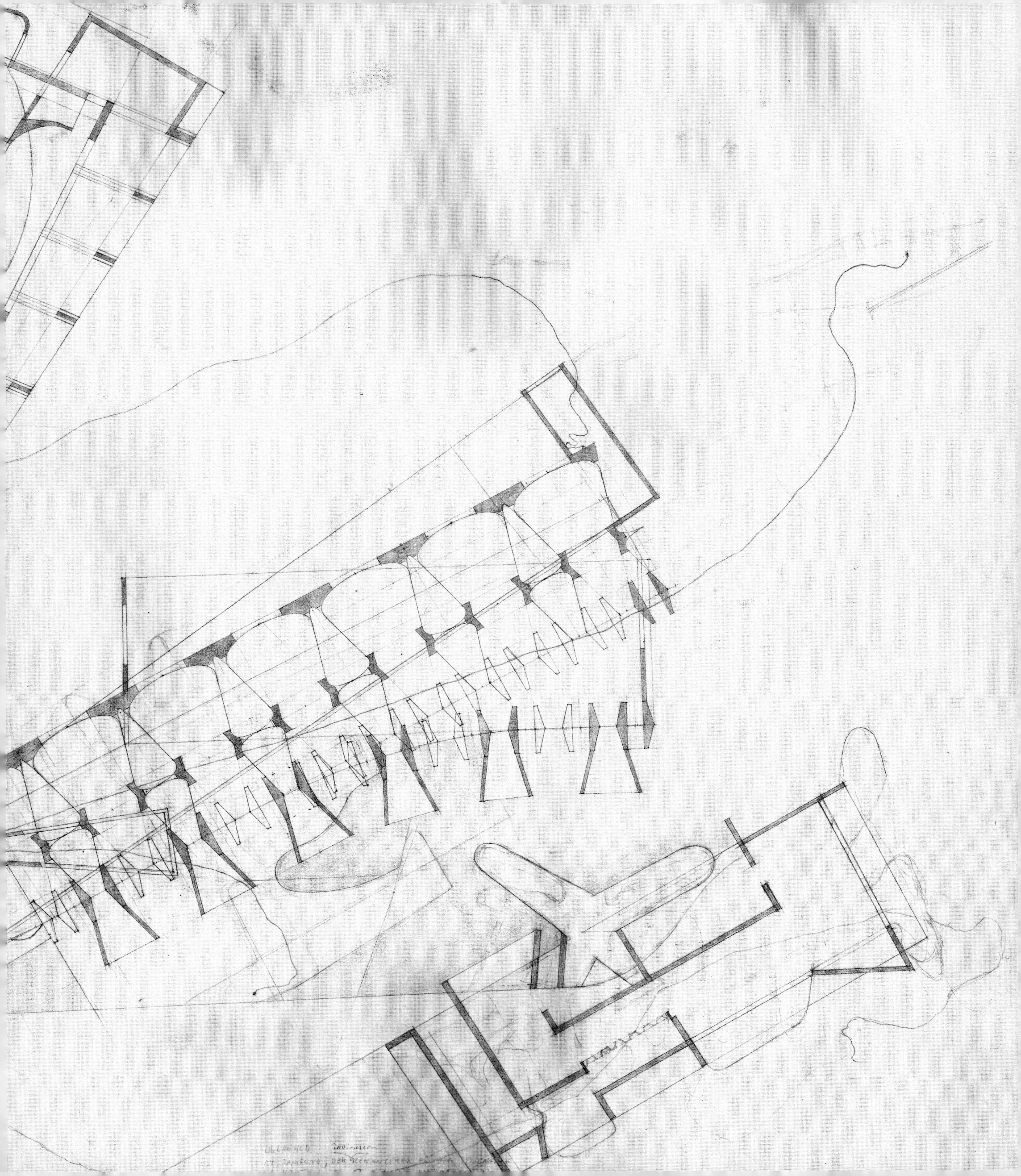

mulations are to be found. In a thin zone around and a little ways into the earth's crust, there is a complex indeterminacy on a level with the haze in the larger distribution's middle – 'unpredictable whirlpools'. Bodies turn up as a determinacy – as a surface distension between two indeterminacies, an inner and an outer. Bodies turn up upon the intervention of an elusive thermocline's very first adumbration of languidness higher than that of the original indeterminacy.

Gravity remains free energy resultants inside of the ligated, which in certain instances influence the focal point in a multitude, while possessing an unorganized surplus of power which is drawn out from the multitude into the void. The gravitational field establishes a thick spherical zone around the multitude. For multitudes of all sizes, the gravitational field has the same thickness, analogous to the unimpeded resultant's action-horizon. Every gravitational vector is a movable center in a spherical field without surface, drawn over time. The gradual dilution of power takes place over the elapse of light years. Does this power ever expire in its constant dilution, as it moves outwards?

Stars are accumulations of matter in a gravitational focal point – a (set-) intersection of resultants, whose glow-horizon has internalized all organizations of substance in white-hot indeterminacy, still held together by a magma cap as in an incandescent pouch - a thermocline of languidness; an inverted soufflé holding the inner gas pressure within its incrustation in the meeting with the universal coolness. The growing internal glacier-like pressure is offset by the liberation of light and heat, out in all directions. When very large stars have thinned out the energy of the gravitational focal point to a certain level, gravitation will let loose of the pouch- body that, like a spherical red-hot spinnaker, will be pushed by the internal pressure and glide outward until it bursts and dissolves in a sudden indeterminacy. An outgoing resultant will, in certain sudden instances, posit an inner body. This body will be able, with its gravitational field, to inflect the resultants inwardly, toward a vacuum facing in toward the center that is more powerful than the corresponding outer. The explosion is turned inward, in a self-generating gravitational field of both body and hole – the extreme monotony's black hole.

The complex indeterminate arises in the meeting between bodies. The bodies have arisen by virtue of a self-organizing which does not build itself up, however, to any critical condition that is far out of balance. The critical system organizes itself away from an equilibrium through a local balancing act, which becomes more and more critical. All vectors are situated in the middle of an all-encompassing landslide resulting from the universal critical catastrophe, The Big Bang. Even in the midst of the landslide, critical ways of organization are locally established.

On the bodies' outer and inner sides, a zone of equalization turns up between the determined and the indeterminate, which locally organizes the formidable powers. This zone constitutes a standstill, on a level with the swamp in the middle of the vast standard distribution between the universe's horizon of expansion and the black hole. In excess of the emission of heat, what is left is distinct body and indeterminacy. In the cessation of power through organizing, local standstill or the utmost degree of rippling can turn up as violent storms. In the cessation's intensely loaded critical state of being, what can appear are bodies and movements, in all sizes from the largest - corresponding to about 1/10 of the largest body's size - and indeterminacy, on either side of the standstill in the current meeting. The great meeting constitutes the summit in a descending hierarchy of logarithms which finds its way down to the smallest scale: fungus spores, viruses and prions enter into infinitely small meetings in the vast indeterminate Pacific. The great meeting elicits, in the adjustments of the balance, mighty forces, which drive the complex indeterminacies of the wind systems and the ocean currents. *The monsoon and the Gulf Stream.* Small and perpetually repeated adjustments and compensations for the tidewaters and the night have stirred up the primeval soup, which has acquired on its surface a skin of disclarity. Beneath this insulating skin, the potassic salts have transformed themselves, under the pulse of day and night, slowly into a ligation. On the other side of this, the salts have developed a self-protection, or a self-maintenance, of their transformational processes, driven by the sun's light. *Campbell's blue bottle, amoebae.*

There where gravitation meets a flat landscape is where the stream most intensely entwines its course. *Meander, Brahmaputra.*

Density is the formal theme, and the increase of density at selected spots is a way of accelerating the system. That the city displays features of complexity - of distinct spillovers - constitutes a testimony about the city's willfulness – an immanence that disposes the city's space as an always already, so that it can all at once be sensed as a landscape-like otherness and be perceived in its disposition's tendencies, albeit flickering tendencies. If the virtual tendencies are too feeble and are characterized by too many corpuses at a complex level that is too low, the city gets into the hyper-referentiality or the image. If the city cannot manage to organize its vectors so that the tendencies will clearly emerge – if it can no longer build itself up toward a self-organized critical contour – then an intervening time within which the city is maintained from one center in its historic contour will supervene. This contour has now become a sedimentary deposit, and from an edge, fissures in what has been meaningful up until now are being opened up. Insisting on a city which through its own history is slowly being saturated with coordinates' pixels is tantamount to insisting on a picture. When the density of coordinates

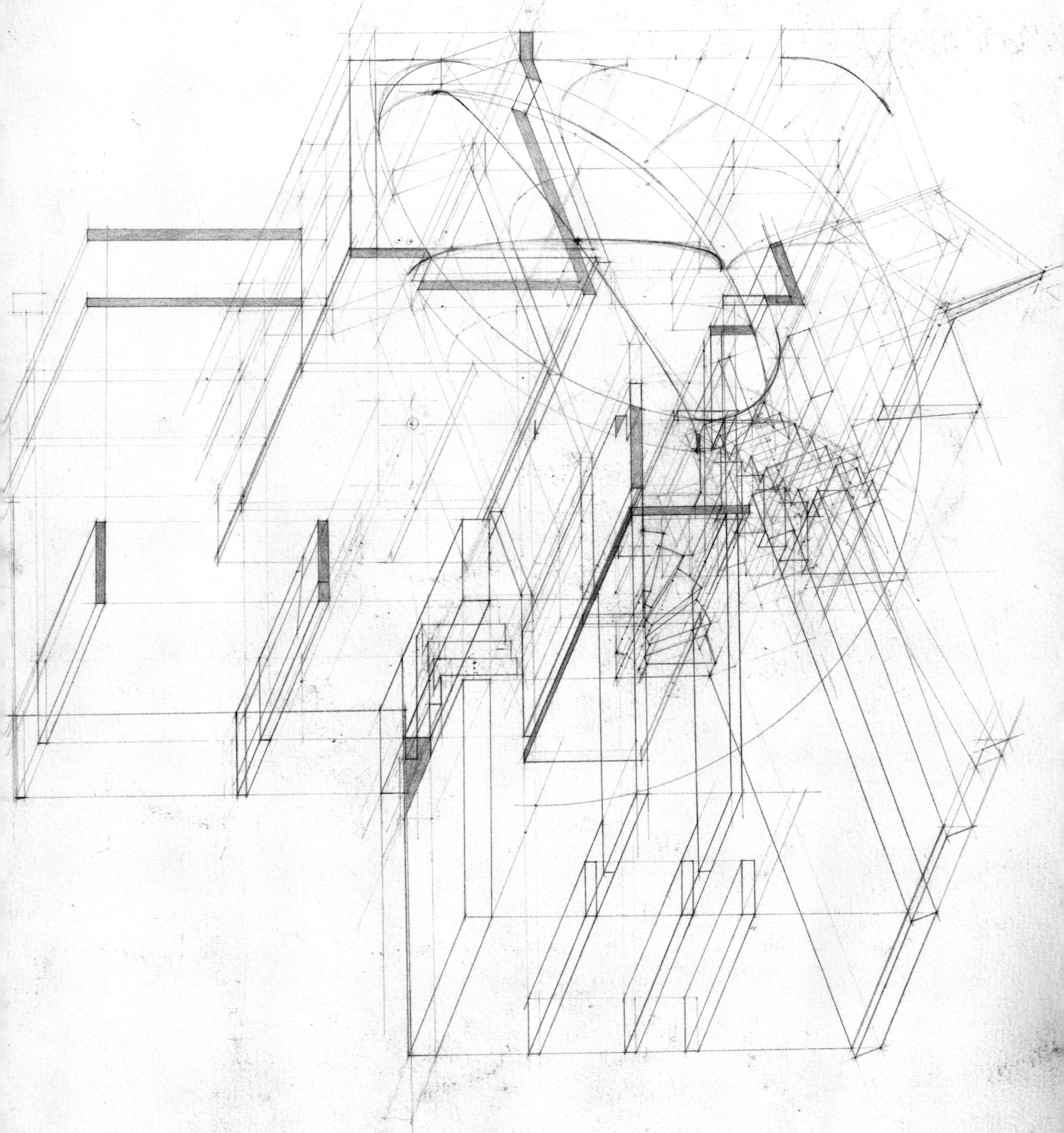

becomes sufficiently great, the city moves from being manifold to being picture, from one point of view. From other places, the picture's clarity is seen as an omen about the hitherto organized contour's impending debacle in the moment of perfection. Building continues to proceed on the picture's consummation, despite the fact that a catastrophe slowly rolling in from another edge is dissolving the city's neighborhoods into complex indeterminacies. *In the indeterminate areas, new bodies will be formed.*

Are the houses bodies, like language in the moment of the spoken and written word, and like the human body / *not conclusively for this/?* They do manage to ligate an inner and an outer room with a delaying languidness. Buildings govern interior and exterior spaces, which they themselves – outwards, toward the city and inwards, towards their own center – are capable of edging so that unpredictable whirlpools form: into indeterminate spaces that are no longer merely chaotic or static, but complex. The bodies in the chaotic are battling to maintain a delay between one particular thing and something else ... *critical discrepancies must be snatched from any dimension that is not already strained to the max* ... with a ligating body, which fashions what are formally the most monotonous substance organizations, where the indeterminate is most chaotic.

Interstellar dust and heavenly bodies. The paper's indeterminate openness and the alphabetical character. Ramifying electric micro-streams and computers. Where the outer points meet one another in a zone that is everything but gray, complex indeterminate milieus with analogously complex bodies come into being. What is the pinnacle of the complexity in the interval between chaos and monotony? Something that is neither firm nor floating – a morass, like the brain's extreme complexity, reaching out for an indeterminate exterior, like this indeterminate's ligating body and ligated interior in one single convolution. Seen from *here*, language is on the side of noise and architecture is further out, on the side of monotony. The delay between the indeterminate interval and the brain-body has established the most complex indeterminate that exists. With high frequency, what arise here are languidnesses, delaying bodies in the complex indeterminate field of slow, organizational pragmatics.

Architecture sets bodies into – and toward – the complex indeterminate – heterotopias, which allow other bodies to turn up. Bottlenecks and ligations. Architecture is the art of the delay.

Thanks to cand.mag. Jacob Lykkegaard, for his commentaries and suggestions for emendations in the manuscript.

1. C. Juel-Christiansen: in "Project theme: Transitions, the introductory draft for the assignment".
2. B. Cache: *Earthmoves*.
3. C. Juel-Christiansen, op. cit.
4. D. Hollier: *Against Architecture*.
5. Weekendavisen, August 7-13, 1998. F. Stjernfelt on the book entitled *How Nature Works. The Science of Self-Organized Criticality*, by Per Bak.
6. ibid.
7. See *Monument og niche*, by C. Juel-Christiansen.
8. W. Benjamin via Peter Madsen: *Semiotik og Dialektik* (Semiotics and Dialectics).
9. S. Kwinter: *Flying the Bullet, or When Did the Future Begin*.

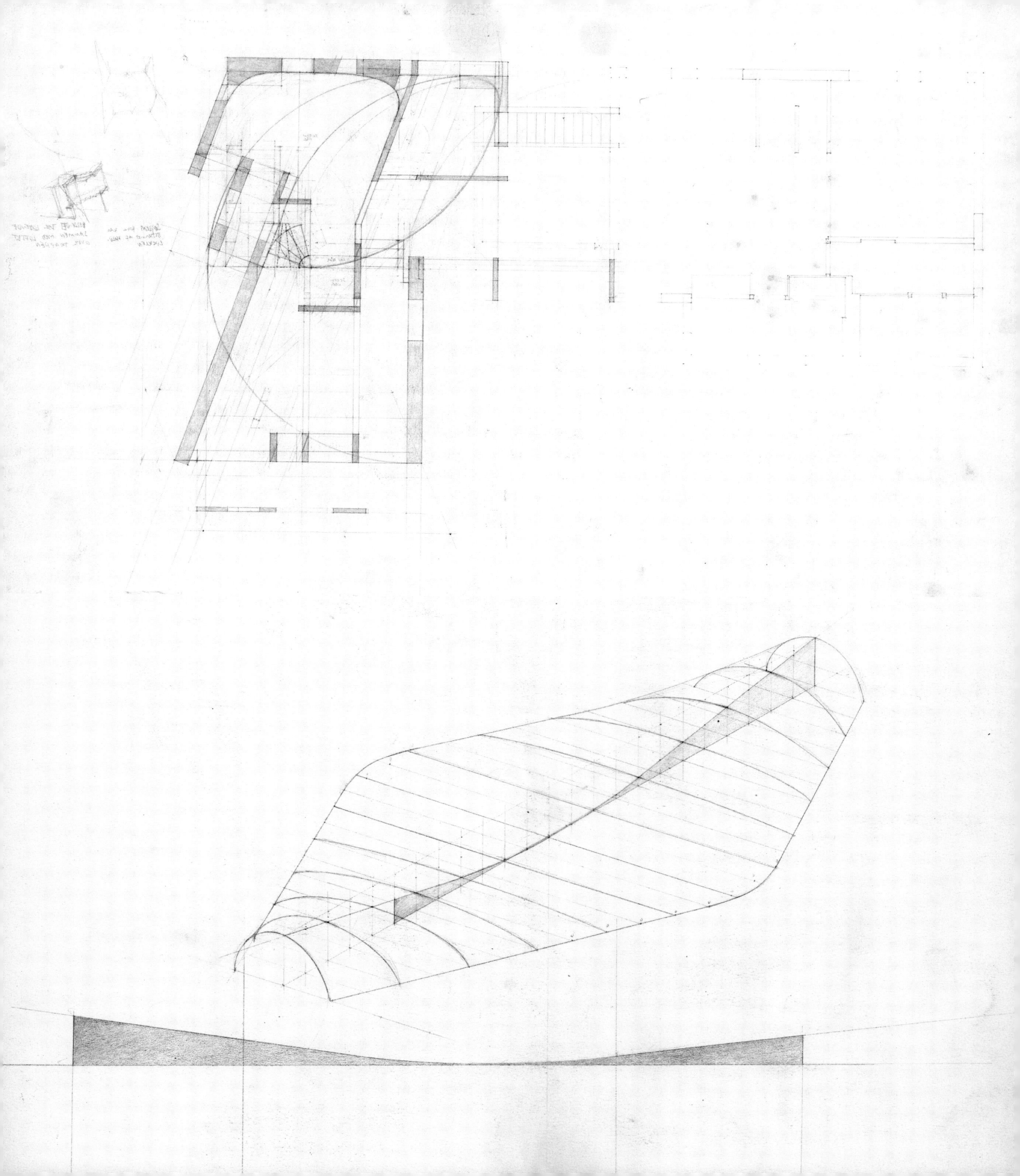

ANDERS ABRAHAM

Conditions – "Nocturnal sands"

"Yet the reality in question is a strictly material one; that is, it is subject to no allegorical interpretation. The reader is therefore requested to see in it only the objects, actions, words, and events which are described, without attempting to give them more or less meaning than in his own life, or death."
Alain Robbe-Grillet, from "In the Labyrinth"

By contemplating an area as a composite and coherent physical, spatial and psychological condition - by understanding it as being assembled from a multitude of conditions and by naming these conditional forms, it is possible to recognize and create sequences and potential narratives in the Composite.
"Nocturnal sands" is a narrative that conjoins the multitude of material from a region south of Copenhagen with the space that arises when the multitude obscures representation.
The project collocates the area's genesis, making, fabrication, materials and space into a new coherent condition of the Night scale, within which the individual is free to navigate in a space between liquid and solid!
The area contains two contradictory processes: a pumping up/ accumulation of sand from the bay and a supply/ assembling, coming in from the north, of pre-cast concrete elements.

From an area south of Copenhagen, the following form-processes, conditions and fixed positions can be observed:
A+C. Sand dredging, B. Assembly ties, D+K+O. Temporary assembly ties, E. Vertical casting forms, F. Sand banks, G. Reinforcement elements, H. Fire-lane mark, I. Component assembly, J. Storage, L. Space between the blocks, M. Agricultural landscape, N. Fixed floor-wall joint, P. Horizontal forms.
(The list in itself does not manifest any particular order or logical coherence.)

A+C. "...five million cubic meters of sandy bottom in the Køge Bay created a beach of seven kilometers and a recreational area of five square kilometers..."(1. p.5).
Behind the artificial sand dunes, six lakes and a harbor were excavated. These were planned according to the need of the inland earthwork projects (establishing roads and building plots). It was a guiding principle that the earthworks to be constructed should be equal to the available excavated materials. At the same time as the artificial dunes were constructed, the jetties were built, and a portion of the needed 70,000 cubic meter of granite for the jetties consisted of lake-stones.
Subsequently, the gravel pits on Sjælland were emptied of their stockpiles of stones, and the rest of the stones were delivered from the fields of a southern Swedish manor house.
B. Assembly ties for non-loadbearing façade from the Jespersen system.
D+K+O. Braces, wedges, mandrils and wall anchors - "...with pre-fabricated floor-slabs and walls, and potentially beams and columns, it is rarely possible to attain fixed joints, and we therefore obtain a building that is assembled of simple construction elements, 'the house of cards type'. Special provisions have to be made in order to ensure the stability of the construction against horizontal forces.
Provisional braces are utilized when installing the wall elements,..."(3. p.76).
E. "The battery-form: the fabrication process - rigging of form, shaping of reinforcement, emplacement of reinforcement and the mold elements, casting, control of hardening, stripping of formwork, finishing work, storage" (2. p.89).
F. "... just off the coast, islands are formed from drifted sand from the surf-zone...these sand islands (have) been deposited by material migrating along the shoreline, and between the islands and the coastline's shallow, lagoon-like areas filled with algae..."(1. p.13).
G. "...the shaped reinforcement from the reinforcement workshop is mounted into the form. In order to secure the needed distance between the form panel and the reinforcement rods, special distancing-blocks are utilized..." (2. p.95).
H. A steel-broom is the marking of a fire lane. The broom is used for putting out a fire breaking out in covered areas of the beach.
It is a symbol of loss and of being on the alert for any latently tragic change in the present condition.
The Composite is full of symbols of the rules that preserve the local conditions. These rules are often of a pragmatic character, and are typically linked to the fundamental preservation of a collective order.
I. "...in the principle of the open system, around app. 80% of floor- and wall-production for buildings projected according to the Jespersen system, are standard components..."(3. p.240).

J. "...during storage the shrinkage of the concrete dies out before final assembling..."
"...wall- and façade elements are usually stored in special storage racks, from where the stored elements can be removed in any order..." (2. p.107).
L. The space between the blocks within the homogeneous, industrially mass-produced areas leaves its mark on the visitor with a sensation of frightful deprivation, of loss and latent malice.
The structures are simple and almost emptied of any narrative, filled up with material and created within a coarse tectonic rationality.
Together, the blocks neither create a space like that of a material reduction and refinement (absence), nor of an articulated presence like that created of plasticity and richness. The building system has consistently reduced the differences through endless repetitions.
Among groups of blocks with different structures without any connections, transitions appear as edges and ruptures. The surfaces between the structures are non-articulated depots of the seabed, which erase the local topography. They are pragmatic plateaus of clay and sand, which replace the collective urban plan. Here are only pragmatic regulations and few humanistic values; the individual is left without collective narratives and without any community. Here, the individual is compelled to create his own marks and his own meaning!
M. "The agricultural landscape is divided up according to natural water boundaries, territorial dividing lines (originally surveyed with measuring rope ("rebning")) and demarcated property lines, for example, stone fences, boundary ditches and hedges" (5. p.36) "...in loamy regions of the countryside, there is often a distance of three kilometers from one village to the next. This distance is, of course, not capricious but is rather determined by the methods of working and the technological possibilities over which the middle ages held sway..." (5. p.34).
N. "...the abutment's forces must be conveyed from floor to wall. Vertical forces in the wall will be conducted through the fixed floor-wall joint, (depositing for concrete horste). The floor-end must be capable of turning around the abutment's edge in response to deflection. Horizontal forces in the floor-slab must be conveyable in both directions. Dilatation between floor elements must be capable of being absorbed. Deviations in measurement between fabrication and assembly must be capable of being absorbed..." (3. s.95).
P. "...a load-bearing façade element (a result of the 'inverted' direction of the span) constitutes among other things that the effective lengthwise floor-slab reinforcement is referred to the interior fixed floor-wall joint, and to the poured joint in the façade line..." (4. p.71) "...the horizontal form consists of a form-board, upon which the element's edge-delimitation are mounted molds for doors, windows and other exigent openings..." (2. p.88) "...in the finished element there are special stainless steel ties between the front plate and the reinforcement of the back wall..." (2. p.97).

1. 'Køge Bugt Strandpark" (Beach-park at Køge Bay), Køge Bugt Strandpark, 1986.
2. 'Betonelementer" (Concrete Elements), Bentonelement-foreningen, 1991.
3. "Montagebyggeri" (Assembly Building), Polyteknisk Forlag, 1984.
4. "Husbygning" (House Construction), Aktuelle Byggerier, 1969-73.
5. "På opdagelse i Kulturlandskabet" (Discovering the Cultured Landscape), Miljø- og Energiministeriet 1995.

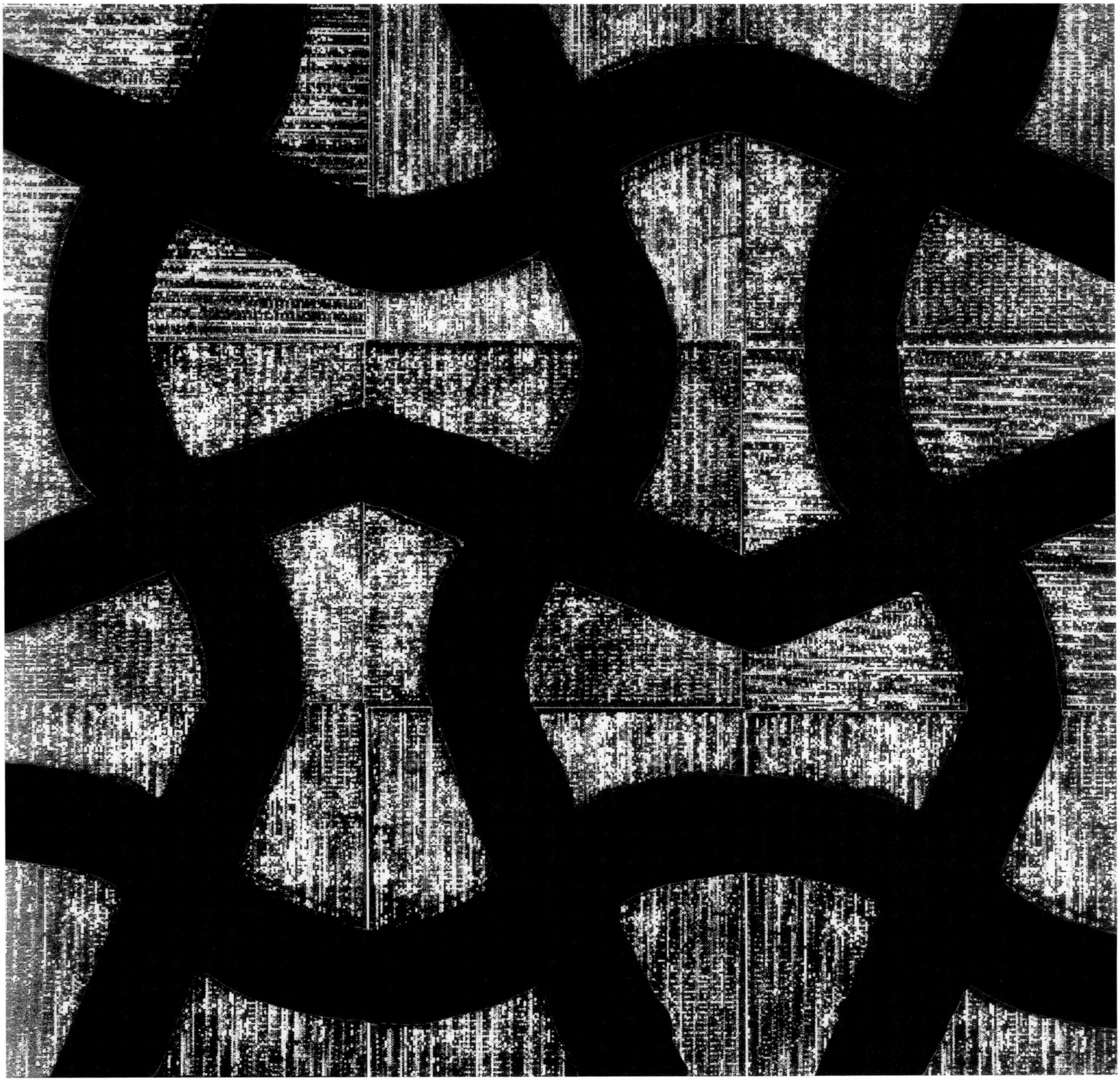

A

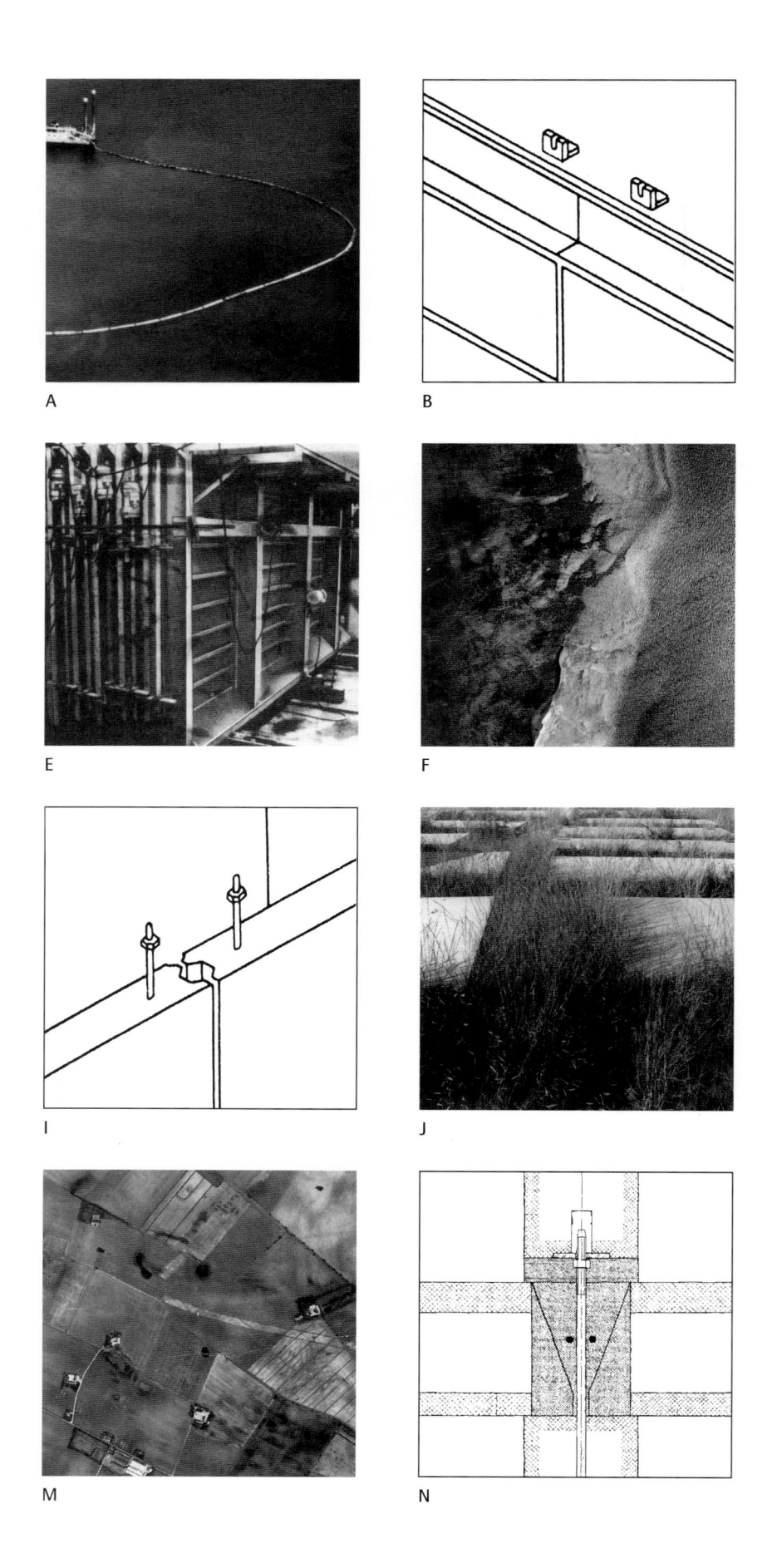

B

E

F

I

J

M

N

C

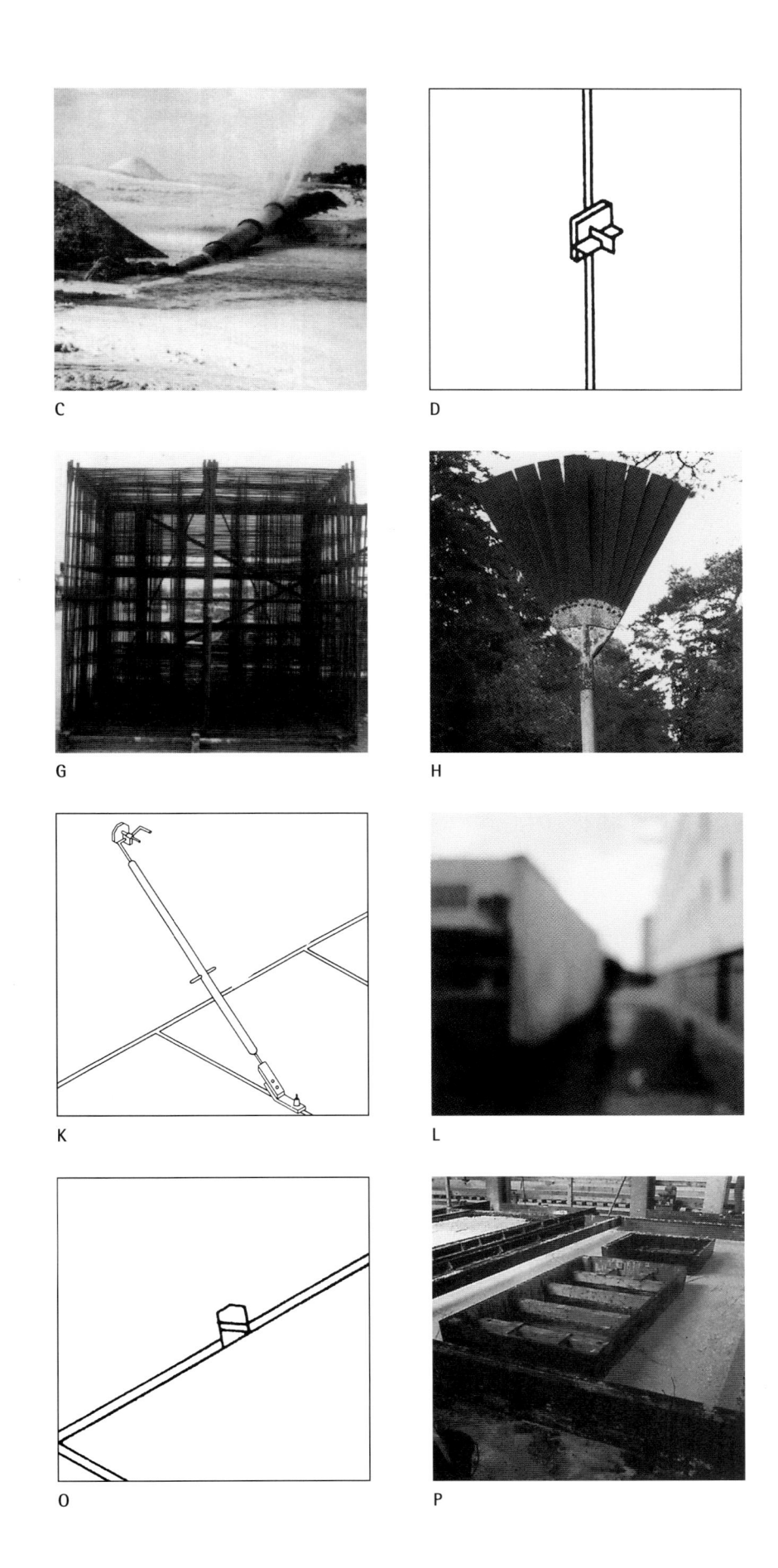

D

G

H

K

L

O

P

165

Night Scale I

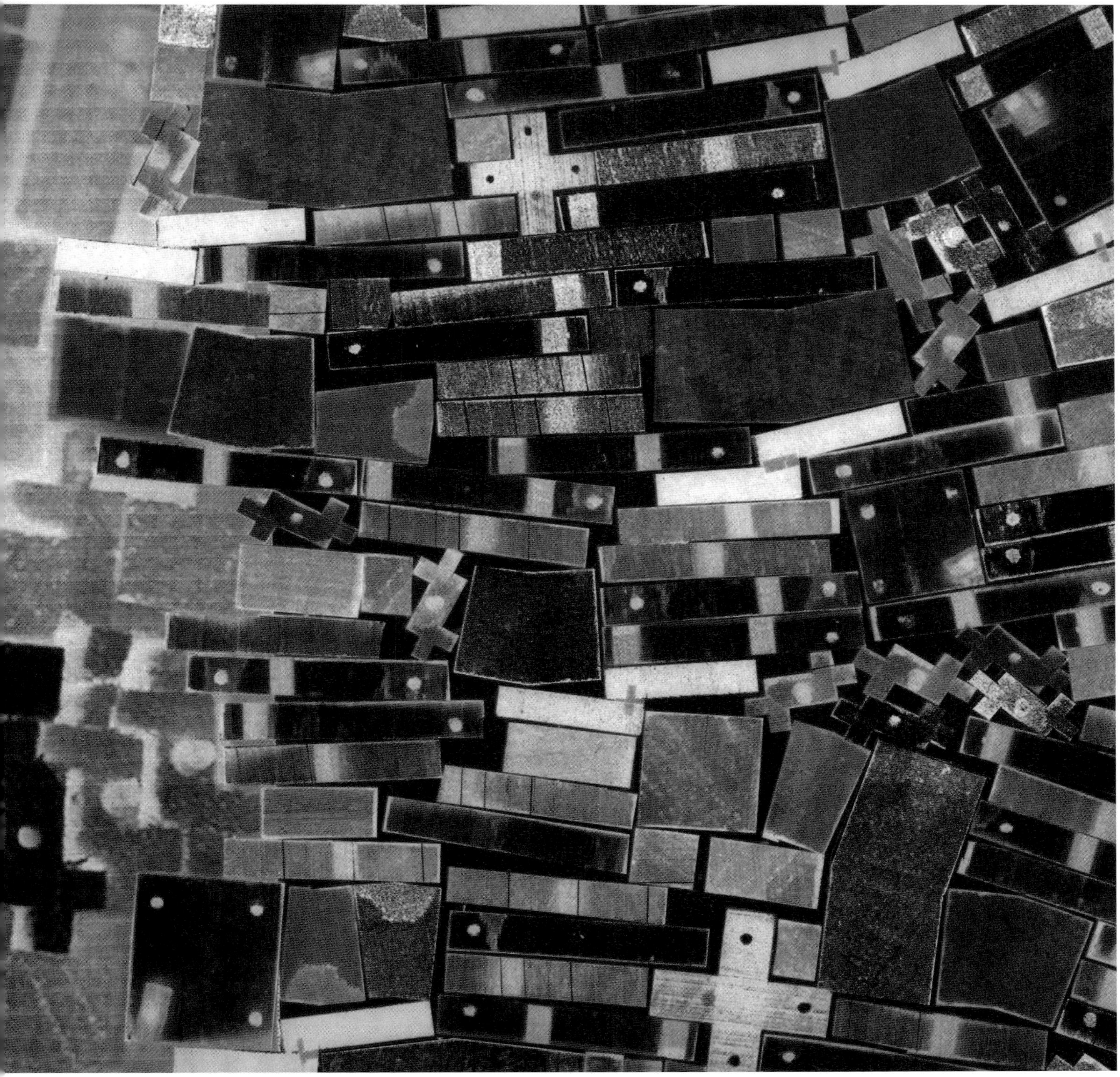

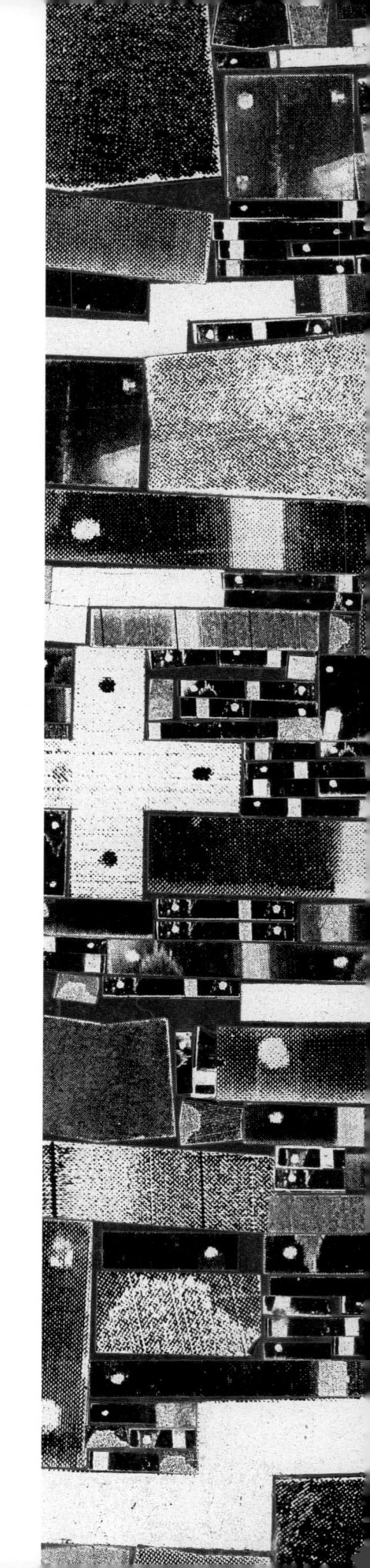

Night Scale II

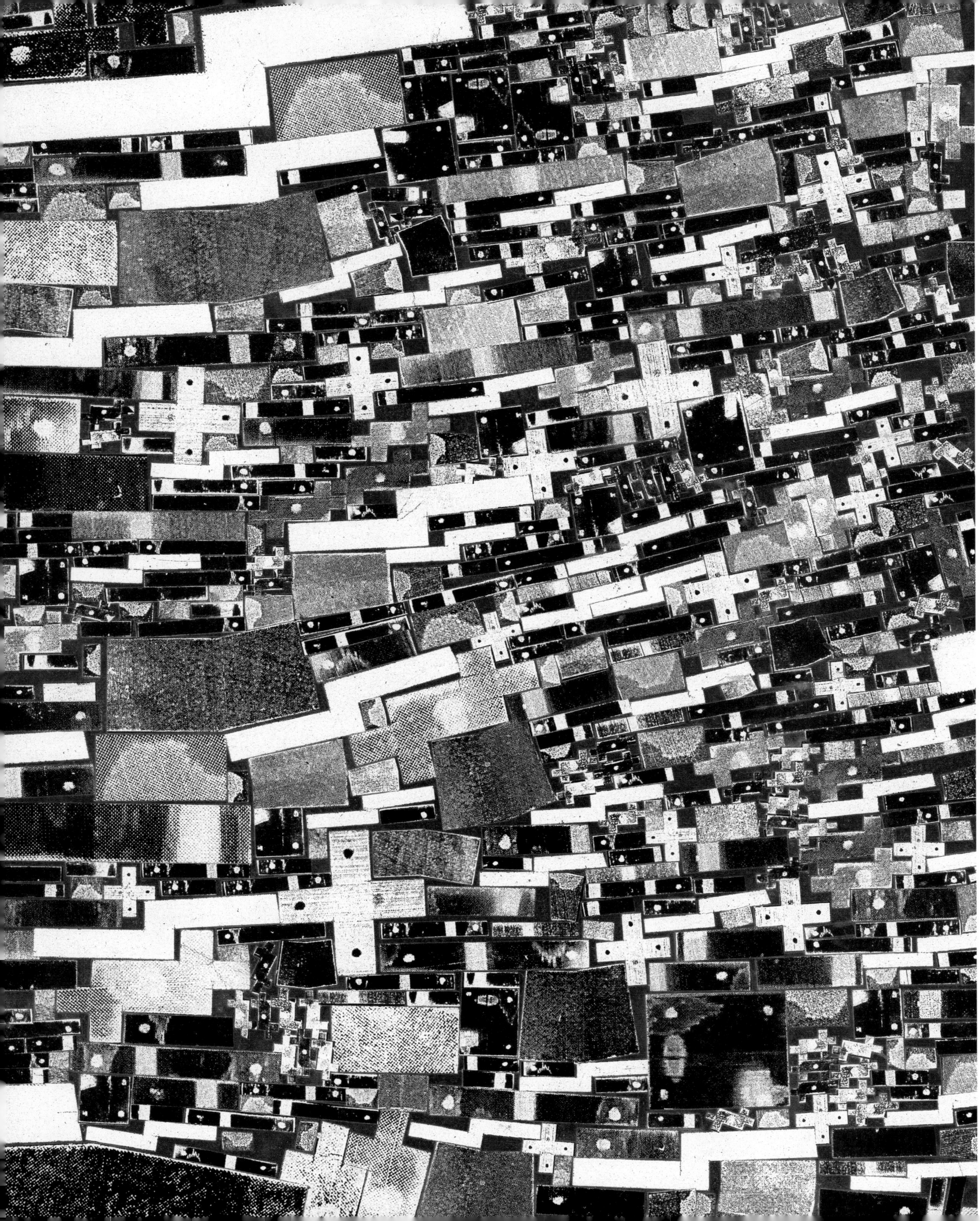

Area

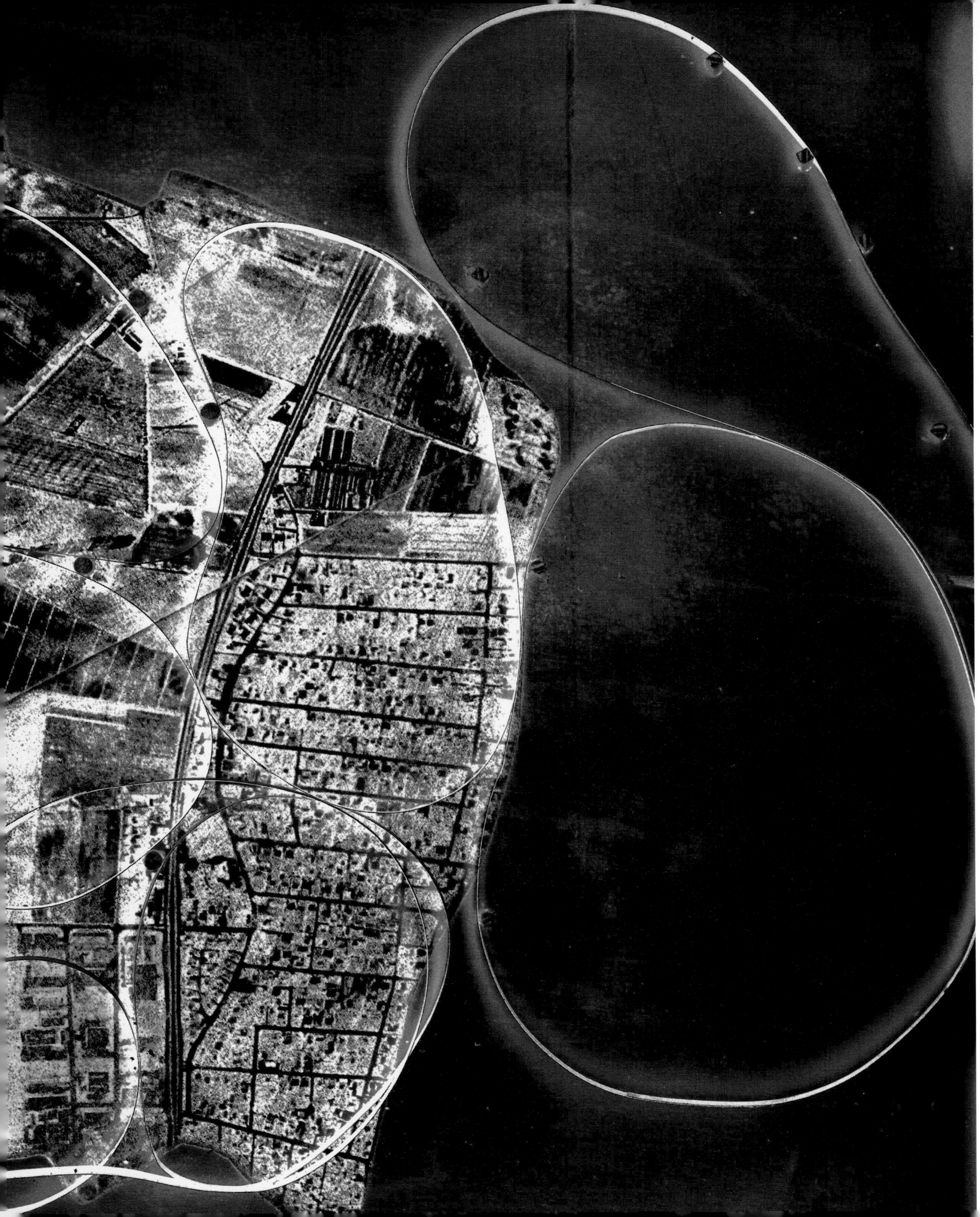

Programs:
1. forked breakwater/sand anchor
2. bay
3. pumped up seabed (sand)

4. fresh-water lake
5. floating tree with lead weight, inhabited by cormorants
6. wooden laths
7. large casted stones

8. epic rock
9. stones
10. gravestone
11. stone fence
12. parish road
13. navigation marks

14. cemetery
15. sepulchral monument
16. lake
17. stones

18. pre-fab concrete factory
19. paving stone depot
20. barn

21. jail
22. factory (clothespins)
23. factory converted into residences (large)

24. drained area
25. residences (simple)
26. parking lot
27. stonecutter and sand blaster
28. parish road/boundary

29. machine pool and warehouse
30. factory
31. workshop
32. drain
33. village pond

34. mosque
35. church
36. collective house
37. magistrate
38. smaller residences

39. studio for a painter (like Asger Jorn)
40. house for a debuting author
41. church (small congregation)
42. shelter
43. deposited material from the excavation in the bay (clay)
44. residences for singles

45. residences
46. information
47. material depot
48. fallow field
49. barn

Gaze

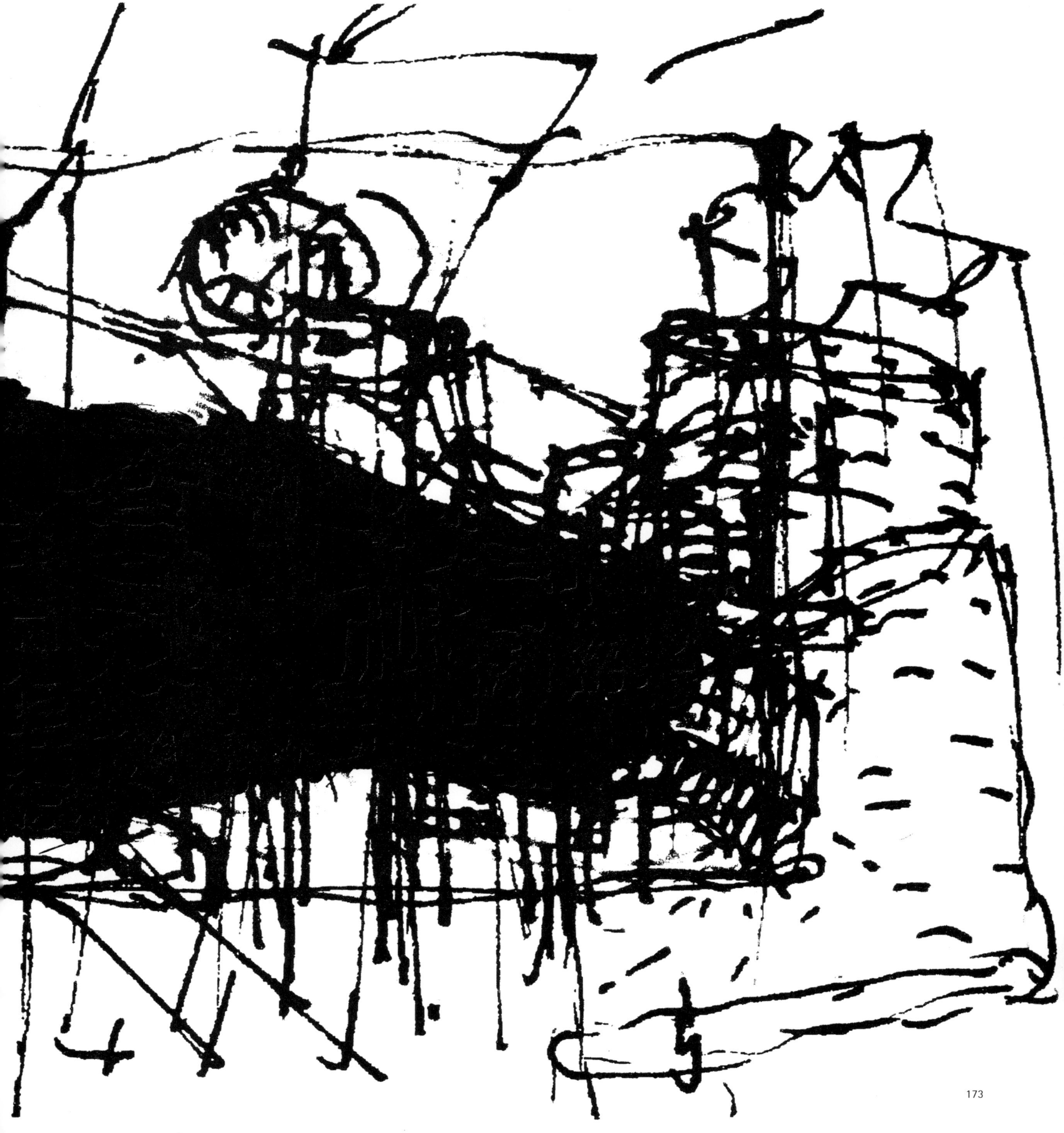

174

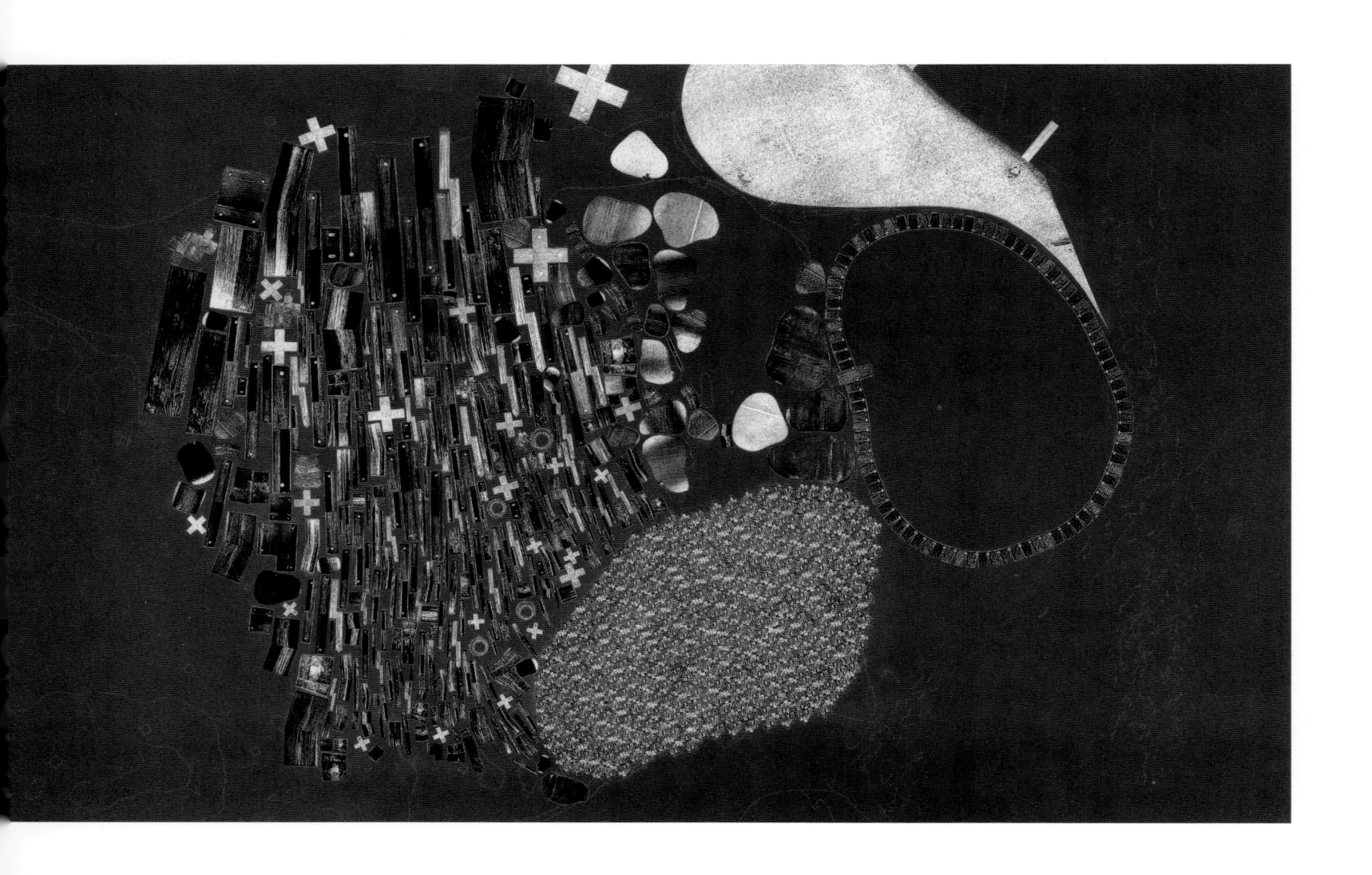

Numbers refer to programs page 172.

29

31

30

32

33

18

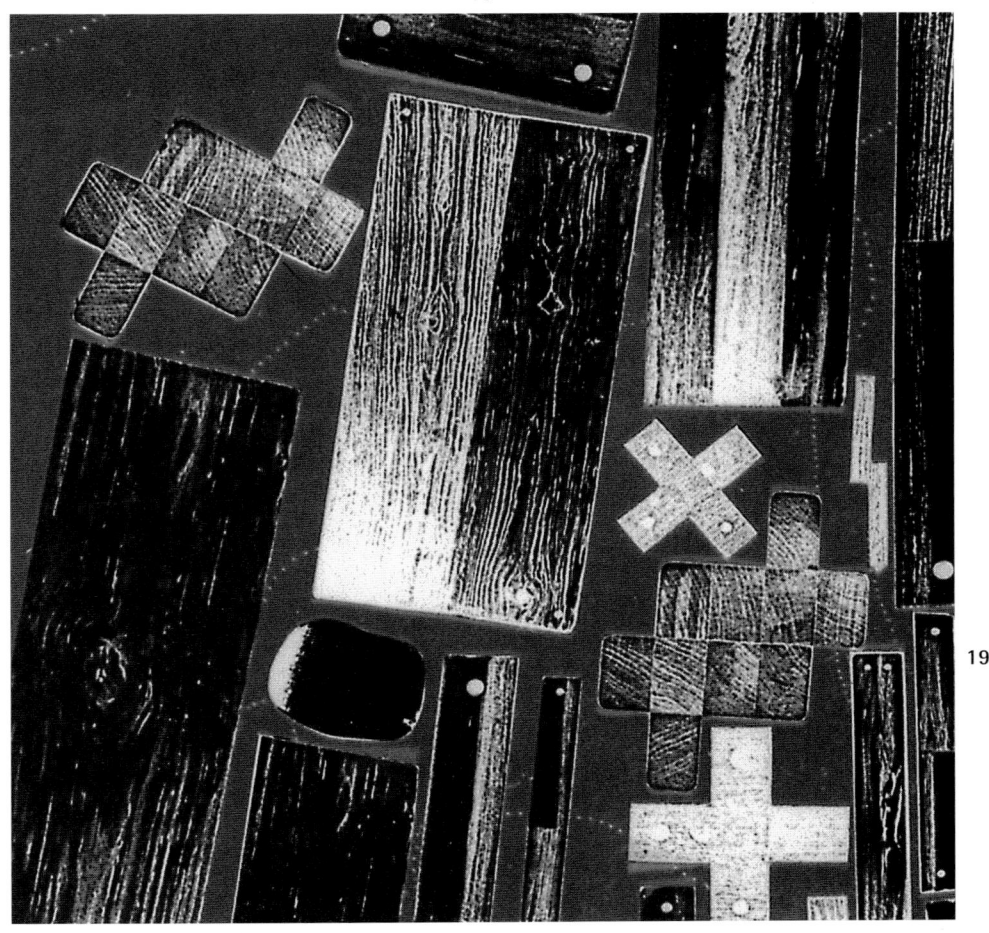

19

20

1

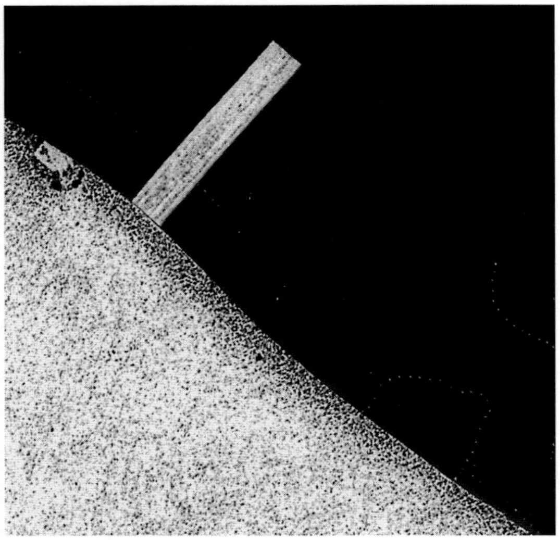

2

3

10

9

8

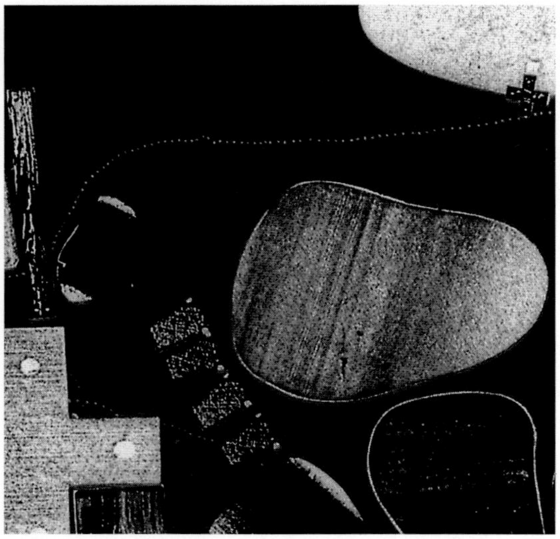

13 12 11

48

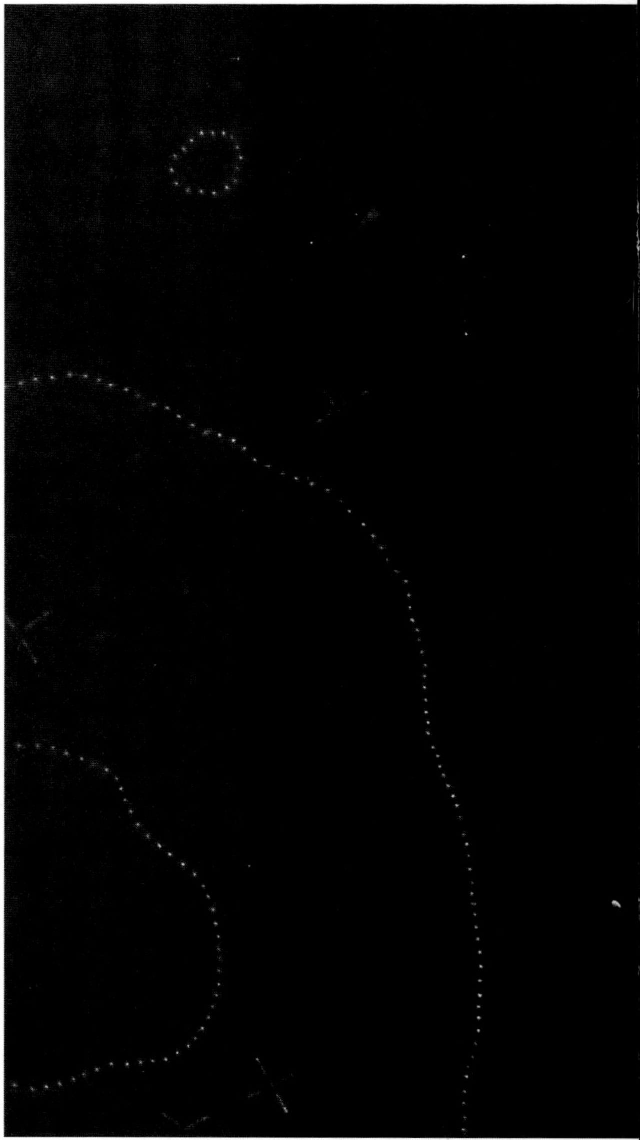

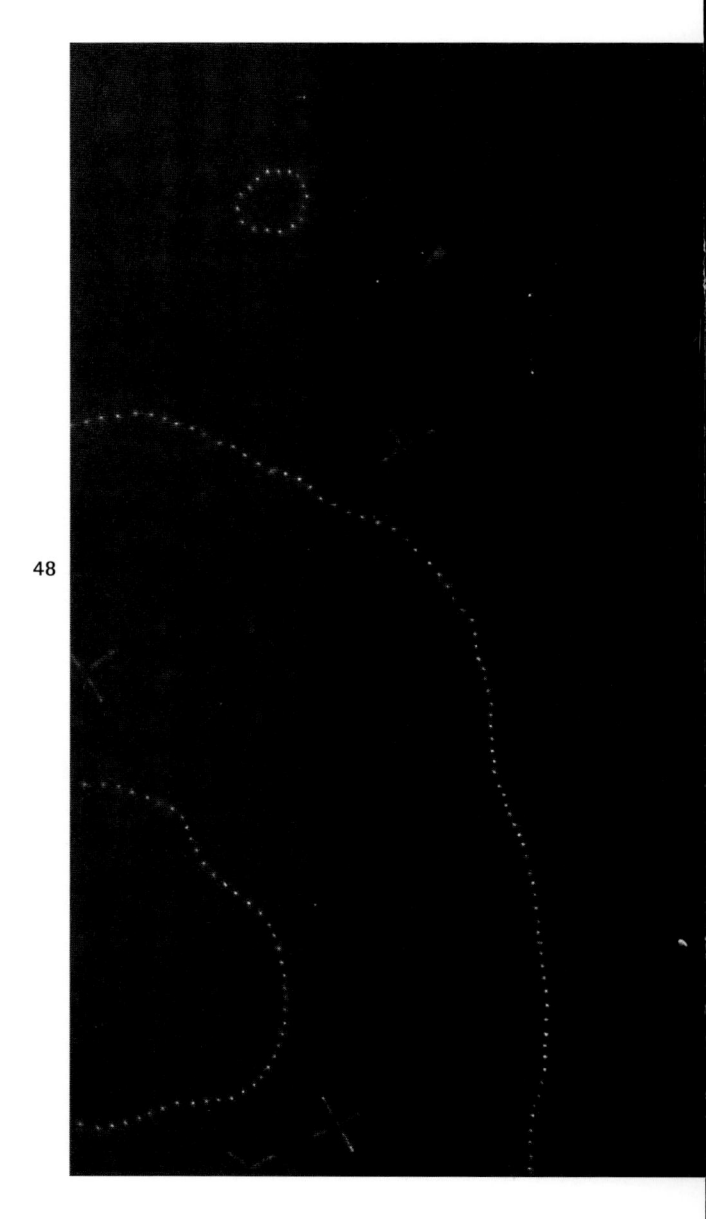

45

49 47 46

34

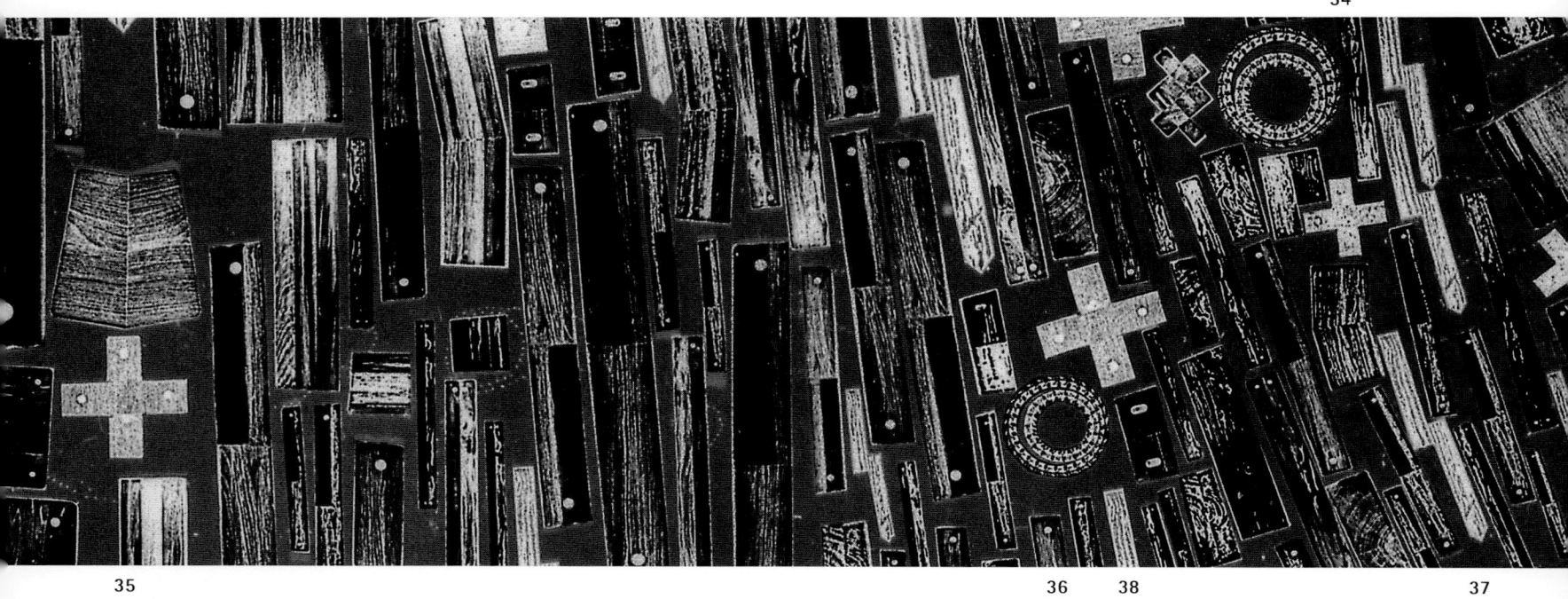

35 36 38 37

40
39
41
42
43
44

6 5

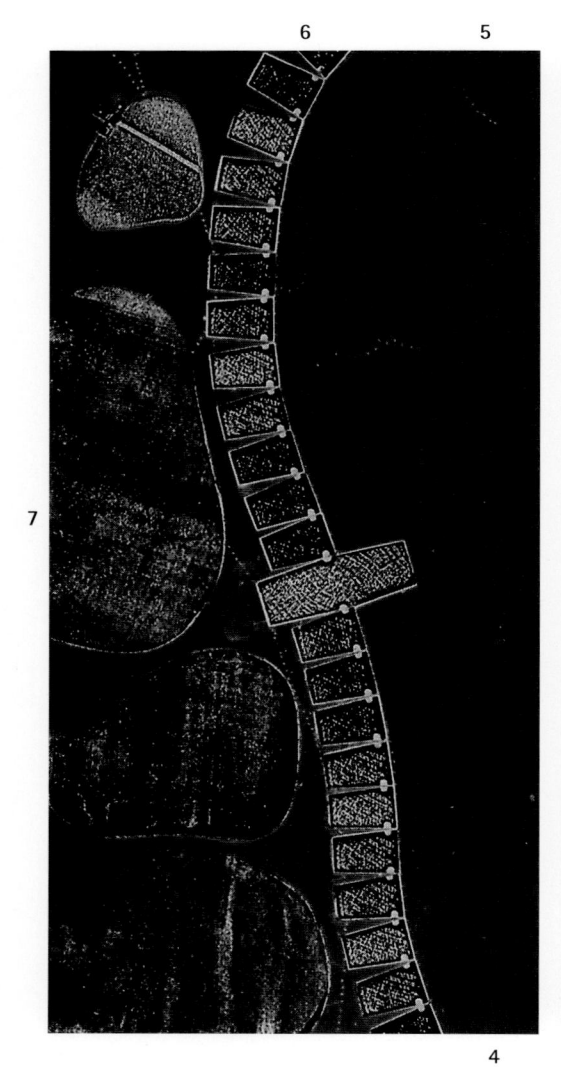

7

4   21 22   23

14 ↑

15

16

17

183

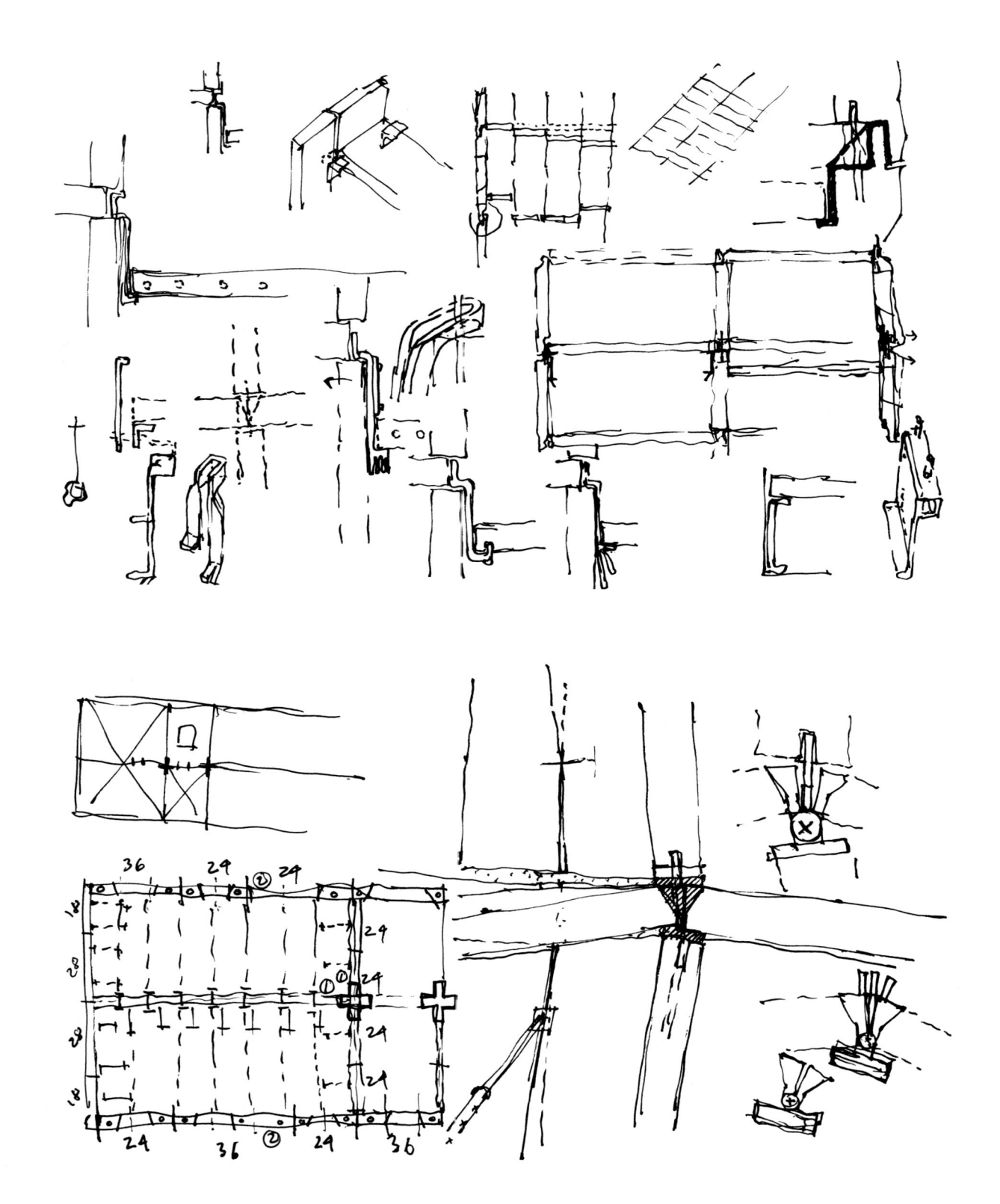

Structural Details –
The ties are structural and symbolic fix-points in the multitude of cast elements.

#6 #6 #6

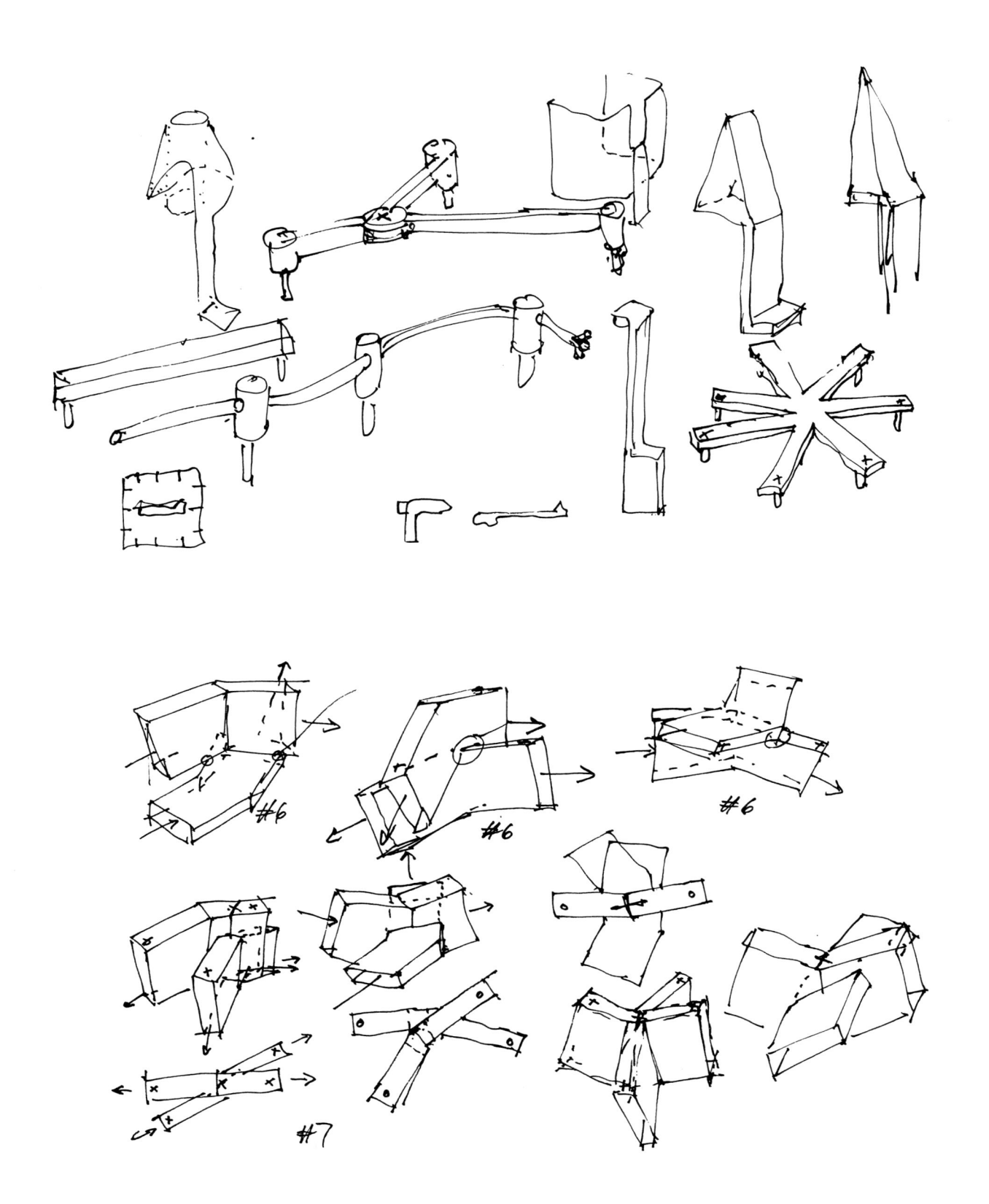

#7

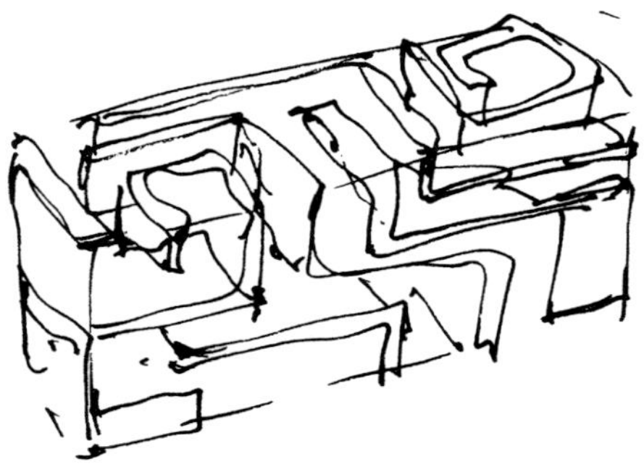
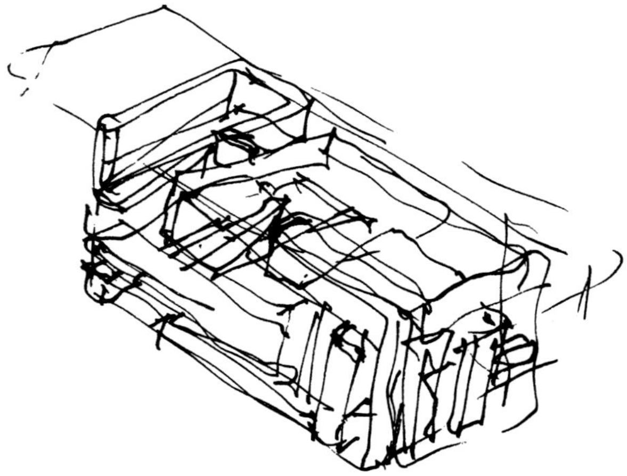
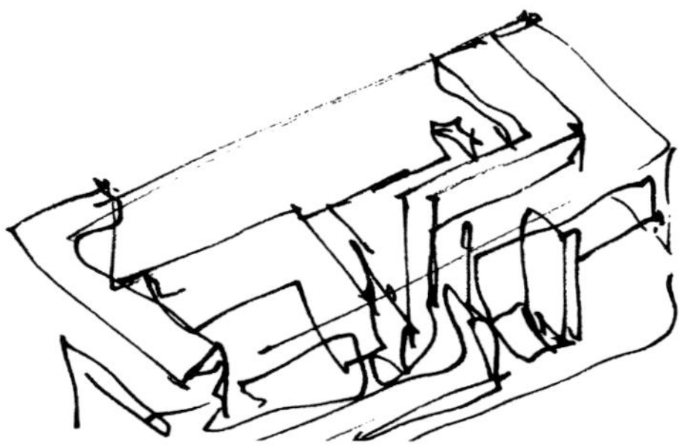
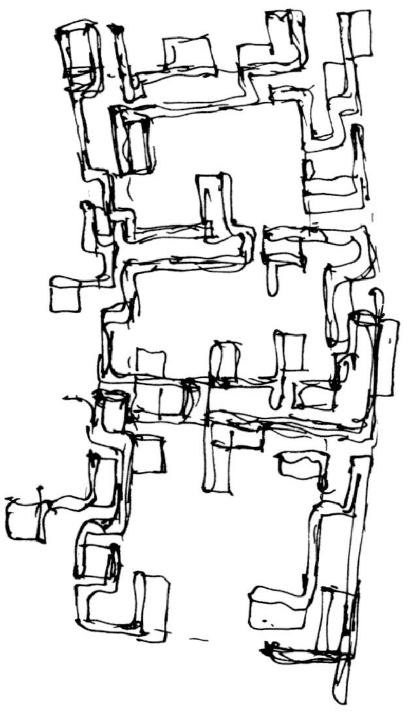
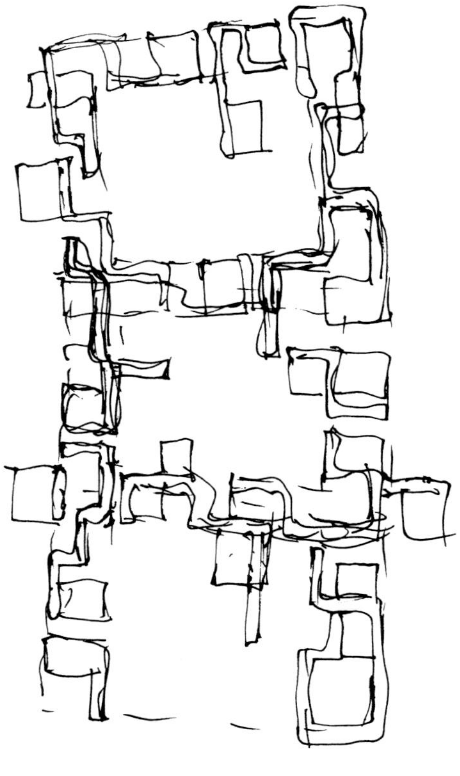

187

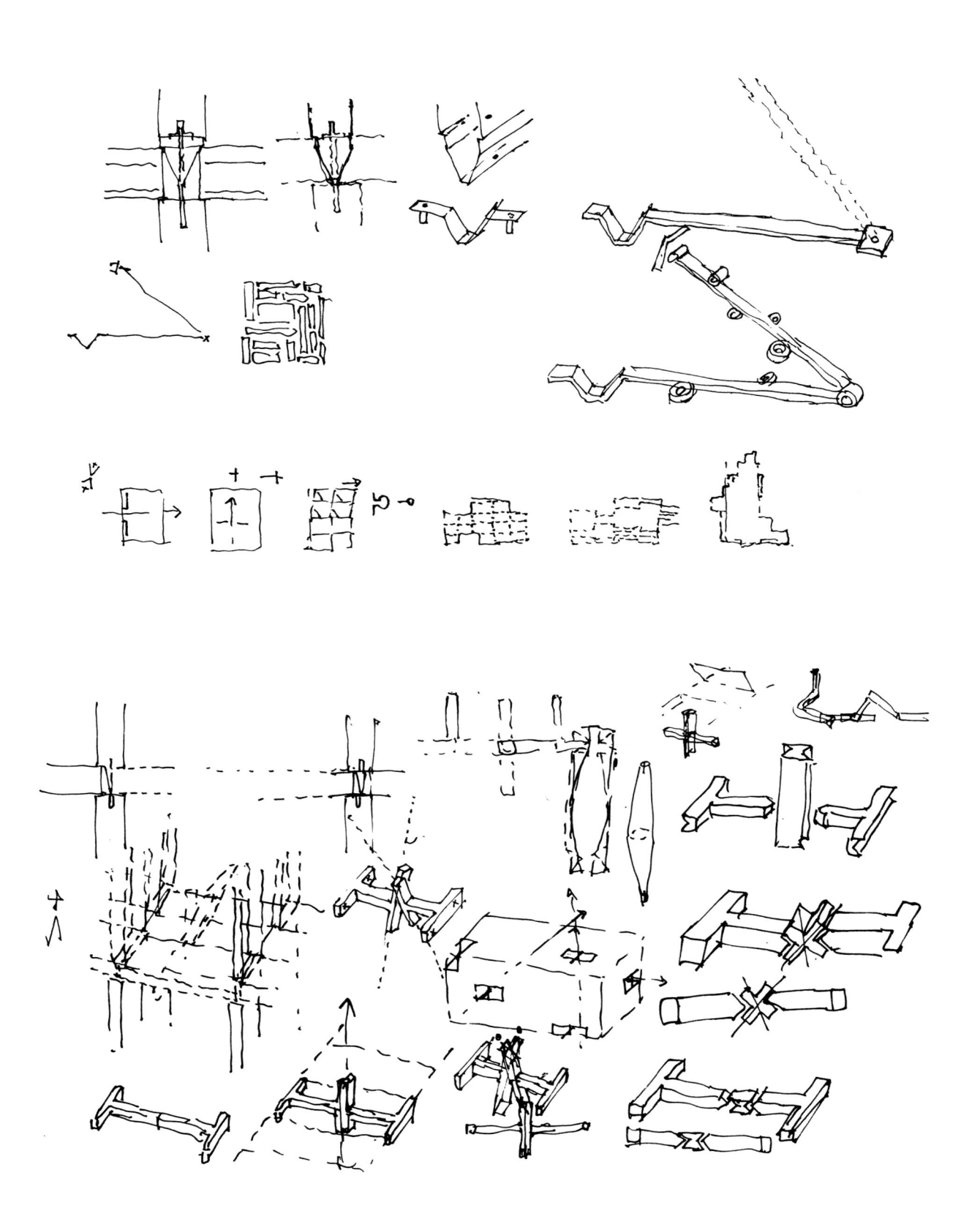

ANDERS MUNCK

28M

The town hall has no façade, no balcony from where proclamations are decried or where the city's heroes can receive their ovation, no ashlar in granite that can resist the disgruntled citizen's torrent of bottles and tomatoes. The municipality's presence is indicated by a sign on the central plaza with an arrow pointing up to the right. The town hall, the shopping center, the metro-train and thus any other municipality in the region of the capital city melt together imperceptibly. In spite of this, the municipal administration is far from being invisible in the urban scene. The town hall is a part of the city's tallest building, which also contains hotels and a fitness center. The entire municipal tower seems to be resting gently on the center's suspended acoustic ceiling - an enormous concrete deck hangs above the open square by a cable, and it is supported by a point further up. You're lured into believing that there is really a constant displacement of support points further up there, as if the building's anchoring issued from above. I visited the technical management office in order to find some drawing material with which to work. The map material is digitalized, and you can choose freely between different kinds of information that have been input: roads, houses, land-register boundaries and technical-supply pathways. The closer you zoom in on a given section, the more information you get and eventually a perfect map delineates itself in the memory of the viewer. Smaller sections of this scale-flexible and fluidly undefined map can be printed out, of course, but then the map's power as one vast infrangible corpus vanishes, and you're left standing there holding a piece of paper. During my visit, it also became clear to me that the architectural drawings that I wanted to use were simply not accessible. Or else they had gotten lost in the files that are kept down in the basement. And maybe they wouldn't be obtainable anyway, because the administration just wouldn't be able to set aside time to look for them. Or even to find out what it might cost to implement the more than likely futile task of attempting to procure them and copy them, if they ever existed at all. The question of bringing to light precisely the drawings which were the very roots of the building within which we were standing, namely the building containing the town hall and also, subsumed under this, the technical management office, was suddenly transformed into a meta-question. It was as if a Renaissance architect who wanted to create meaning in his building by allowing the building's geometric order to represent the universe was asked the subtle question, "Where in this universe is your own building situated?" The city was created in a big bang, and details about its emergence must therefore remain swathed in a mist. The plan keeps to a stringent functionality: primary, secondary and tertiary production, recreation and reproduction of the manpower, everything is kept separate in an utterly traffic-separated network of pathways and roads. The hierarchical center-structure, with several local shopping areas and one vast shopping center, was created on the basis of a thoroughly planned utopia, which boils trade and service down to issues of saving time and maximum efficiency. Places that cannot be neatly inscribed into this functionality are more difficult to catch sight of. The cemetery ought to be such a place, but no new burial places have been established in connection with the development of the city. It is, instead, the old parish church that has had to call in more terrain in order to make room for the growth. The cemetery is far from the city, and if you're on foot, you've got to walk through several tunnels in order to get there. At one child's grave site, instead of a cross, there is a pinwheel, with eight aluminum-foil propellers. It stands there in all its mass-produced anonymity. Every child has had a windmill like this one. Maybe this child was especially fond of this one. Maybe the parents just felt that the form, with the solitary stick and its constant movement when the wind blows through it, belonged here at the spot. However, even if the pinwheel, by virtue of its proximity to a traditional symbol-praxis, almost manages to become a new sign, the instinctive impression of a collective loss of common speech and a missing urban backing is haunting. When the single entity that speaks most distinctly to an observer of personal utterances in the public space - is 40 grams of Chinese-fabricated plastic, this also has to do with the fact that the item is registered in one of the few spaces within the municipality that still contains a symbolic charge, instituted and maintained by a diminutive and hard-working Romanesque parish church. In order to understand the modern public space, we must consider, in the midst of the massive loss of meaning, the cursors that establish the meanings by which we orient ourselves and which, in spite of everything, specify the buildings and impart to them recognizability and identity.

On the following pages, there is a series of drawings and notes made about buildings that characterize the architecture of the *public life* around the Køge Bay.

ISHØJ	**ISHØJ**	**ISHØJ**	**AVEDØRE**
Grill bar: Red & Yellow	Bilka: Pick-up Dock	Local police station	Large building: back side
AVEDØRE	**ISHØJ**	**ISHØJ**	**BRØNDBY**
Adventure playground: the rainbow	 Bilka: Parking lot	Ishøj Motor Center	Brøndby Stadium
BRØNDBY	**ISHØJ**	**BRØNDBY**	**ISHØJ**
Brøndby Strand church	Ilva: entrance façade	Allotment garden cabin	Industrial area: kilns

Ishøj. Grill bar. scale 1:50
The grill bar is centrally situated between the apartment houses in the northern section of the Ishøj plan. Along with two larger ball-cages and the local supermarket, this establishment constitutes the public space of the local milieu. The name "Red & Yellow" refers to the grill bar's function as a hotdog stand, where mustard and ketchup once played a bigger role than they do today. The menu has now been expanded to include pizza and kebab. The name possesses no utopian dimension and does not refer to some locality in distant climes. Its distinctly here-and-now presence establishes an autonomous place. This self-referentiality is underscored by the fact that the sign posting has been executed in red, with yellow letters and stripes.

Ishøj. Bilka: Pick-up dock. Scale 1:50
It doesn't seem reasonable to ask customers to carry certain items up to the cash register. If you've just sprung for a TV, you need not haul a 100-lb. cardboard box around the shopping center. What you do instead is to drive around the building and pick up the appliance at the pick-up dock. Unfortunately, you've also got to do this if you're on foot and you've just purchased a cell phone that weighs less than half a pound. You've got to cross the parking cellar, through the approach driveway, out on the traffic lane and into a yard where the pick-up dock comes into view at the end of a sequence of unloading ramps and garbage containers. The video cameras just above the door are positioned centrally in the yard and the sign that calls attention to their watchful attendance is somehow superfluous, although it serves to remind us that it is not exclusively customer service that conditions this maneuver.

Ishøj. Local police station. Scale 1:50
Even though the local police station in Ishøj Station's Center shoots its way into the parking lot; its primary petition is toward the shopping center. The video camera mounted on the wall is turned toward the police station and not out toward the parking lot. The two windows have each been bestowed with an extra frame, with an impact-resistant acrylic plate, mounted with four large shiny bolts, which cannot be loosened from the outside. This form of safeguarding corresponds to the trelliswork on the constabulary's buildings in classic architecture, but here it is cleansed of any symbolic charge, and the windows' total of eight shiny bolts and the acrylic's distorted reflection stands, along with the parking reservations for the two squad cars, as the only physical expression of the building's use.

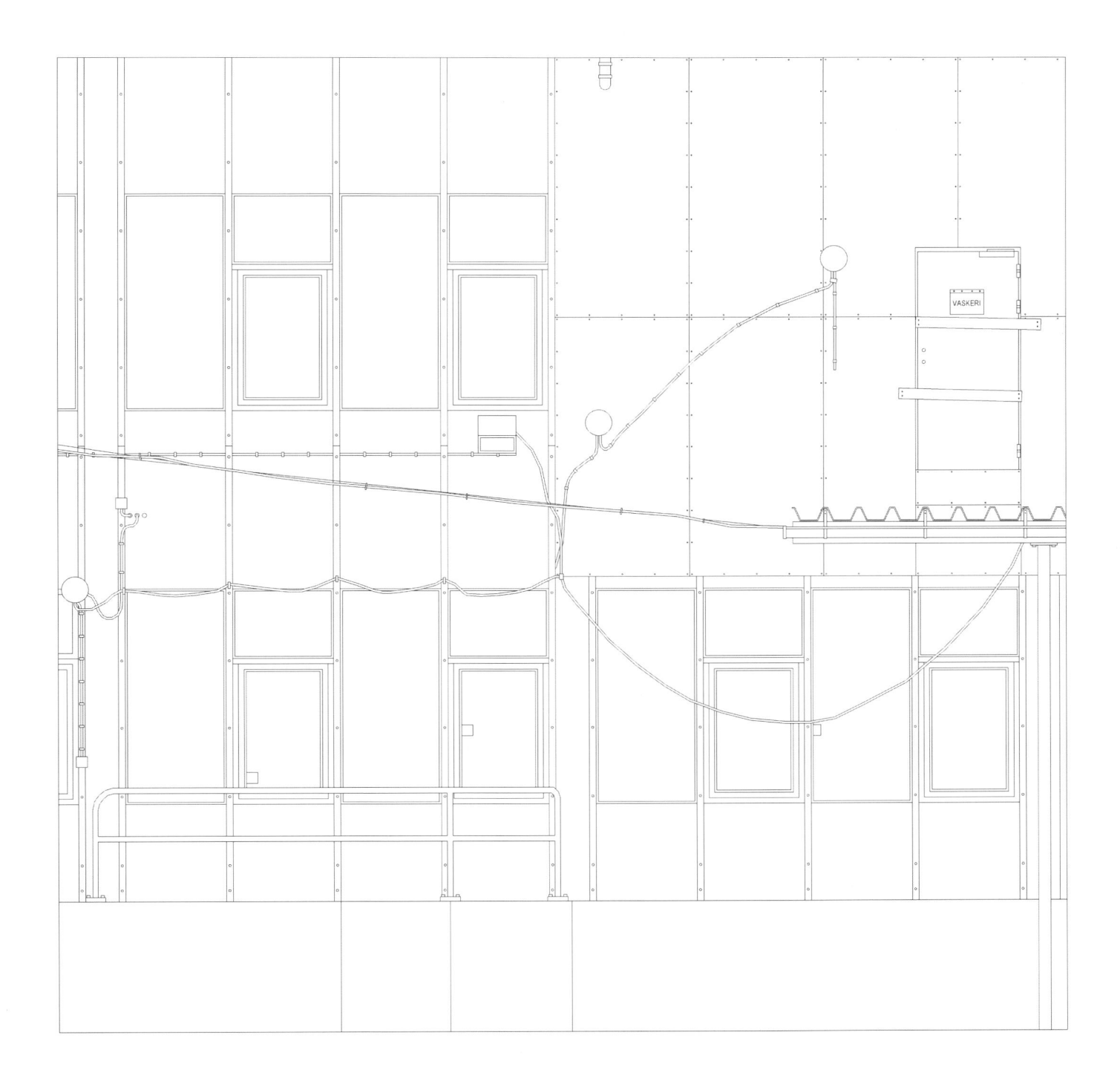

Avedøre. Large building. Scale 1:50
Together with this urban development's position in between the Hvidovre barracks and the western ramparts, Avedøre Junction's medieval planning scheme - the basis for the town wall-like ribbon development, which delimits a densely populated public space – imparts a very special character to the place. As in the classical defenses, vast grounds have been invested. Here, they establish traffic separation. On the exterior of this large building, a supply-moat supplies the shops on the other side with their avenues of access. The parking lot is conjoined with the large building by concrete ramps, which cross over the moat like drawbridges. The provisional installations attest to the fact that this exterior is not the façade but rather the back of the building, and these installations play their part in clarifying the ligation of the space.

Avedøre. Adventure Playground. Scale 1:50
Outside of the town wall in Avedøre Junction, certain odd-sized objects that cannot find any place for themselves inside the wall are gathered together. The adventure playground possesses an architectonic surfeit, which manifests itself partly in the plan for the aggregate facility, arranged with a compactness around the central open area, where a small stage is encircled by small trees, and partly in the simple constructions where, as we see here, a two-story house has been constructed with a columnar façade on the second floor, which faces out to the central open area, and a footbridge leading over to the annex. This gangway encases a small tree, which is given the room it needs to grow up through the construction.

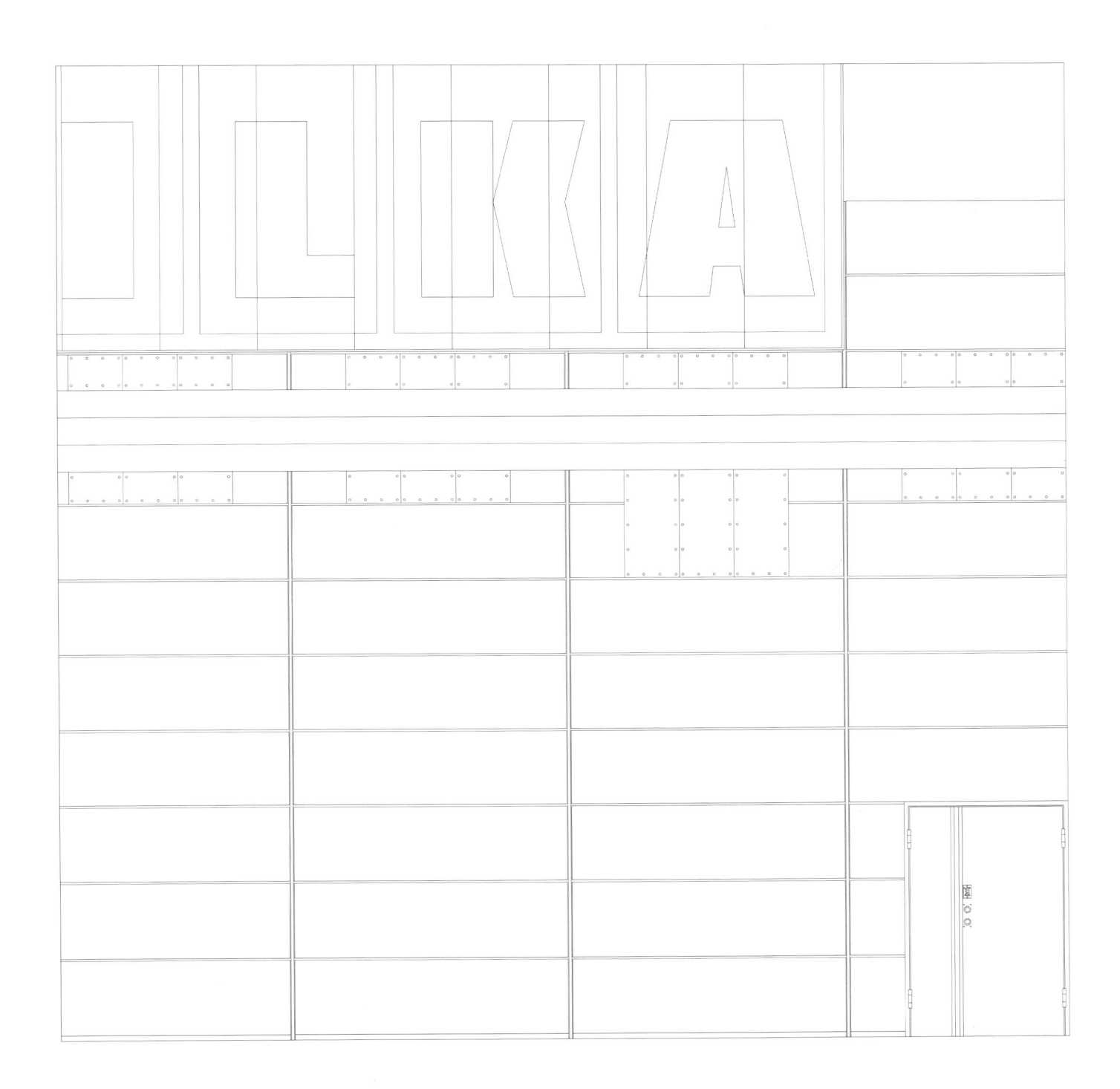

Ishøj. Bilka: Parking lot. Scale 1:50
The endless series of concrete elements, the absolute lack of initiative toward any detailed treatment of the façade, the horizontal blue-white strips with the sign that reposes at the top, provides an unequivocal acknowledgement that we should not expect to find an entrance here. The deliberate maintenance of the place's closed nature is seen in the boarded up windows and the emergency exit that has no handle on the outside. Nothing divulges the scale of this façade and consequently it establishes a vacuum in the heart of the city.

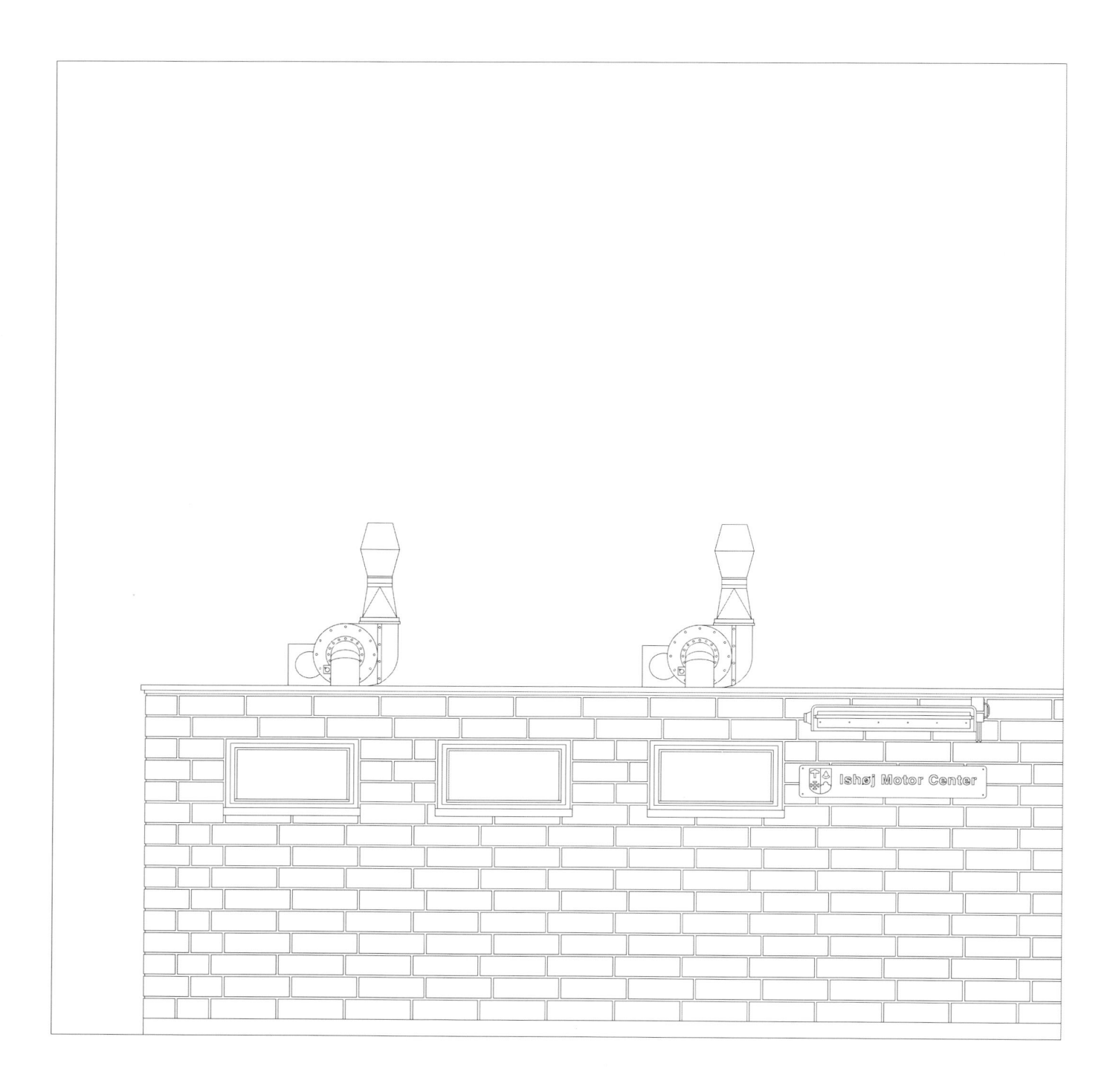

Ishøj. Ishøj Motor Center: Scale 1:50
Motor-cross and go-cart lanes constitute a miniature closed circulatory system consisting of muddy mounds and asphalt loops flanked by worn-out tires and workshops for repairing the vehicles. This facility has been placed right in between the highway and the industrial quarter. The very location accordingly plays its part in imparting a special kind of "model" character to the place, while also anchoring its socializing role in connection with a modern transportation- and production-society.

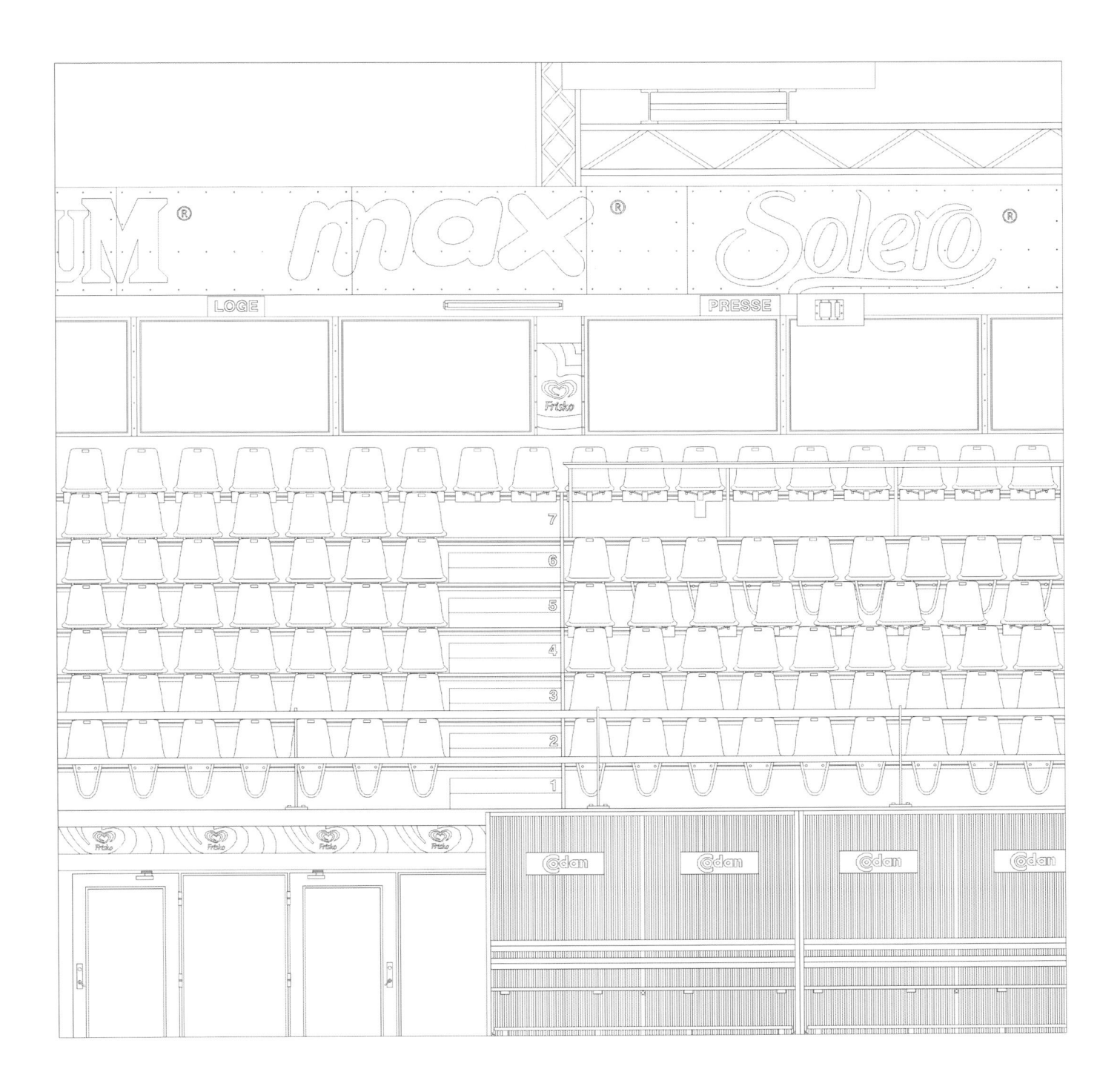

Brøndby. Brøndby Stadium. Scale 1:50
While a portion of the advertising space on the lengths of lath addresses itself directly to the public at the stadium and refers to what can be bought in the stadium's kiosks, the home-team's reserve-bench is endowed with the chief sponsor's trademark. The execution of the logo is very restrained, since it primarily addresses itself to close-ups on TV-broadcasts and has also been conceived as merging with the rest of the players' uniforms. Without the team, the bench looks somehow like an empty cross in the church and merely calls attention to the absence of the players, each of whom bears the trademark upon his breast.

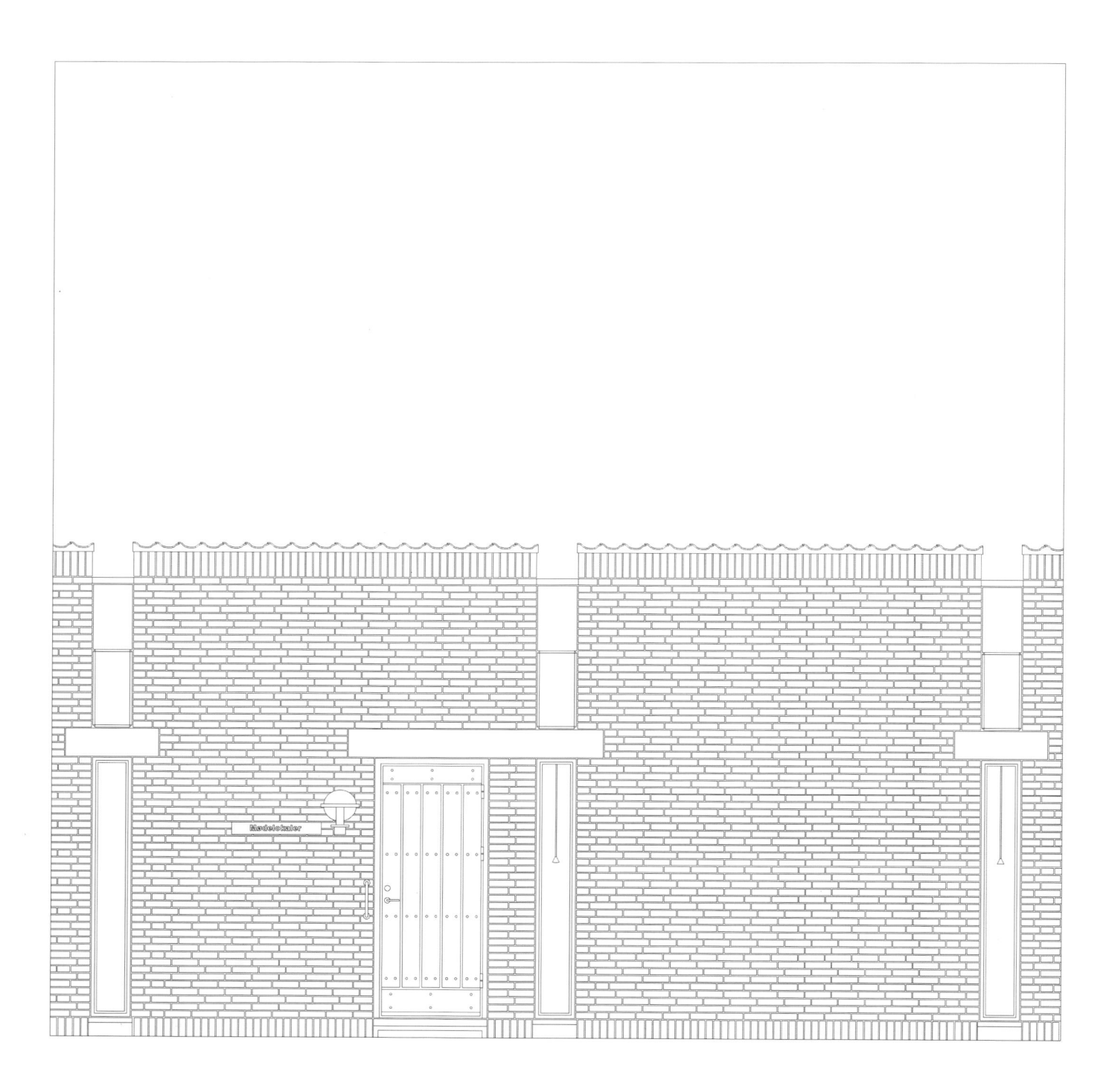

Brøndby. Brøndby Strand Church. Scale 1:50
The entrance to the congregation's conference rooms opens up the steady rhythm in the side façade by elongating the concrete lintel in such a way that also makes room for a door which, by virtue of its size and execution in solid wood with rivets, imparts a solemn expression. In this way, the door finds its rightful place in the apparently unbreakable rhythm.

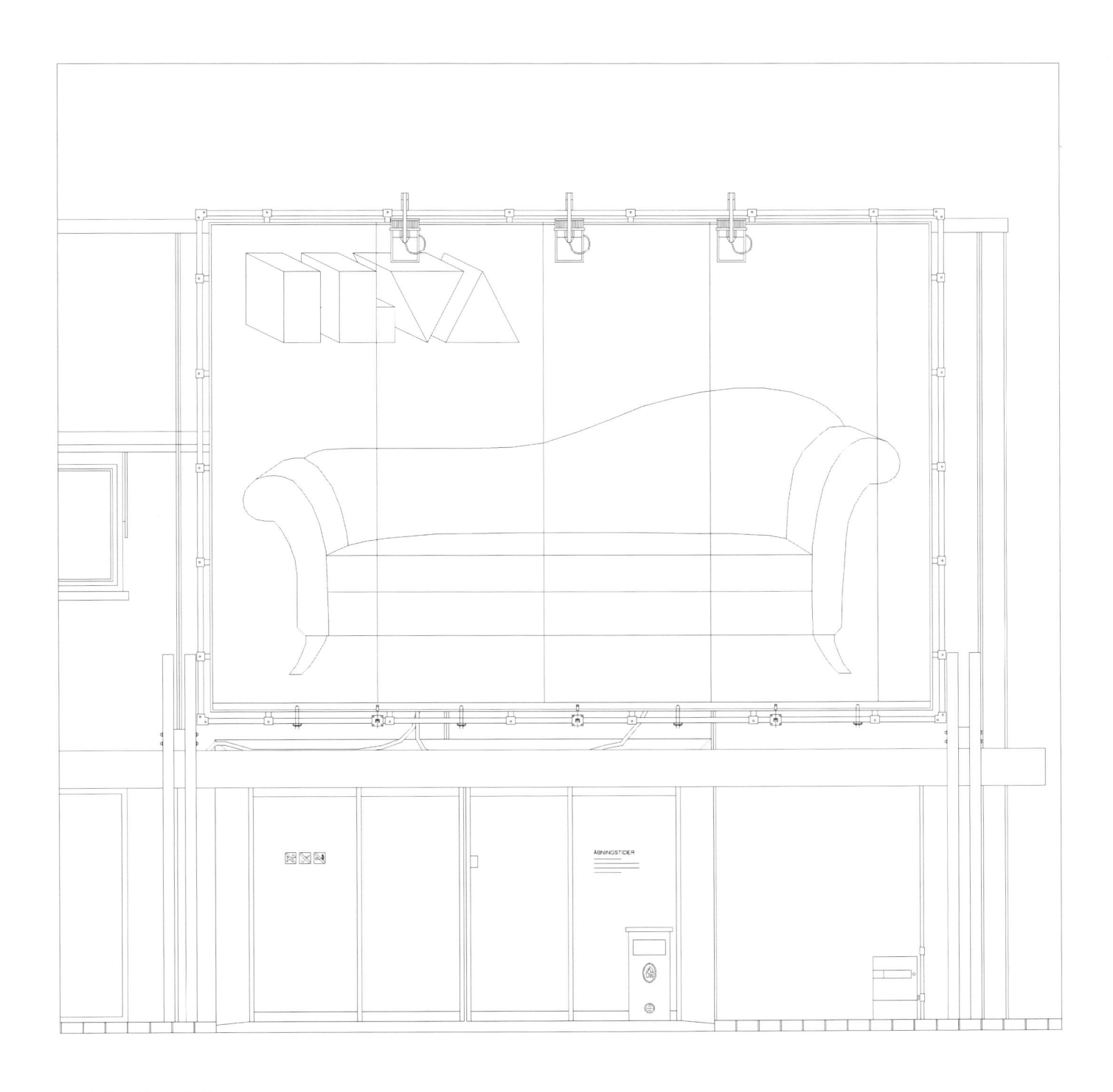

Ishøj. Ilva. Scale 1:50
Standing at the parking lot in front of this furniture store, you find yourself to be standing on the same level as a completely straight section of the Køge Bay Highway. There is no baffle wall and only a very low and dense shrubbery. The buildings lie there side by side and look directly out on to the highway's passing traffic. On a scaffolding of pipes and fittings, a large picture of a sofa has been stretched out and above the image, the name of the firm is added. The sign contains no further information about any terms of sale and serves solely to localize the place.

Brøndby. Allotment garden cabin. Scale 1:50
The cabin has been assembled out of different boards and plates, which have all been bestowed with the unifying feature of a wall-to-wall covering of orange paint. The left side can be locked up, while the right side is an unroofed shelter-construction. These two sections are conjoined by a gate, which imparts a symmetric aspect. The long boards in the left side and the shorter ones in the right side provide the façade with a hierarchy that underscores the two different functions. The interior of the yard is painted with a powerful yellow hue which, upon being intensified through reflections in the small yard, appears to be powerfully luminescent.

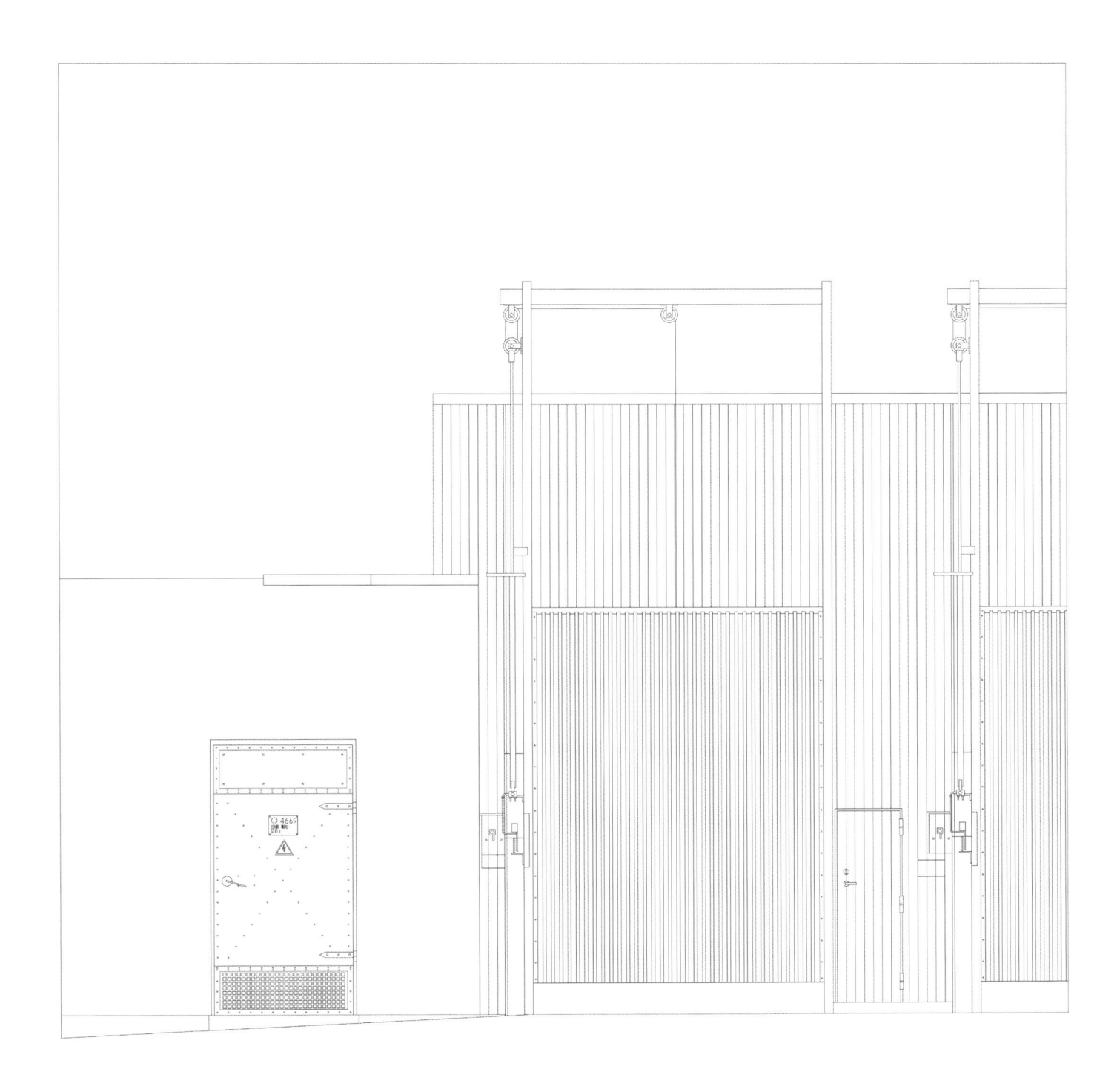

Ishøj. Kiln. Scale 1:50
After wood is impregnated, and thus rendered waterproof, it has to be dried out in a kiln. The outer paneling on the oven-section on the right side of the construction is executed in compregnated wood. The doors, executed in metal plates, and the section with all the technical facilities on the left are polished up in a light-green color that corresponds to the area's many stacks of compregnated wood and with the rest of the building. The building bears the mark of many years of use. This is the quarter's "mother building", which has generated the material for all the other buildings. The building is itself an offshoot of another place but, at the same time, it is the bearer of one particular culture, since it has been fabricated itself out of compregnated wood.

POUL INGEMANN

Six brief conversations

1st conversation
A: I read somewhere that one of the three tenors, José Carreras, once stated, "We're not afraid that other people have sung the same songs before. We're using our talent, personality and feelings to instill something new into the music. In pop music, it's a whole different kind of thing. If you make a song into a hit, it becomes your own. But the opera singer knows that on every single night, there is someone out there singing the very same song somewhere - on some another stage"
B: Or a suitor sings for the bride of his choice the very same words that are being heard, at the very same instant, by the gala-dressed public at the Metropolitan Opera.
A: Exactly, it's the same material, and it doesn't have to be inside the darkness of the opera house that the most intense feelings are enunciated.
B: It is thought provoking, however, that when he stands there on the stage, it becomes an echo of every suitors' song.

2nd conversation
A: Have you ever experienced the silence that emerges after you one night, at high speed and without much rest in your body, go driving beneath phosphorescent lights through the desolate land-

scapes encircling the city and then, because you thought you could keep awake, you are suddenly awakened by metal being grinded against the traffic divider's concrete, glass being shattered and the motor with a crescendo speeds up only to thereafter in silent flight send the vehicle forth between small factories and worlds that you didn't even know were there?
B: Sure, that kind of night can be real peaceful.

3rd conversation
A: What do you call your dogs?
B: Nóstos and Álgos.
A: That makes me think of the guy – I can't remember his name – who, upon being asked, from where do you come, answered: "From my childhood."

4th conversation
A: With the knife and the dusty dirt as implement and element, we used to play "country". A combination of calculation and chance determined the extent of land possession. When all these intersecting lines are viewed from the air, from our child-eyes' low approach, the internal glance could localize here a castle, and there a fortress, a church, a school, even the whole little society, where there were, once again, small houses with little doors and small windows.
B: Yes, I can remember that liberating state of mind, when chance was a fellow player whenever the land had to be parceled out. In this grid-net of lines and capriciously selected geometric plots, there was an incentive to do something anarchistic and dangerous. The elements were few, and so were the rules of the game – two guys, the soil and the knife, the bird's-eye-view and the good fling.
A: The marking off of pioneer territory had something so incontestably special about it. It was the same every time. It was like a new beginning. The fraction of a second was observed in silence, as if flinging the knife into the virgin earth required courage and surmounting.
B: I believe that it was only us who could see the cities, the roads, the many lights and the darkness over the country. It was like flying. From that altitude, everything was beautiful. It was so quiet down there. You couldn't separate the unhappy from the happy. You could feel the nothingness on the other side, from the universe's unfathomable endlessness to the city's labyrinths of nooks and folds.
A: We'll have to teach the map reader and the pilot to unite the geometric glance with the experience that tells us that there are map readers and pilots hidden in the lights which, like mirror images, reveal to us the starry skies.
B: It is indubitably more gentle to measure and describe the elephant man's cowl than to move into that darkness that lies beneath the fold and deeply down in the hollow of the eye.

5th conversation
A: We don't have nature anymore. That's why it's being replaced by another kind of nature. Not nature in a naturalistic reproduction, but rather in the form of nature's impersonal-ness and lack of meaning. We're not building cities outside the cities, as you might well imagine, but rather new landscapes, which volunteer themselves with ravines and infinite plains.
B: Where you are alone with your heartbeat and where the sudden assault is filmed by the fluorescent glimmering's dispassionate light.
A: Or from all the illuminated internal worlds, which as mirages beguile like some femme fatale in the night. It is the sight's penetration that has the first claim. Everything is laid bare, and only centimeter-thin glass separates the worlds.
B: Worlds which, by hook or by crook, must be united through the vision. Hygienically defensible, we have the opportunity of settling ourselves as witnesses.
A: Yes, there is something ill-mannered about the way the modern manifests itself. In much the same way that we played "country", we are seized by a savageness whenever the earth becomes disfigured by our knife. There is no place that the knife should not have been; suddenly it was the surface and not the point that set our brains on fire.

6th conversation
A: Would you have ever imagined that this country would become pioneer territory? That places could be scratched out from real space, earth for the indisposed. Not out of compassion, but because there is a need for the pioneer, for the ear and the eye in the night, out there on the edge.
B: A place of changeover, where the one crosses over the trails of the many.
A: In much the same way as those coat pockets that have an extra hole and you can put your hand down into the warm pants pockets?
B: You could say that.
A: Yeah, with a little ingenuity, you could call the coat pocket a bulging out of the public space, whereas there, a little bit further in, there is more than cap and gloves. It's almost as if you would willingly allow strangers to dive down into the coat pocket, but then not any further.

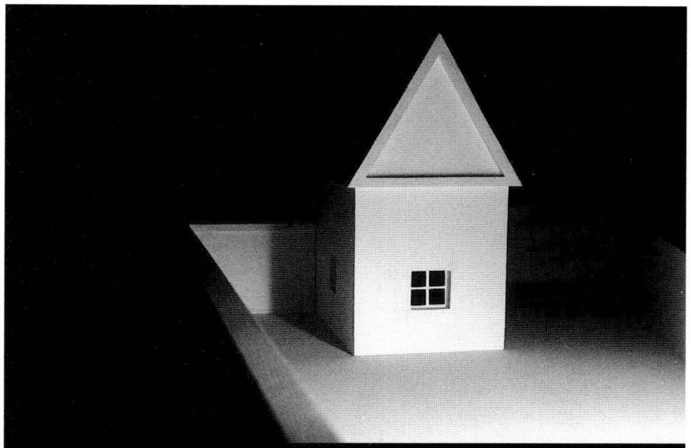

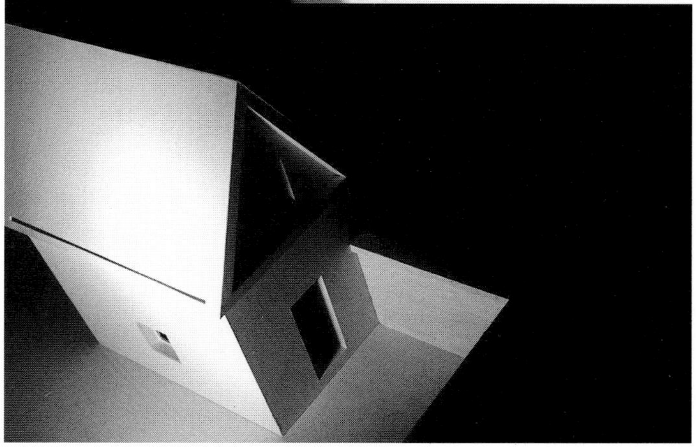

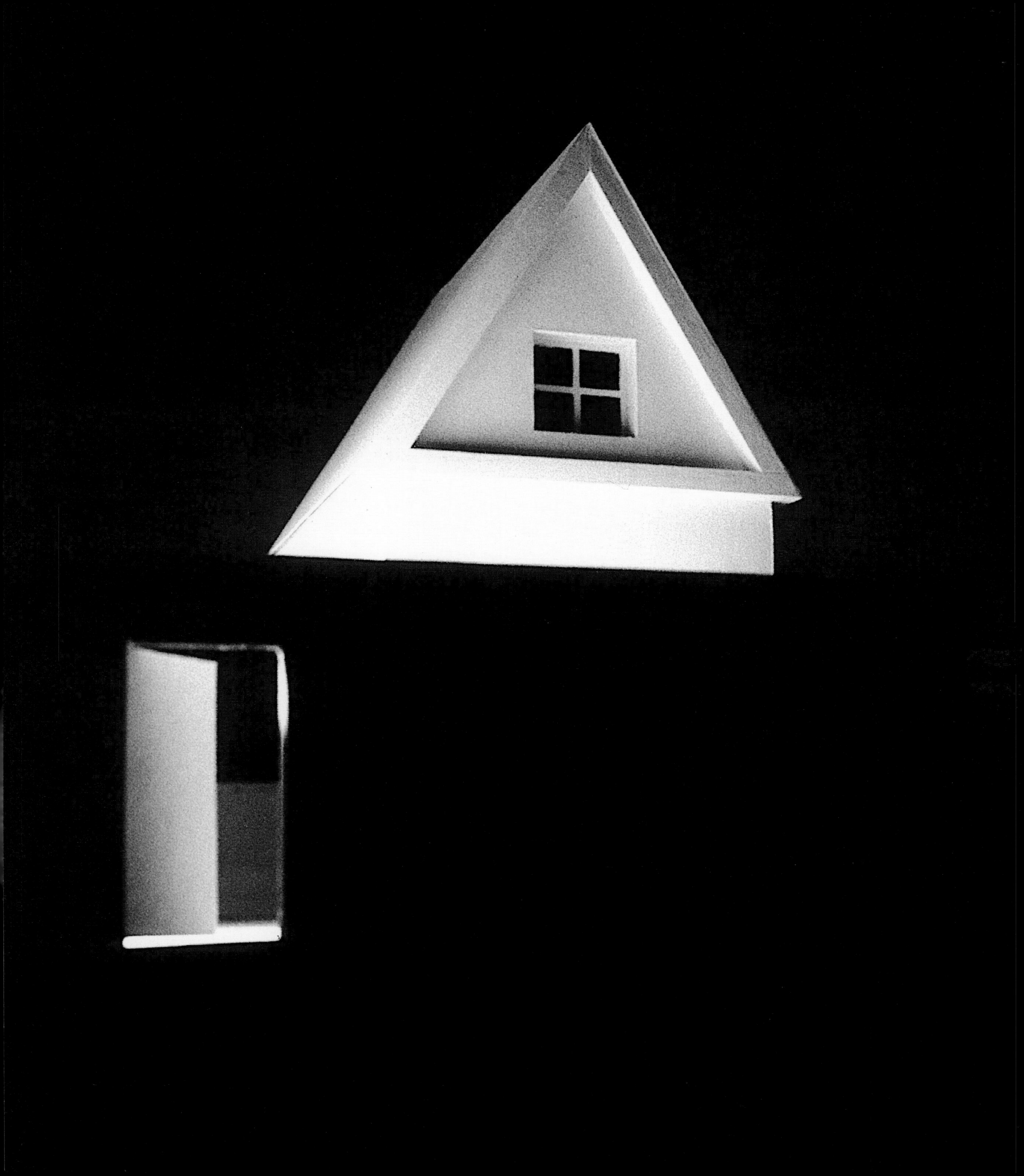

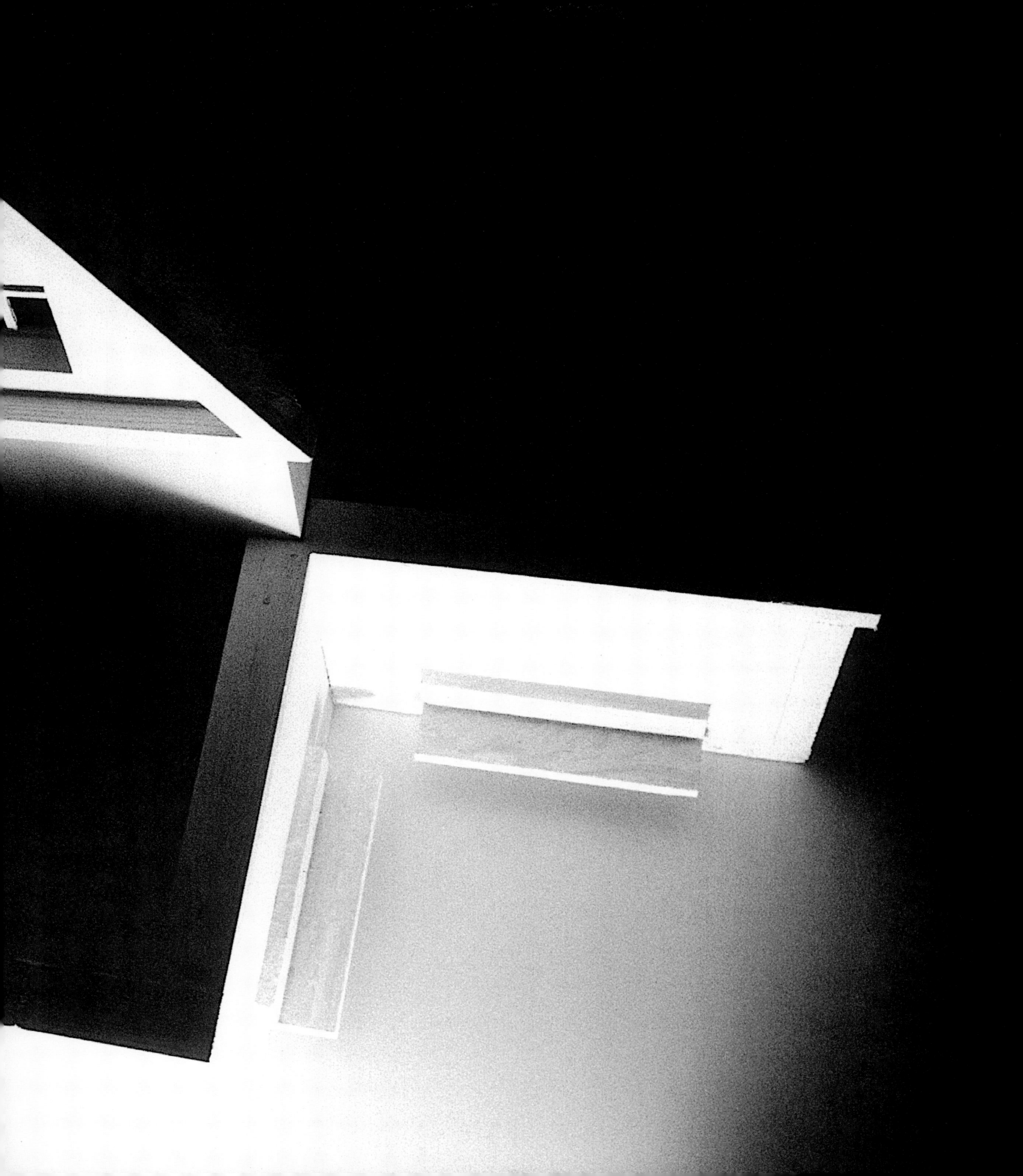

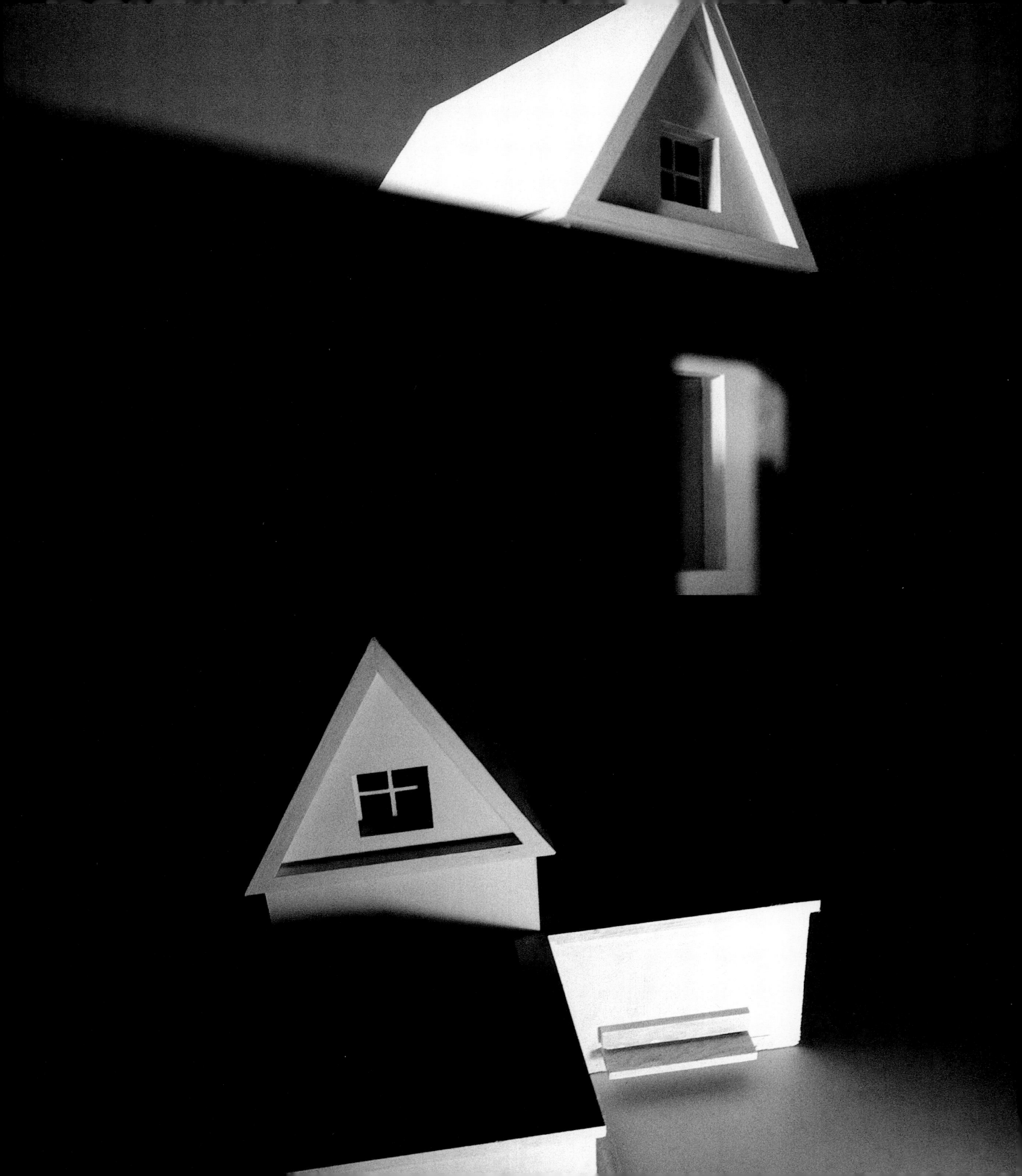

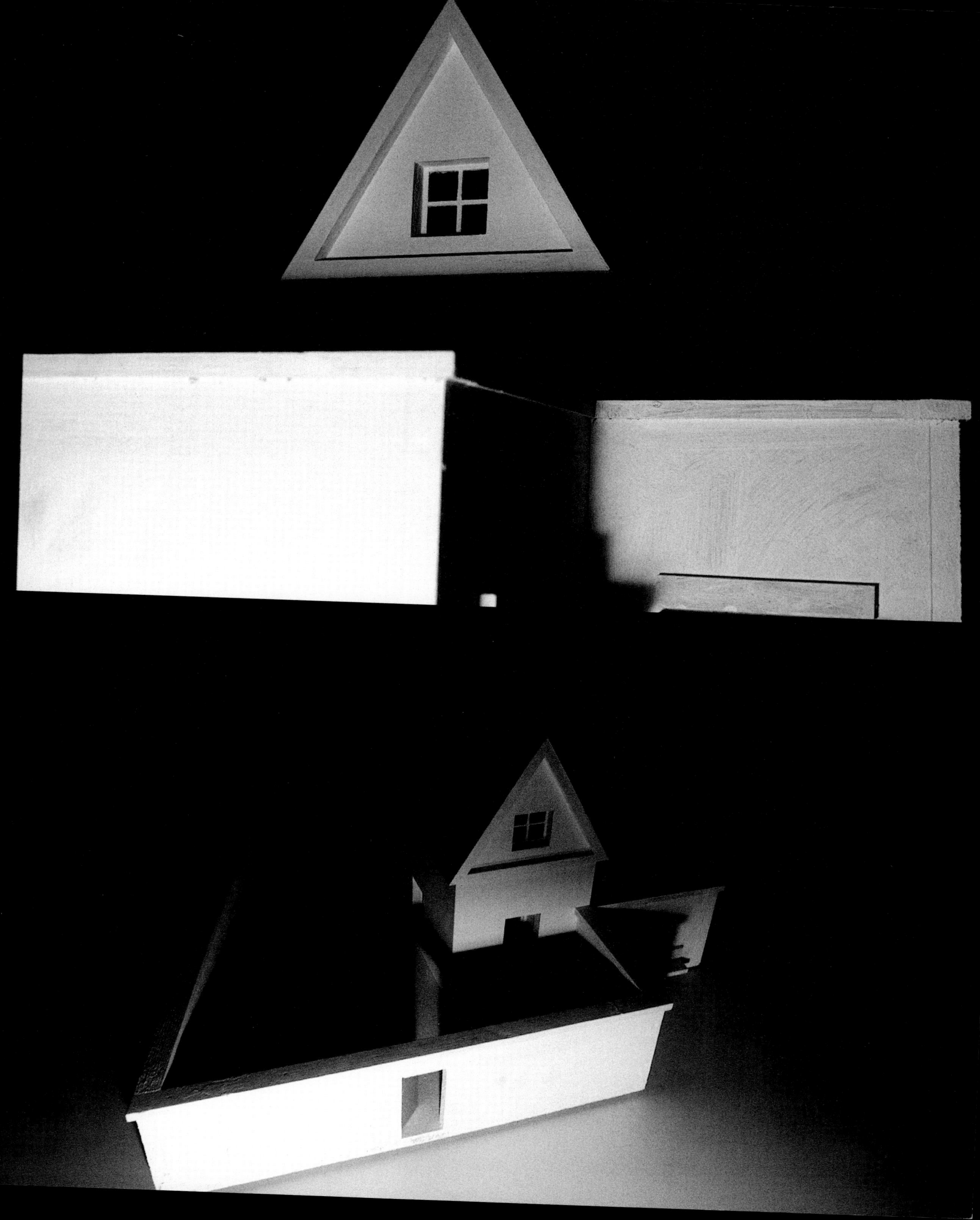

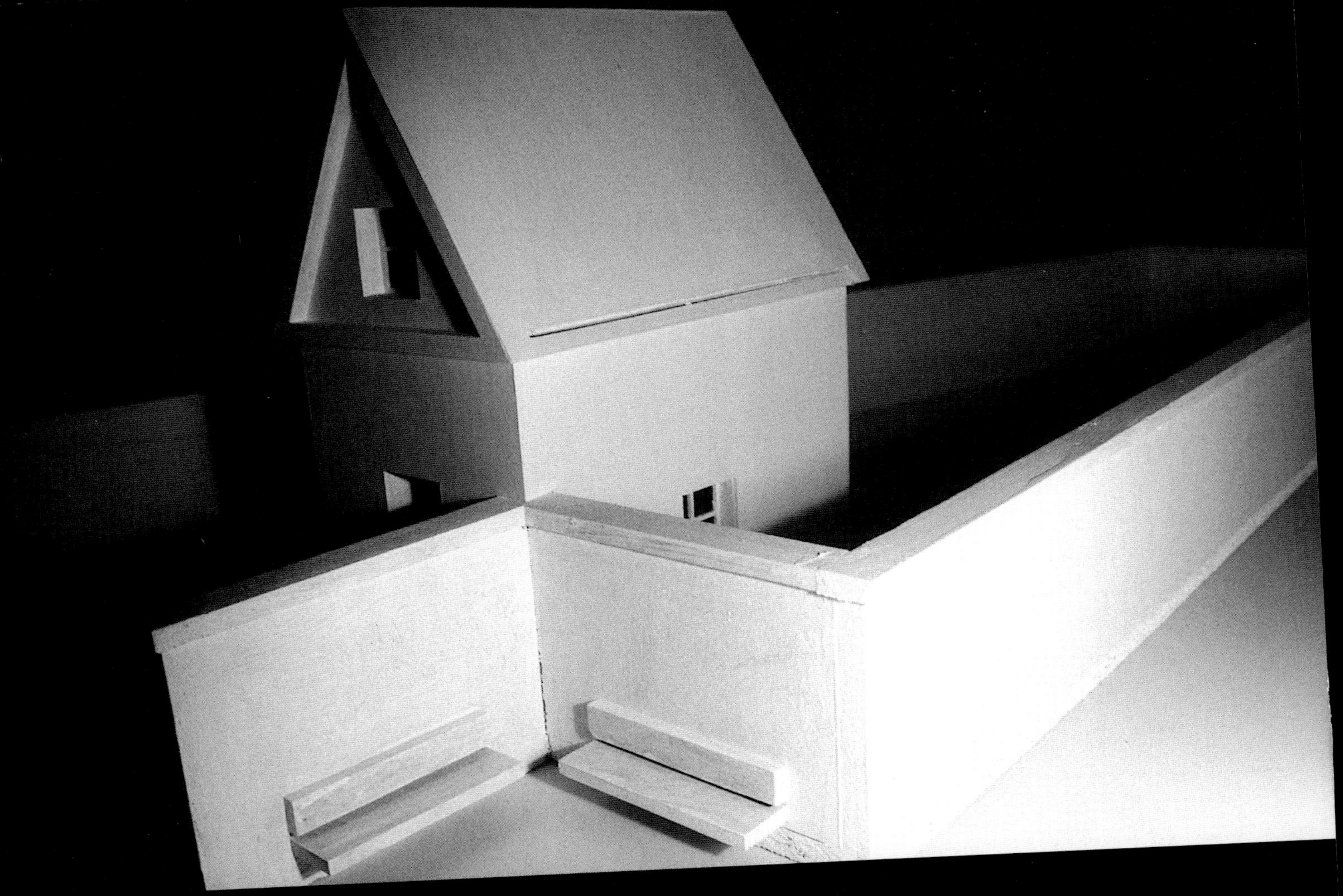

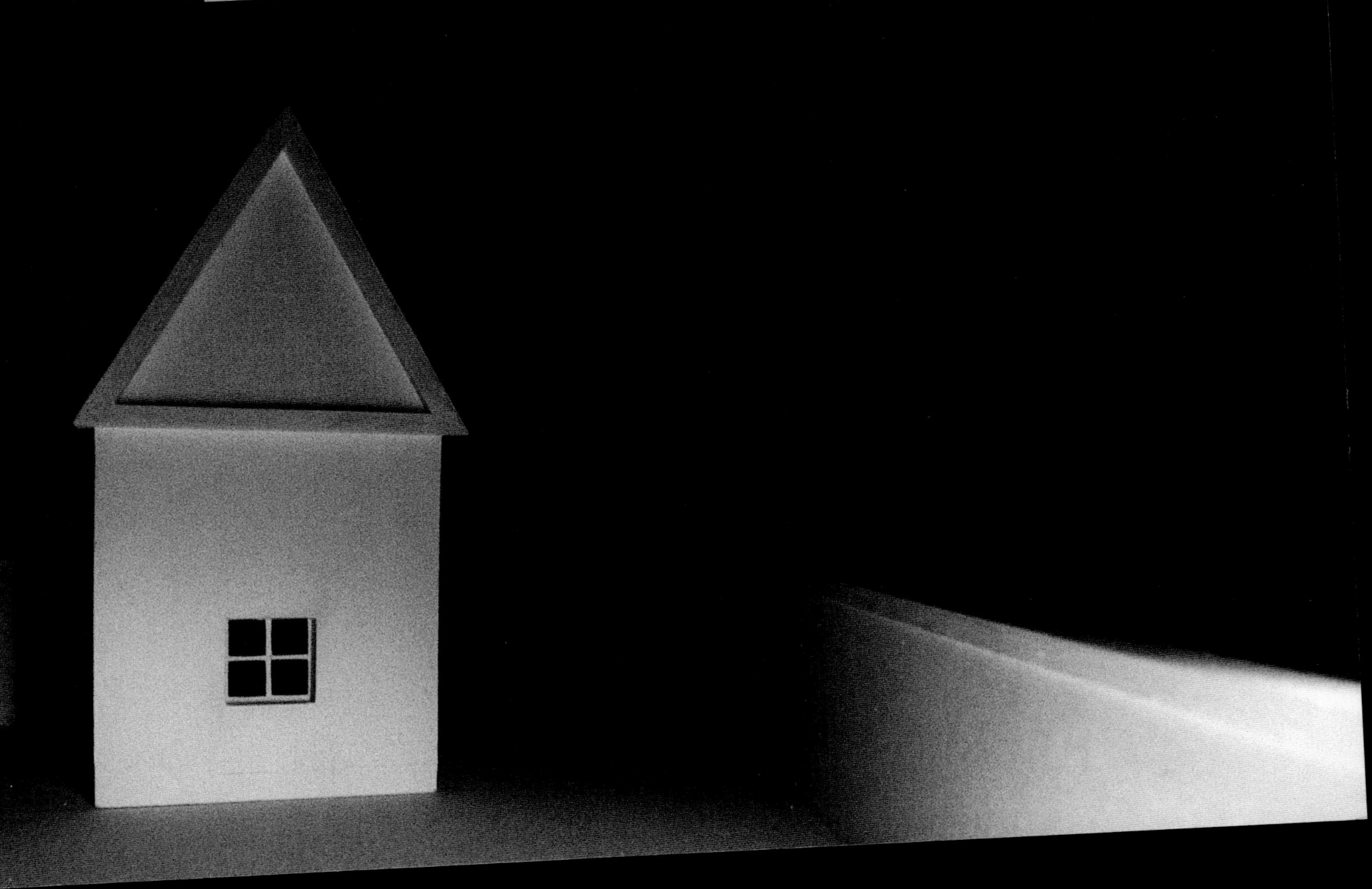

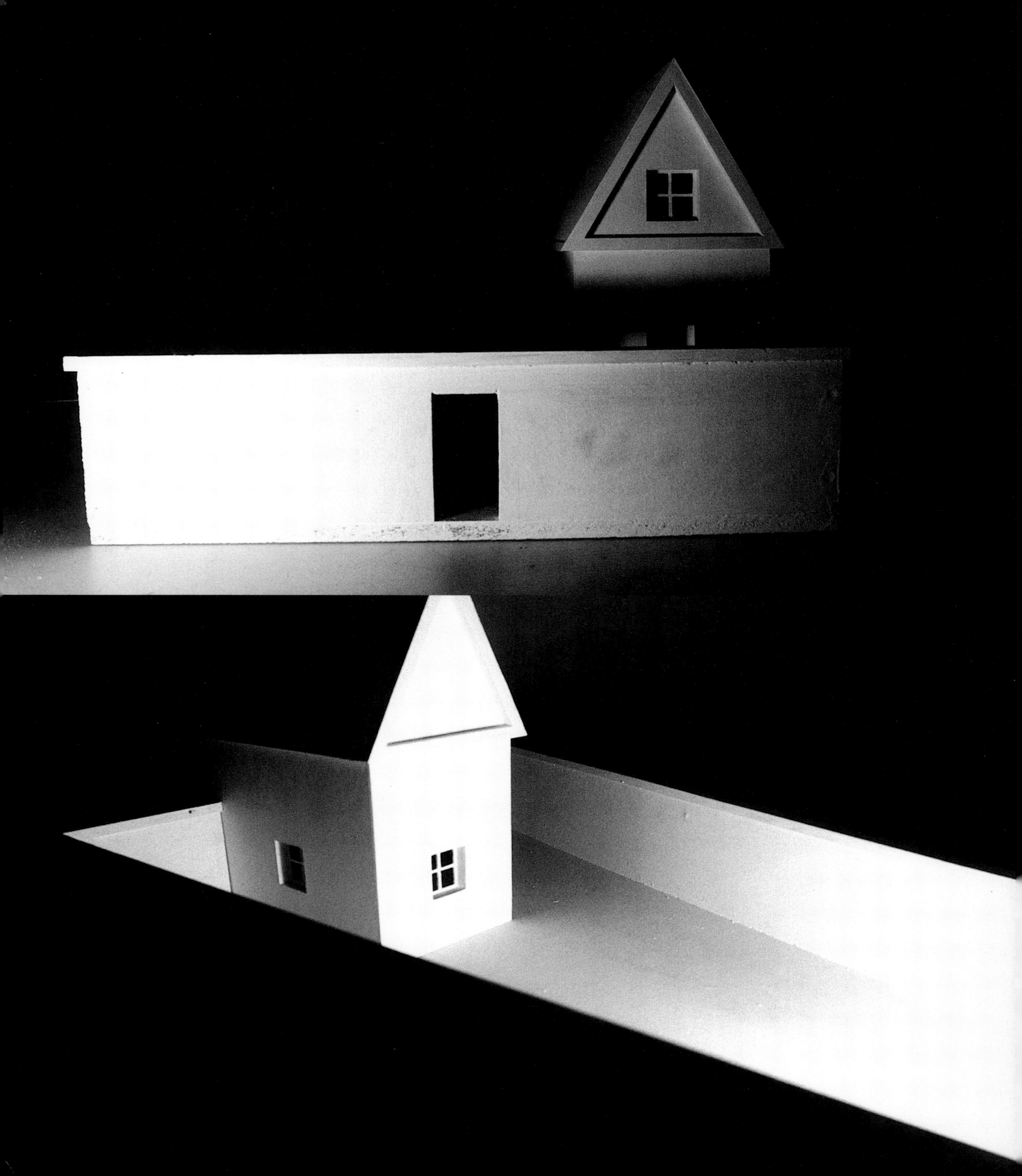

RESUME - THE WORKS SET INTO PERSPECTIVE

Carsten Juel-Christiansen

The Collective Space

In Steen Høyer's work, it is the landscape - the coherent, partitioned and built-upon surface - that constitutes the collective space. The surface acquires its spatial character through being delimited by the sea, through its meeting with the light from above and with its traces of geological genesis from beneath. The everyday landscape is framed in by temporal dimensions, by infinitude and the moment, which are manifest physically in the sea, the terrain's forms and the light. Construction upon the surface is not regarded by Steen Høyer as culture in contradistinction to nature but rather as an integral element within a conception of nature that subsumes growth, metabolism, the transformation of the surface and where the local conditions are always influencing the design. If this aggregate organism is to be visible, the currently prevailing divisions of the landscape, established according to aesthetic considerations, will have to be put aside. The focus is to be aimed at the transformational processes in general and in this connection, it is not historic images of completeness that will be used as references but rather the entire arsenal of architecture's and landscape architecture's spatial effects which are to be employed in a free manner in order to mark out our bodily presence in the space.

Jens Kvorning observes the urban space and sees an evolution which is gradually but steadily rubbing out the space's differences. Strøget, the pedestrian promenade running through the heart of downtown Copenhagen, and the Lyngby shopping mall situated in a suburban area north of Copenhagen, are indeed two different localities. Nonetheless, they give forth a nagging impression of being identical, due to the fact that the very same wares are being sold in both places and by virtue of the codes that control the proceedings. In terms of consciousness, we find ourselves within one space where the codes' enforced orthodoxy outdoes the physical differences and where, it might be said, there is no time to waste in the space's predictable program. In relation to this homogenous space, Kvorning defines the collective space as a free space, where one can experience both the city's and life's nuanced differences as the factors that keep the space open. He apprehends the assignment's sites as instances of islands of otherliness, and he proposes planning strategies for fortifying their resistance to the homogenization of the space. The city's inaccessible areas, like the railway's terrain in the center, are viewed by Kvorning as dream-like oases that will become confiscated into the city's homogeneous space as soon as they can be built upon in a profitable manner if they are not solidified with a utility which can keep a tight grip on their specific character and also assign them a function within the city's organism.

For Tage Lyneborg, it is the site's plan-figurative order which arranges the parts of the urban plane that are spread out and provides the foundation for the locality's meaning. Just as, in its day, "the finger plan" furnished an iconographically clarifying coherence among the parts of Greater Copenhagen - its center, its residential areas and its recreative landscapes - Lyneborg is thinking today, as the Øresund Bridge is about to open up the region in all directions, that two intersecting axes, a north-south and an east-west, can be marked out in the city's organization. The purpose is to re-establish a hierarchical coherence in the space among the city's center, its periphery and the surrounding landscape. The locality's greater spatial order is built up in prepared contexts of the site's materials: land, water and city. These are articulated sporadically alongside and parallel to the city's axes. What is employed in this re-adaptation is a wide range of urban functions, ranging from energy landscapes, beach and club facilities to expansive elevated urban terraces and roofed halls. In Lyneborg's proposal, the axes are, primarily, mentally forming pictures. They need not be realized in their entirety, but they cut across the existing urban space and are established as fragments, each of which establishes wholeness and acquires its very own urban identity.

As far as the three works in the collective space are concerned, what matters is that the site, that which is outside of or precedes the city, is apprehended as that which can represent common values. This has to be expressed through a special architectonic effort which is to be set into motion in opposition to the global functionality that organizes the space into systems that make everything identical. The global systems' transparency has to be veiled or deformed by something which in its specific character is not transparent and which turns the site into a focal point - for us.

In Høyer's work, it is the distinctive Danish landscape, which with its light and presence comes to a standstill, that creates a slower rhythm of events in relation to progress's technical dynamics. This landscape is articulated in such a way that it comes to represent an undisturbedness while also allowing a presentiment of its inherent powers to take over the whole scenery. With Kvorning, it is the Central Station - the place where the trip ends, or begins - which is monumentalized as a complex plaza formation, interlaced with accessible and inaccessible areas, surrounded by near and remote urban horizons. What we see in Lyneborg's contribution is the distinct connection between the historic center and the surrounding periphery that binds the region's free-flowing parts together into one site and accentuates the site's history as a repository of meaning.

In these three works, the relationship to the horizon, be it visible or perceptual, plays a crucial role as a meaningful framing of the site: "Here". The natural elements' manifest attendance at the city's central plaza in Høyer's project; the exposure of the train's tranquilly gliding movement along dense edges of the city in Kvorning's work; urban modules of solar cell islands which move, in Lyneborg's proposal, from the mainland out over the face of the water. *Each contribution, in its own way, expresses an underlying wish to mark out continuous connections to a horizon that carries significance that runs across the high-frequency highway system and in contradistinction to the city's partitions.*

The Space's Middle Ground

For Kristine Jensen, the space's middle ground is a threshold, which she specifies in two ways: as the site where the locality's identity is characterized and as a free space in comparison with the city's detail-controlling functional program. That which holds the two conceptions together is the thought that the middle ground is the place in architecture where the meeting between people and the world obtains its finely nuanced expression. It is the place where new actions and new techniques braid themselves into cultural experiences that are represented in the urban space's form elements. In Kristine Jensen's work, the middle ground is elaborated as a bounded condensation of an unbounded surrounding space. Running parallel with the architectonic intention is the thought that the meeting between people at one spot can be elevated into articulating the fundamental solidarity that binds people together.

In Svein Tønsager's work, the city's space is seen as an imprint of and a casting mold for the city's functionality and social organization. The existing city's hierarchically organized spatial coherence, from its public central plaza to its individuals' private quarters, sets firm frames around public and private life, even though technology and culture have brought about new relations between these spheres. In the city's plan, a number of lesser established functions are marginalized. Frequently, these are recreational spaces, social spaces, spaces for play and experimentation and spaces for the establishment of a new functionality. In the ongoing march of economic development, these spaces are ousted from the center and referred instead out to the areas' periphery. Tønsager views these functions as being vital elements in a prospective praxis which he imagines could entail a new organization of the urban space. What is characteristic of Tønsager's way of organizing is that the urban functions are not merely dispersed in relation to one another by the streets' extension, but are also brought closely together inside an urban space with many levels, connected by ramps, elevators, etc. What we have here is a tolerant co-existence of complex functions and urban spaces which fashions the space's middle ground and establishes close connections between private and public spaces and between productive and recreative exertions. The notion is that such a co-existence will be both possible and imperative when the individual's day is no longer regulated by a set time schedule.

Niels Grønbæk experiences the space's middle ground as a 'narrative space', which we know from the movies, from literature, from visual sequences where the camera follows one person's movement through the city's space and from the author's reflection on his distance from and his connection to the people among whom he lives. Grønbæk regards this movable subjective point of view in the context of that distinctive dissociation between the city's space and its inhabitants which is the direct result of urban dispersal. Living in the city today is being a traveler. Great distances are covered every day merely in order to navigate through the functional patterns that fasten existence together. The city assumes form as an image on the windshield, and the buildings become set pieces in a course of movement, but the meaning of the life that they are framing can barely be sensed. The person himself is the storyteller; it is he who gives form to the meanings inside this space, where meaning is so bleak. The person's relationship to the surrounding space has changed, while the city's relation to itself has also changed. Urban dispersal entails an inversion of the contracting forces that created the city and in this inversion, the city's inventory of type forms, streets and blocks, etc. is put out of play. The dispersed developments no longer contain any form-creating power that might extend beyond the individual parcelling of lots and therefore, they fail to designate any line of development for a city. In conformity with a number of the other contributors to this book, it is necessary for Grønbæk to turn this development in toward other avenues in order to free up resources that can be found in the city and in its inhabitants. His suggestion is that this can proceed by turning the city's expansion inward and by entwining the urban neighborhoods' middle ground in a more concentrated urban development. Grønbæk is working with a form of building that has the character of a woven fabric which braids its way around and through the city's fixed block structure, its detached buildings and its open areas without questing for any fixed form. It is the density in itself that is the form. The woven fabric is characterized by an intersection between smaller and larger space-creating elements which refer simultaneously to the individual person as a center and to the social exchange that creates the city's space.

The body plays a central role for the three contributions that work with the space's middle ground, both the city's body and the bodies that live in and move through the city - the space as body, as a modulated, unbroken coherence or maybe most of all as a density, an inextricably bound context of different parts that touch each other, shape one another and operate together. Kristine Jensen places her spaces in left-over patches of ground. By designing them as accessible islands in the midst of a stream of railway lines and roadways, which differentiate the city's dense space from the harbor's open industry landscape, these disparate elements are fastened together into an apprehensible urban body. Tønsager extends an urban field to the harbor in such a way that the bridge element brings the city and the commons together. In the constructed field, the city's geometry is altered by having the harbor's and the commons' free spatial sequence shape the urban space's organization. In Grønbæk's work, the density possesses an organic character. His urban web evolves slowly, without really being sure of its own end. This is a double body, situated in between city and house, which unfurls a connection between the separated bodies.

The Edge of the Space

Anders Abraham moves into the dispersed urban space which was engendered by the industrialization process that construction was subjected to. The urban areas in the city's periphery are not densely built up but they are typically characterized by large-scale transformations, by the regulation of the terrain, by changes in the land-use pattern and by building systems. Abraham perceives this space as being desolate without being empty and as being plentiful without being meaningful. He views the space's leveled or 'entropic' character as a consequence of a simplified set of standardized solutions in the buildings which are revised and recapitulated in connection with simple plan schemes that seem to have the capacity of propagating themselves interminably and predictably in the space. Abraham calls attention to the edge of the space by developing another space from a position inside the entropic space, a space which might have been had other perspectives been incorporated into the systems' design while allowing the same transformative force to be effective, anyhow. By engrafting these perspectives onto his plan images, he delineates a space that can be conceived as being contained in the presently existing space as a lost possibility or a dream. In doing this, he re-opens the industrially erected space as a building site and places the building site's open space around its forms, materials and potential meanings. The portions of the plan that he shows articulate the city as an aggregate multitude of individual differences. Every individual element, which might be a plot or a building, possesses its own firmly defined form while being simultaneously inserted into its place in the surrounding multitude. Where the constructed element-city seals its expectations to the outer horizon with the natural space's light is where Abraham induces into this imagined element-city an inner horizon which is delineated in the city's substance in the meeting between living space and building processes, in between the host of personal identities and the city's identity.

For Anders Munck, the modern public space is a space without any history. It is a space that refers only to the functionality which the space fulfills and which remains blind to the world of life encompassed by the space. The individual's world is more finely-meshed than what is manifest in the space's expansive toy bricks and it is also characterized by other relations, by a breadth of life situations for which the space's architecture cannot provide the perspective. A space filled with traces of homelessness. It is by catching hold of a span of variation of these traces that he indicates the edge of the space. Munck registers the absence of intimacy, of openness, of frames of mind and of personality in the space. It is precisely by focusing so sharply on their absence that he gets them to emerge, as repressed elements. His framed observations of the surrounding space constitute fissures leading to another world - a world with another scale, a psychic scale, which has not yet vanished entirely or which has not yet reported itself. Munck's way of focusing brings this a jolt closer.

To Poul Ingemann, the space of existence is the first space. The space that is surrounded by darkness on all sides. He similarly perceives individuality as a space, a second space, that is linked up with the first. It is the space of existence which, as a common condition, makes all men equal, but this equality does not have a human subject. It has only the single individuals, each of whom exists in his/her very own space. Ingemann apprehends the edge of the space as a play that takes place in between the limits of these two spaces. His project circles around giving expression to that which is all at once absolutely common and absolutely individual, as being two sides of the same coin. Ingemann erects a house at the edge of the space. It is surrounded by darkness. Its exterior is a plaza and its interior an atrium. The private space is manifest in the most ordinary forms. In the contemporary, transparent space, the difference between the space's exterior and its interior is annulled. This transparency is perceived by Ingemann as being bared to reflection on fragility as a basic human condition and he calls attention to the edge of the space by setting forth the most general as being the most remotely situated.

What is common to the projects that deal with the edge of the city is that they have a conception of the contemporary space as being reduced. They view the urban space's evolution as a progressive loss of identification-points for the people who live inside its circumference. In Abraham's project, what is indicated is the lack, or the absence, of solicitude in the manner the substance is adapted and in the detailing of the space. The connection which craftsmanship engenders between the body and the building is simply not attendant in the industrially generated surroundings and there has not been enough thought given to how this absence influences the space's value. Through his contribution, Abraham demonstrates that there is an importunate need to transform the building robot, whose powers far surpass the human body, and to develop this robot with a sensitivity that correspondingly surpasses the narrow rationality which brought it forth. With Munck, it is the space's symbolic content and language that are reduced to being signs for simple functional relations. The modern public space is depicted in Munck's optics as a machine with a simple behavioral program. By virtue of this, it removes itself from a human content matter, since the identification between machine and man is inverted, and as it is suggested, the more perfectly a machine functions, the less it comes to resemble the human circumstances. For Ingemann, the individual's place and mark in the space has been rubbed out. The individual, who with his feelings and understanding has access to the immeasurable dimensions, who is the genuine standard of value for the entire development, is represented more and more faintly in the space's architecture. *By making a display of the reduced contents in the contemporary urban space, the contributions that work with the edge of the space are pointing toward another space and toward points of orientation which will possess the capability of turning the city's development inward, on other pathways.*

In the past half a century, when the urban space has expanded so vehemently, it has been a bearing idea, with respect to the progress of society, that the material conditions be improved and that the sense of social confidence among the population be raised. Have these goals formulated themselves into any recognizable urban image? Perhaps this is precisely the case. Perhaps the urban space has unfurled the dimensions that dwell behind its development while simultaneously taking in the entire landscape. The urbanized space is about to be closed into its own form. The projects in the book move into the border zones and ruptures between the urban space's different parts. In doing so, they offer an attempt to show that architecture has the capacity to open the space toward new dimensions by elaborating the urban space's transitions and by condensing its internal coherence.